Brilliant Microsoft® Excel 2003

Steve Johnson

Perspection, Inc.

PEARSON
Prentice Hall

Harlow, England • London • New York • Boston • San Francisco • Toronto
Sydney • Tokyo • Singapore • Hong Kong • Seoul • Taipei • New Delhi
Cape Town • Madrid • Mexico City • Amsterdam • Munich • Paris • Milan

Pearson Education Limited
Edinburgh Gate
Harlow
Essex CM20 2JE
England

and Associated Companies throughout the world

Visit us on the World Wide Web at:
www.pearsoned.co.uk

Original edition, entitled SHOW ME MICROSOFT OFFICE EXCEL 2003, 1st edition, 0789730057 by
JOHNSON, STEVE; PERSPECTION, INC., published by Pearson Education, Inc, publishing as
Que/Sams, Copyright © 2004 Perspection, Inc.

This edition is manufactured in the USA and available for sale only in the United Kingdom,
Europe, the Middle East and Africa.

The right of Steve Johnson to be identified as author of this work has been asserted
by him in accordance with the Copyright, Designs and Patents Act 1988.

ISBN-10: 0-13-200132-2
ISBN-13: 978-0-13-200132-8

British Library Cataloguing-in-Publication Data
A catalogue record for this book is available from the British Library

10 9 8 7 6 5 4 3 2
09 08 07 06 05
Printed and bound in the United States of America

The publisher's policy is to use paper manufactured from sustainable forests.

Brilliant Guides

What you need to know and how to do it

When you're working on your PC and come up against a problem that you're unsure how to solve, or want to accomplish something in application that you aren't sure how to do, where do you look?? Manuals and traditional training guides are usually too big and unwieldy and are intended to be used as an end-to-end training resource, making it hard to get to the info you need right away without having to wade through pages of background information that you just don't need at that moment – and helplines are rarely that helpful!

Brilliant guides have been developed to allow you to find the info you need easily and without fuss and guide you through the task using a highly visual, step-by-step approach – providing exactly what you need to know when you need it!!

Brilliant guides provide the quick easy-to-access information that you need, using a detailed index and troubleshooting guide to help you find exactly what you need to know, and then presenting each task on one or two pages. Numbered steps then guide you through each task or problem, using numerous screenshots to illustrate each step. Added features include "See Also ..." boxes that point you to related tasks and information in the book, whilst "Did you know?..." sections alert you to relevant expert tips, tricks and advice to further expand your skills and knowledge.

In addition to covering all major office PC applications, and related computing subjects, the *Brilliant* series also contains titles that will help you in every aspect of your working life, such as writing the perfect CV, answering the toughest interview questions and moving on in your career.

Brilliant guides are the light at the end of the tunnel when you are faced with any minor or major task!

a

Acknowledgements

Perspection, Inc.

Brilliant Microsoft Excel 2003 has been created by the professional trainers and writers at Perspection, Inc. to the standards you've come to expect from Que publishing. Together, we are pleased to present this training book.

Perspection, Inc. is a software training company committed to providing information and training to help people use software more effectively in order to communicate, make decisions, and solve problems. Perspection writes and produces software training books, and develops multimedia and Web-based training. Since 1991, we have written more than 60 computer books, with several bestsellers to our credit, and sold over 4.5 million books.

This book incorporates Perspection's training expertise to ensure that you'll receive the maximum return on your time. You'll focus on the tasks and skills that increase productivity while working at your own pace and convenience.

We invite you to visit the Perspection Web site at:

www.perspection.com

Acknowledgements

The task of creating any book requires the talents of many hard-working people pulling together to meet impossible deadlines and untold stresses. We'd like to thank the outstanding team responsible for making this book possible: the writer, Steve Johnson; the editor, Holly Johnson; the technical editor, Nicholas Chu; the production team, Kate Lyerla, Joe Kalsbeek, and Ryan Suzuki; the proofreader, Beth Teyler, and the indexer, Michael Brackney.

At Que publishing, we'd like to thank Greg Wiegand for the opportunity to undertake this project, Sharry Gregory for administrative support, and Sandra Schroeder for your production expertise and support.

Perspection

Dedication

Most importantly, I would like to thank my wife Holly, and my three children, JP, Brett, and Hannah, for their support and encouragement during the project.

About The Author

Steve Johnson has written more than twenty books on a variety of computer software, including Microsoft Office XP, Microsoft Windows XP, Macromedia Director MX and Macromedia Fireworks, and Web publishing. In 1991, after working for Apple Computer and Microsoft, Steve founded Perspection, Inc., which writes and produces software training. When he is not staying up late writing, he enjoys playing golf, gardening, and spending time with his wife, Holly, and three children, JP, Brett, and Hannah. When time permits, he likes to travel to such places as New Hampshire in October, and Hawaii. Steve and his family live in Pleasanton, California, but can also be found visiting family all over the western United States.

Contents

C

$0.45
$0.45
$0.35
$2.35
$2.20
$2.40
$0.50

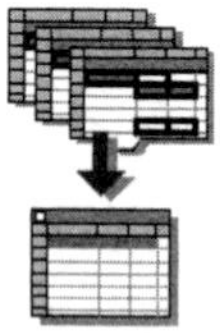

=SUM(B4:B10

Introduction

Welcome to *Show Me Microsoft Office Excel 2003*, a visual quick reference book that shows you how to work efficiently with Microsoft Office Excel 2003. This book provides complete coverage of basic and intermediate Excel 2003 skills.

Find the Best Place to Start

You don't have to read this book in any particular order. We've designed the book so that you can jump in, get the information you need, and jump out. However, the book does follow a logical progression from simple tasks to more complex ones. Each task is no more than two pages long. To find the information that you need, just look up the task in the table of contents, index, or troubleshooting guide, and turn to the page listed. Read the task introduction, follow the step-by-step instructions along with the illustration, and you're done.

What's New

If you're searching for what's new in Excel 2003, just look for the icon: New!. The new icon appears in the table of contents so you can quickly and easily identify a new or improved feature in Excel 2003. A complete description of each new feature appears in the New Features guide in the back of this book.

How This Book Works

Each task is presented on no more than two facing pages, with step-by-step instructions in the left column and screen illustrations in the right column. This arrangement lets you focus on a single task without having to turn the page.

Step-by-Step Instructions

This book provides concise step-by-step instructions that show you "how" to accomplish a task. Each set of instructions include illustrations that directly correspond to the easy-to-read steps. Also included in the text are timesavers, tables, and sidebars to help you work more efficiently or to teach you more in-depth information. A "Did You Know?" provides tips and techniques to help you work smarter, while a "See Also" leads you to other parts of the book containing related information about the task.

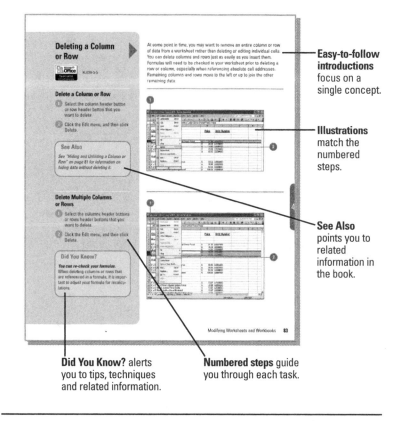

Easy-to-follow introductions focus on a single concept.

Illustrations match the numbered steps.

See Also points you to related information in the book.

Did You Know? alerts you to tips, techniques and related information.

Numbered steps guide you through each task.

Real World Examples

This book uses real world examples to help convey "why" you would want to perform a task. The examples give you a context in which to use the task. You'll observe how *Home Sense, Inc.*, a fictional home improvement business, uses Excel 2003 to get the job done.

Real world examples help you apply what you've learned to other tasks.

Troubleshooting Guide

This book offers quick and easy ways to diagnose and solve common Excel 2003 problems that you might encounter. The troubleshooting guide helps you determine and fix a problem using the task information you find. The problems are posed in question form and are grouped into categories that are presented alphabetically.

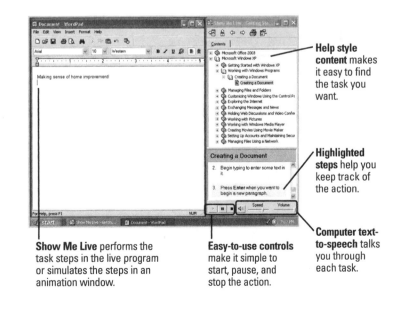

Troubleshooting points you to information in the book to help you fix your problems.

Help style content makes it easy to find the task you want.

Highlighted steps help you keep track of the action.

Computer text-to-speech talks you through each task.

Show Me Live performs the task steps in the live program or simulates the steps in an animation window.

Easy-to-use controls make it simple to start, pause, and stop the action.

Show Me Live Software

In addition, this book offers companion software that shows you how to perform most tasks using the live program. The easy-to-use VCR-type controls allow you to start, pause, and stop the action. As you observe how to accomplish each task, Show Me Live highlights each step and talks you through the process. The Show Me Live software is available free at *www.perspection.com or www.quepublishing.com/showme.*

Microsoft Office Specialist

This book prepares you fully for the Microsoft Office Specialist exam at the specialist and expert levels for Microsoft Office Excel 2003. Each Microsoft Office Specialist certification level has a set of objectives, which are organized into broader skill sets. To prepare for the certification exam, you should review and perform each task identified with a Microsoft Office Specialist objective to confirm that you can meet the requirements for the exam. Throughout this book, content that pertains to an objective is identified with the Microsoft Office Specialist logo and objective number next to it.

Microsoft Office Specialist

About the Microsoft Office Specialist Program

The Microsoft Office Specialist certification is the globally recognized standard for validating expertise with the Microsoft Office suite of business productivity programs. Earning an Microsoft Office Specialist certificate acknowledges you have the expertise to work with Microsoft Office programs. To earn the Microsoft Office Specialist certification, you must pass one or more certification exams for the Microsoft Office desktop applications of Microsoft Office Word, Microsoft Office Excel, Microsoft Office PowerPoint, Microsoft Office Outlook, or Microsoft Office Access. The Microsoft Office Specialist program typically offers certification exams at the "specialist" and "expert" skill levels. (The availability of Microsoft Office Specialist certification exams varies by program, program version, and language. Visit *www.microsoft.com/officespecialist* for exam availability and more information about the program.) The Microsoft Office Specialist program is the only Microsoft-approved program in the world for certifying proficiency with Microsoft Office programs.

What Does This Logo Mean?

It means this book has been approved by the Microsoft Office Specialist program to be certified courseware for learning Microsoft Office Outlook 2003 and preparing for the certification exam. This book will prepare you fully for the Microsoft Office Specialist exam at the specialist and expert levels for Microsoft Office Excel 2003. Each certification level has a set of objectives, which are organized into broader skill sets. Throughout this book, content that pertains to a Microsoft Office Specialist objective is identified with the Microsoft Office Specialist logo and objective number below the title of the topic:

 XL03S-1-1
XL03E-2-2

Logo indicates a task fulfills one or more Microsoft Office Specialist objectives.

327

Getting Started with Excel

Introduction

Microsoft Office Excel 2003 is a spreadsheet program that you can use to track and analyze sales, create budgets, and organize finances—both business and personal. You can also use Excel to manage inventory, setup investment reports or create loan amortizations. Microsoft Excel is a financial tool for performing calculations and other tasks automatically, which allows you to accomplish a variety of business or personal tasks in a fraction of the time it would take using pen and paper.

This chapter introduces you to the terminology and the basic Excel skills you can use in the program. In Excel, files are called **workbooks**. Each new workbook contains a default setting (which you can change) of three **worksheets**, which are similar to the pages in an accountant's ledger. You can format the work-sheets for your specific project at hand, or you can download pre-made templates from Microsoft's Web site.

You navigate through various tasks with a click of the mouse, or by using short-cut keys on your keyboard. Microsoft Excel is set up with a variety of menus and dialog boxes that assist you in getting the job done right. Toolbars help you when you need to quickly perform a task, such as formatting text. When working with your worksheets, you can view more than one, or resize the window to compare data.

The Office Assistant, along with Excel's extensive on-line Help, can point you in the right direction. When you finish the design of your worksheet you can save it in various formats, a Web page for example, to use in another office program. Should something happen to your workbook or worksheets, Excel has a recovery feature designed to help recover your worksheet.

Starting Excel

Before you can begin using Excel, you need to start the program. The easiest way to start Excel is to use the Start menu, which you open by clicking the Start button on the taskbar. When Excel starts, it displays a new workbook so that you can begin working immediately.

Start Excel from the Start Menu

1. Click the Start button on the taskbar.

2. Point to All Programs, and then point to Microsoft Office.

3. Click Microsoft Office Excel 2003.

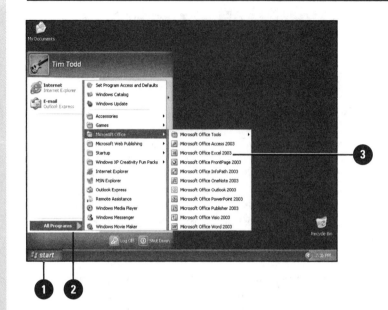

Viewing the Excel Window and Task Panes

When you start Excel, the Excel program window opens with a blank workbook—ready for you to begin working.

Cell address
Each cell has a unique address determined by the column letter and row number. For example, the cell B4 is the intersection of column B and row 4.

Title bar
The title bar contains the name of the active workbook.

Menu bar
The nine menus give you access to all Excel commands.

Formula bar
Any data contained in the active cell appears in the formula bar.

Select All button

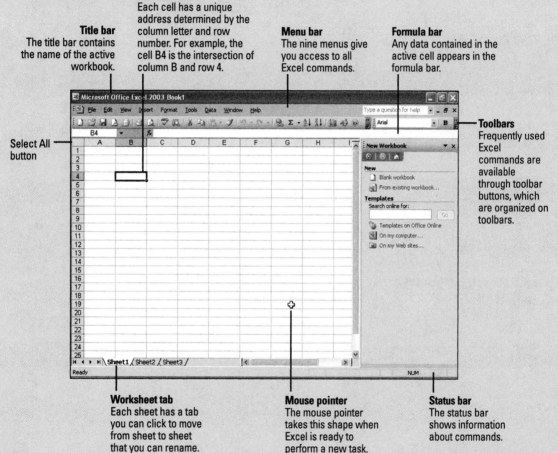

Toolbars
Frequently used Excel commands are available through toolbar buttons, which are organized on toolbars.

Worksheet tab
Each sheet has a tab you can click to move from sheet to sheet that you can rename.

Mouse pointer
The mouse pointer takes this shape when Excel is ready to perform a new task.

Status bar
The status bar shows information about commands.

Starting a New Workbook

When you start Excel, the program window opens with a new workbook so that you can begin working in it. You can also start a new workbook whenever Excel is running, and you can start as many new workbooks as you want. Each new workbook displays a default name ("Book1," "Book2," and so on), numbered according to how many new workbooks you have started during the work session until you save it with a more meaningful name.

Start a New Workbook from the Task Pane

1. Click the File menu, and then click New.

2. Click Blank Workbook.

   A blank workbook is opened.

3. Click the Close button on the task pane.

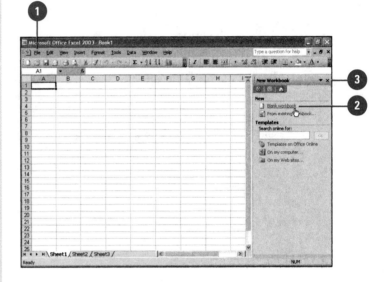

Start a New Workbook from the New Button

1. Click the New button. Excel opens a blank workbook.

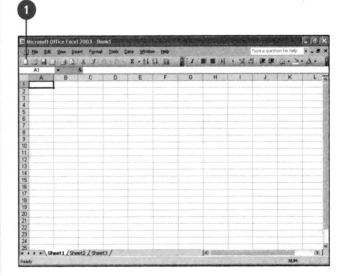

Create a File Using a Template or Wizard

1. Click the File menu, and then click New.

2. Click On My Computer.

3. Click the tab for the type of document you want to create.

4. Click the icon for the template or wizard you want to use.

5. Click OK.

6. If you choose a wizard, follow the step-by-step instructions. Click Next to move to the next wizard dialog box.

7. When you reach the last wizard dialog box, click Finish.

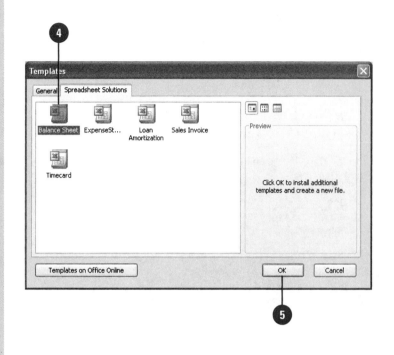

Get Templates on the Web

1. Click the File menu, and then click New.

2. Click Templates On Office Online to open the Microsoft Web site in your browser.

3. Click the link to the template you want.

4. Click Download Now, and then follow the online instructions.

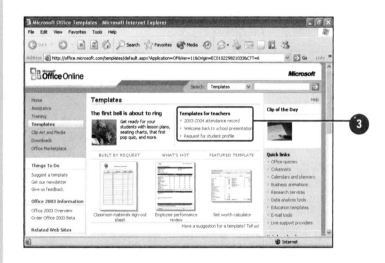

Opening an Existing Workbook

When you want to use a workbook you have previously created, you must first open it. You can open an Excel workbook and start Excel simultaneously, or you can open an Excel workbook file or file created in another spreadsheet program after you start Excel. If you can't remember the workbook's name or location, Excel even helps you find files.

Open a Workbook from the Excel Window

1. Click the Open button on the Standard toolbar.

2. Click one of the icons on the Places bar for quick access to frequently used folders.

3. If the file is located in another folder, click the Look In list arrow, and then select the drive or folder containing the file you want to open.

4. If necessary, click the Files Of Type list arrow, and then click the type of file you want to open (click Microsoft Excel Files to see workbook files).

5. Click the name of the workbook file.

6. Click Open.

Did You Know?

You can change the default file location of the Open dialog box. Click the Tools menu, click Options, click the General tab, and then enter a new location in the Default File Location box.

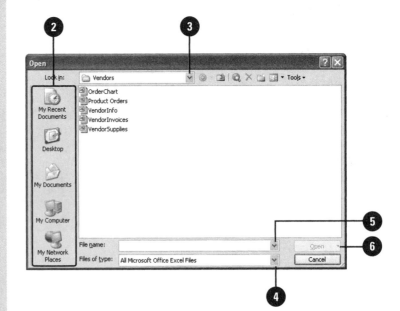

Open a Recently Opened Workbook from the Start Menu

 Click the Start button on the taskbar.

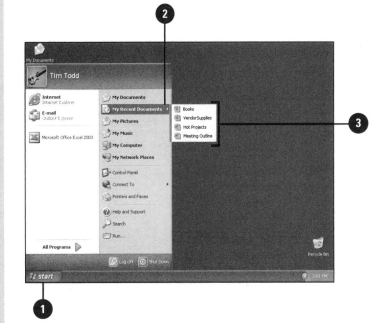 Point to My Recent Documents. The Documents menu displays a list of recently opened documents.

3 Click the Excel workbook you want to open.

Did You Know?

You can see recently opened files on the File menu. If you have recently opened and closed a workbook file, you can click the File menu, and then click the file name at the bottom of the File menu to open the file.

You can change the number of recently opened files that appear on the File menu. Click the Tools menu, click Options, click the General tab, and then change the number in the Recently Used File List box.

You can find a file when you're not sure of its name. In the Open dialog box, click the Look In list arrow, and then select the drive where the file might be located. If you know any characters contained in the file name, type them in the File Name box. Click the Tools menu, click Search, click to select the Search Subfolders check box, and then click Find Now.

Moving Around the Workbook

XL03S-1-2

You can move around a worksheet using your mouse or the keyboard. You might find that using your mouse to move from cell to cell is most convenient, while using various keyboard combinations is easier for covering large areas of a worksheet quickly. Or, you might find that entering numbers on the keypad, that Enter is a better method. Certain keys on the keyboard—Home, End, and Delete to name a few—are best used as shortcuts to navigate in the worksheet. However, there is no right way; whichever method feels the most comfortable is the one you should use.

Use the Mouse to Navigate

Using the mouse, you can navigate to:

◆ Another cell

◆ Another part of the worksheet

◆ Another worksheet

Did You Know?

Microsoft IntelliMouse users can roll from cell to cell with IntelliMouse. If you have the new Microsoft IntelliMouse—with the wheel button between the left and right buttons—you can click the wheel button and move the mouse in any direction to move quickly around the worksheet.

You can quickly zoom in or out using IntelliMouse. Instead of scrolling when you roll with the IntelliMouse, you can zoom in or out. To turn on this feature, click the Tools menu, click Options, click the General tab, click to select the Zoom On Roll With IntelliMouse check box, and then click OK.

To move from one cell to another, point to the cell you want to move to, and then click.

When you click the wheel button on the IntelliMouse, the pointer changes shape. Drag the pointer in any direction to move to a new location quickly.

To see more sheet tabs without changing the location of the active cell, click a sheet scroll button.

To move from one worksheet to another, click the tab of the sheet you want to move to.

Use the Keyboard to Navigate

Using the keyboard, you can navigate to:

◆ Another cell

◆ Another part of the worksheet

Refer to the table for keyboard shortcuts for navigating around a worksheet.

Keys For Navigating in a Worksheet	
Press This Key	**To Move**
Left arrow	One cell to the left
Right arrow	One cell to the right
Up arrow	One cell up
Down arrow	One cell down
Enter	One cell down
Tab	One cell to the right
Shift+Tab	One cell to the left
Page Up	One screen up
Page Down	One screen down
End+arrow key	In the direction of the arrow key to the next cell containing data or to the last empty cell in current row or column
Home	To column A in the current row
Ctrl+Home	To cell A1
Ctrl+End	To the last cell in the worksheet containing data

Go To a Specific Location

1 Click the Edit menu, and then click Go To.

2 Type the cell address to the cell location where you want to go.

3 To go to other locations (such as comments, blanks, last cell, objects, formulas, etc.), click Special, select an option, and then click OK.

4 Click OK.

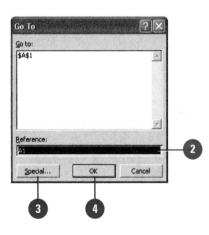

Working with Menus and Toolbars ▶

All Excel commands are organized on menus on the menu bar, and each menu contains a list of related commands. A **short menu** displays often used commands, and an **expanded menu** displays all commands available on that menu. A menu command followed by an ellipsis (...) indicates that a **dialog box** opens, so you can provide additional information. An arrow to the right of a command indicates that a submenu opens, displaying related commands. An icon to the left means a toolbar button is available for that command. Toolbars contain buttons you can click to carry out commands you use frequently. A keyboard combination to the right of a menu command indicates a **shortcut key** is available for the command.

Choose a Command Using a Menu

1. Click a menu name on the menu bar to display a list of commands.

2. If necessary, click the expand arrow to expand the menu and display more commands, or wait until the expanded list of commands appears.

3. Click the command you want, or point to the arrow to the right of the menu command to display a submenu of related commands, and then click the command.

Choose a Command Using a Toolbar Button

1. If you're not sure what a toolbar button does, point to it to display a ScreenTip.

2. To choose a command, click the Toolbar button or click the list arrow.

    When you select a button from the list arrow, the button appears on the toolbar, showing only the buttons you use most often.

Choose a Command Using a Shortcut Key

◆ To choose a command using a shortcut key, press and hold the first key, and then press the other key. For example, press and hold Ctrl, and then press S to perform the Save command.

Shortcut key

Display or Hide a Toolbar

1 Click the View menu, and then point to Toolbars.

2 Click the unchecked toolbar you want to display or the checked toolbar you want to hide.

Did You Know?

You can move and reshape a toolbar. To move a toolbar to another location, click a blank area of the toolbar (not a button), and then drag the toolbar to a new location. To change the shape of a floating toolbar, position the mouse pointer over the edge of the toolbar, and then drag to reshape it.

The commands and buttons on menus and toolbars respond to your work habits. As you select menu commands or toolbar buttons, those commands and toolbar buttons are promoted to the short menu and shared toolbar if they were not already there.

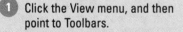

Working with Dialog Boxes

A **dialog box** is a special window that opens when Excel needs additional information from you in order to complete a task. You indicate your choices by selecting a variety of option buttons and check boxes; in some cases, you type the necessary information in the boxes provided. Some dialog boxes consist of a single window, while others contain **tabs** that you click to display more sets of options.

Choose Dialog Box Options

All Excel dialog boxes contain the same types of options, including:

- **Tabs.** Click a tab to display its options. Each tab groups a related set of options.

- **Option buttons.** Click an option button to select it. You can usually select only one.

- **Spin box.** Click the up or down arrow to increase or decrease the number, or type a number in the box.

- **Check box.** Click the box to turn on or off the option. A checked box means the option is selected; a cleared box means it's not.

- **List box.** Click the list arrow to display a list of options, and then click the option you want.

- **Text box.** Click in the box, and then type the requested information.

- **Button.** Click a button to perform a specific action or command. A button name followed by an ellipsis (...) opens another dialog box.

- **Preview box.** Many dialog boxes show an image that reflects the options you select.

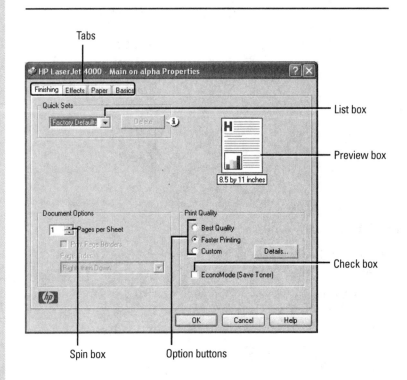

Tabs

List box

Preview box

Check box

Spin box

Option buttons

Using Task Panes

When you start an Office program, a **task pane** appears by default on the right or left side of the program window. The task pane displays various options that relate to the current task. There are several types of options available in the task pane. You can search for information, select options, and click links, like the ones on a Web page, to perform commands. You can also display different task panes, move back and forward between task panes, and close a task pane to provide a larger work area.

Open and Close Task Panes

1. Click the View menu, and then click Task Pane.

2. To open another task pane, click the down arrow on the task pane title bar, and then click the task pane you want.

3. To switch between task panes, click the Back and Forward task pane buttons.

4. Click the Close button on the task pane.

Use the Task Pane

1. When you open any Office program, the task pane appears on the right or left side of your screen.

2. Click an option on the task pane.

Arranging Windows

 XL03S-5-6

Every Office program and workbook opens inside a **window**, which contains a title bar, menus, toolbar and work area, which is where you create and edit your data. Most often, you'll probably fill the entire screen with one window. But when you want to move or copy information between programs or documents, it's easier to display several windows at once. You can arrange two or more windows from one program or from different programs on the screen at once. However, you must make the window active to work in it. You can also click the buttons on the taskbar to switch between open workbooks and other Office documents.

Resize and Move a Window

All windows contain the same sizing buttons:

◆ **Maximize button.** Click to make a window fill the entire screen.

◆ **Restore Down button.** Click to reduce a maximized window to a reduced size.

◆ **Minimize button.** Click to shrink a window to a taskbar button. To restore the window to its previous size, click the appropriate taskbar button.

◆ **Close button.** Click to shut a window.

Use the Mouse to Move a Window

1 Point to the window's title bar.

2 Drag the window to a new location, and then release the mouse button.

Did You Know?

You can quickly switch between Office documents. Each open Office 2003 document displays its own button on the Windows taskbar. You can click the icons on the taskbar to switch between the open Office documents.

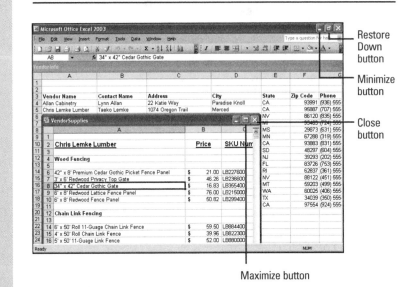

Restore Down button

Minimize button

Close button

Maximize button

Use the Mouse to Resize a Window

1 If the window is maximized, click the Restore Down button.

2 Move the mouse over one of the borders of the window until the mouse pointer changes into a two-headed arrow.

The directions of the arrowheads show you the directions in which you can resize the window.

3 Drag the window border until the window is the size you want.

Arrange Multiple Windows

1 Open up both worksheets.

2 Click the Window menu.

3 Click a window command:

◆ **Compare Side By Side With...** click a workbook, and then click OK to tile two windows.

◆ **Arrange** click an arrange window option (Tiled, Horizontal, Vertical, or Cascade), and then click OK.

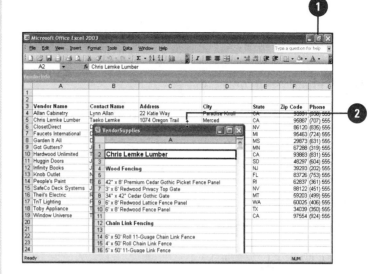

Compare two worksheets vertically

Getting Help

At some point, everyone has a question or two about the program they are using. The Office online Help system in Excel provides the answers you need. You can search an extensive catalog of Help topics using a table of contents to locate specific information, or get context sensitive help in a dialog box.

Get Help Without the Office Assistant

1. Click the Help button on the Standard toolbar.

2. Locate the Help topic you want.

   ◆ Type one or more keywords in the Search For box, and then click the Start Searching button.

   ◆ Click Table Of Contents.

   The topic you want appears in the right pane.

3. Read the topic, and then click any hyperlinks to get the information on related topics or definitions.

4. When you are done, click the Close button.

5. Click the Close button in the task pane.

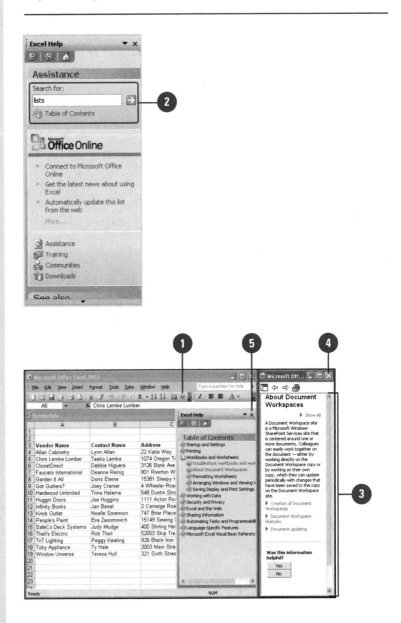

Get Help While You Work

1. Click the Type A Question For Help box.

2. Type your question, and then press Enter.

3. Click the topic in which you want to read.

4. When you're done, click the Close button.

5. Click the Close button on the task pane.

Get Help in a Dialog Box

1. Display the dialog box in which you want to get help.

2. Click the Help button.

3. Read the information in the Help window, and then click any links to display additional information.

4. When you're done, click the Close button.

Getting Help from the Office Assistant

Often the easiest way to learn how to accomplish a task is to ask someone who knows. Now, with Office, that knowledgeable friend is always available in the form of the Office Assistant. Tell the Office Assistant what you want to do in the same everyday language you use to ask a colleague or friend, and the Office Assistant walks you through the process step by step. If the personality of the default Office Assistant—Clippit—doesn't appeal to you, choose from a variety of other Office Assistants.

Ask the Office Assistant for Help

1. Click the Help menu, and then click Show Office Assistant.

2. Click the Office Assistant if necessary, to display the help balloon.

3. Type your question about a task you want help with.

4. Click Search.

5. Click the topic you want help with, and then read the help information.

6. After you're done, click the Close button in the task pane.

7. To refine the search, click the Search list arrow, select a search area, and then click the Start Searching button.

8. Click the Help menu, and then click Hide the Office Assistant.

Did You Know?

You can use the Office Assistant to get help at any time. When you begin to create a type of worksheet the Office Assistant appears and offers you help. You can have the Office Assistant walk you through the process or complete the task alone.

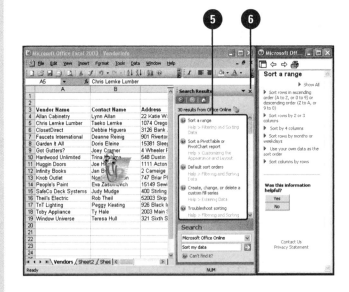

Choose an Office Assistant

1. Right-click the Office Assistant, and then click Choose Assistant.

2. Click the Gallery tab.

3. Click Next and Back to preview different Assistants.

4. Leave the Assistant you want to use visible.

5. Click OK.

   If you are prompted, insert the Office 2003 CD-ROM in your drive, and then click OK.

Turn Off the Office Assistant

1. Right-click the Office Assistant, and then click Options, or click the Options button in the Office Assistant window.

2. Click the Options tab.

3. Clear the Use The Office Assistant check box.

4. Click OK.

Did You Know?

You can hide the Office Assistant.
When the Office Assistant is turned on, you can hide the Office Assistant. To hide the Office Assistant, right-click the Assistant, and then click Hide.

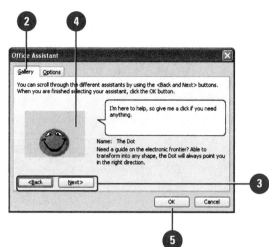

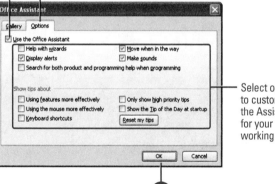

Select options to customize the Assistant for your working style.

Saving a Workbook

 XL03S-5-9

When you create a new Excel workbook, the title bar displays a default title, such as Book1 or Book2. When you save a workbook for the first time, you need to give it a meaningful name and specify where you want to store it. Once you have saved a workbook, you should continue to save it as you work so that changes you make are saved in the file. If you want to make changes to a previously saved workbook, but keep the original version intact, you need to save the changed workbook with a different name; then you will have the original workbook and one with the changes. If necessary, you can also change the file format so you can use the workbook file with a different program.

Save a Workbook for the First Time

1. Click the Save button on the Standard toolbar.

2. Click one of the icons on the Places bar (quick access to frequently used folders) to select a location to save the workbook file.

3. If you want to save the file in another folder, click the Save In list arrow, and then select the drive and folder in which you want to store the workbook file.

4. Type the file name for the new workbook name.

5. Click Save.

   The new name appears in the title bar of the workbook.

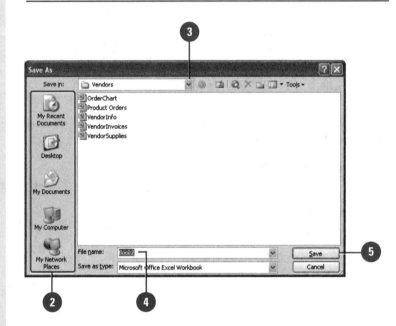

Save a File with Another Name

1. Click the File menu, and then click Save As.

2. Click an icon on the Places bar or click the Save In list arrow, and then click the drive or folder where you want to save the file.

3. Type a new file name.

4. Click Save.

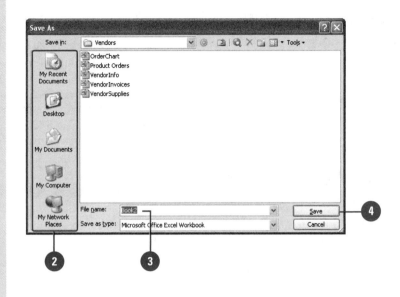

Save a File in a New Folder

1. Click the File menu, and then click Save As.

2. Locate and select the drive and folder where you want to create the new folder.

3. Click the Create New Folder button.

4. Type the new folder name, and then click OK.

5. Type a name for the file, or use the suggested one.

6. Click Save.

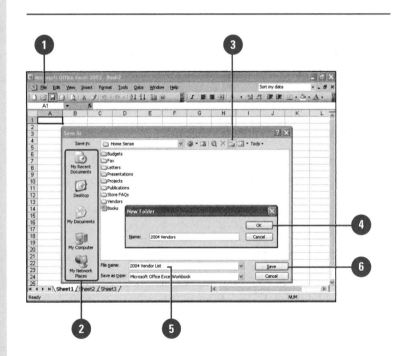

Did You Know?

You can rename a folder in the Save As or Open dialog box. In the Save As or Open dialog box, right-click the folder you want to rename, click Rename, type a name, and then press Enter.

Saving a File with Different Formats

XL03S-5-10

A file type specifies the document format (for example, a template) as well as the program and version in which the file was created (for example, Office Excel 2003). You might want to change the type if you're creating a custom template or sharing files with someone who has an earlier version of a program. You can use the Save As dialog box to change the file type for a document. The Save As Type list arrow displays a list of the available formats, such as Template, XML, Web Page, Text (Tab delimited), Text (MS-DOS), or CSV (Comma delimited), for the program or current selection.

Save a File as a Different Type

1. Click the File menu, and then click Save As.

2. Click the Save As Type list arrow.

3. Click the file type you want.

   You can select file types for previous versions of Office programs.

4. Click Save.

Did You Know?

You can delete or rename a file in a dialog box. In the Open or Save As dialog box, click the file, click the Tools list arrow, and then click Delete or Rename.

You can move or copy a file quickly in a dialog box. In the Open or Save As dialog box, right-click the file you want to move or copy, click Cut or Copy, open the folder where you want to paste the file, right-click a blank area, and then click Paste.

Create a Template

① Click the File menu, and then click Save As.

② Click the Save As Type list arrow, and then click a template.

③ Type a name for the new template, and then click Save.

④ In the new template, add the text and graphics you want to appear in all new office documents that you base on the template, and then delete any items you don't want to appear.

⑤ Make the changes you want to the margin settings, page size, and orientation styles, and other formats.

⑥ Click the Save button on the Standard toolbar.

⑦ Click the Close button.

Did You Know?

You can save multiple versions of a document in Excel. Click the File menu, click Versions, click Save Now, enter comments about the workbook, and then click OK. In the Versions dialog box, you can also open, delete, and view comments from saved versions.

See Also

See "Changing a Template" on page 90 for information on customizing the template you have created.

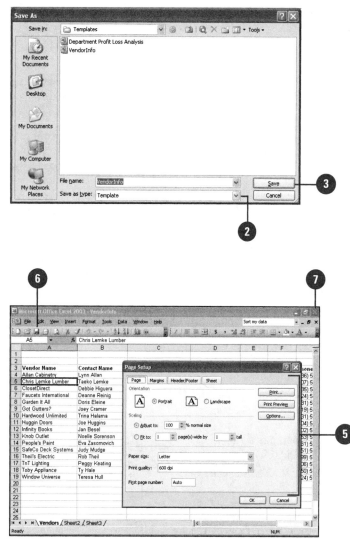

Getting Excel Updates on the Web ▶

Microsoft continues to improve Office 2003 programs with new features, security patches, or bug fixes. Microsoft Office Update allows you to keep your programs up-to-date with the latest software releases over the Internet. Microsoft Office Update scans your computer for any software components or fixes that need to be installed. Critical updates are important to install for your Office programs to run properly. By keeping your Office program updated with the latest security patches, you can protect your computer from the latest Internet threats.

Get Office Updates on the Web

1. Click the Help menu, and then click Check For Updates to open the Microsoft Online Web site.

2. Click Check For Updates to scan your system for any updates.

3. If necessary, click Yes to a security warning.

4. Follow the online instructions to download and install any updates.

Did You Know?

You can get Office information on the Web. Click the Help menu, and then click Microsoft Office Online. Your Web browser opens, displaying the Microsoft Office Online Web site.

You can get critical security updates on the Web. You can also check out Microsoft's Security's Web site for new announcements on the latest threats: *http://www.microsoft.com/security/*

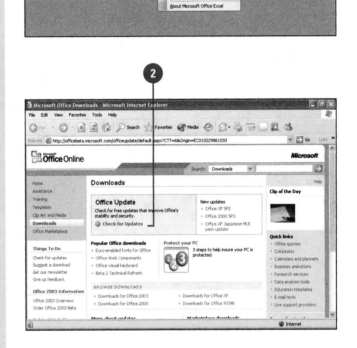

Recovering a Workbook

If Excel encounters a problem and stops responding, the program tries to recover the file the next time you open Excel. The recovered files appear in the Document Recovery task pane, which allows you to open the files, view what repairs were made, and compare the recovered versions. Each file appears in the task pane with a status indicator, either Original or Recovered, which shows what type of data recovery was performed. You can save one or all of the file versions. You can also use the AutoRecover feature to periodically save a temporary copy of your current file, which ensures proper recovery of the file.

1

Recover a File

1. When the Document Recovery task pane appears, click the list arrow next to the name of each recovered file, and then perform one of the following:

   ◆ Click Open to view the file for review.

   ◆ Click Save As to Save the file.

   ◆ Click Delete to close the file without saving.

   ◆ Click Show Repairs to find out how Excel fixed the file.

2. When you're done, click Close on the task pane.

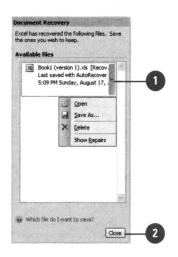

Use AutoRecover

1. Click the Tools menu, and then click Options.

2. Click the Save tab.

3. Select the Save AutoRecover Info Every check box.

4. Enter in the number of minutes or click the up and down arrows to adjust the minutes.

5. Click OK.

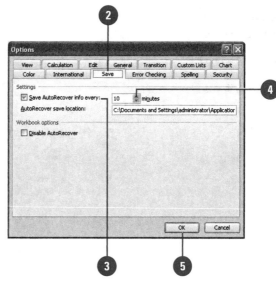

Exiting Excel

After you finish working on a workbook, you can close it. Closing a workbook makes more computer memory available for other processes. Closing a workbook is different from quitting Excel: after you close a workbook, Excel is still running. When you're finished using Excel, you can quit the program. To protect your files, always quit Excel before turning off your computer.

Close a Workbook

1. Click the File menu, and then click Close, or click the Close button on the worksheet window title bar.

   If you have made any changes to the workbook since last saving it, the Office Assistant asks if you want them saved.

2. Click Yes to save any workbook changes; click No to close the workbook without saving any changes; or click Cancel to return to the workbook without closing it.

Quit Excel

1. Click the Close button on the Excel program window title bar, or click the File menu, and then click Exit.

   If any files are open and you have made changes since last saving, a dialog box opens asking if you want to save changes.

2. Click Yes to save any workbook changes, click No to ignore any changes, or click Cancel to cancel the save.

Basic Workbook Skills

Introduction

Creating a Microsoft Office Excel 2003 workbook is as easy as entering data in the cells of an Excel worksheet. Each cell has a **cell address** which is made up of it's column and row intersection. Cells on a worksheet contain either labels or values, a formula or remain blank. Cell entries can be modified using the keyboard or mouse. You can select cells in ranges that are **contiguous** (selected cells are adjacent to eachother) or **noncontiguous** (selected cells are in different parts of the worksheet). Selected cells are used in formulas, to copy and paste data, to AutoFill, to apply date and time and other formatting functions.

If you accidentally make a change to a cell, you can use the Undo feature to "undo" your last change. Excel remembers your recent changes to the worksheet, and gives you the opportunity to undo them. If you decide to Redo the Undo, you can erase the previous change. This is useful when moving, copying, inserting and deleting cell contents.

In addition, Excel offers a Find and Replace feature that allows you to look for labels and values and make changes as necessary. When you need to spell check your worksheet, Excel can check and suggest spelling corrections. You can even customize the spelling dictionary by adding company specific words into AutoCorrect so that the spell checker doesn't think it's a misspelled word.

The Smart Tags feature works with other Microsoft Office 2003 programs to enhance your worksheets. Contact information can be pulled from your address book in Outlook, to your worksheet in Excel. Stock symbols can trigger a Smart Tag choice to import data on a publicly traded company.

Making Label Entries

There are three basic types of cell entries: labels, values, and formulas. A **label** is text in a cell that identifies the data on the worksheet so readers can interpret the information. Excel does not use labels in its calculations. For example, the label *price* is used as a column header to identify the price of each item in the column. A **value** is a number you enter in a cell. Excel knows to include values in its calculations. To enter values easily and quickly, you can format a cell, a range of cells, or a column with a specific number-related format. Then, as you type, the cells are formatted automatically.

To perform a calculation in a worksheet, you enter a formula in a cell. A **formula** is a calculation that contains cell references, values, and arithmetic operators. The result of a formula appears in the worksheet cell where you entered the formula. The contents of the cell appears on the formula bar. Entering cell references rather than actual values in a formula has distinct advantages. When you change the data in the worksheet or copy the formula to other cells (copying this formula to the cell below), Excel automatically adjusts the cell references in the formula and returns the correct results.

The formula entered in cell C6 appears here.

Active cell address

The result of the formula

Label

Value

Selecting Cells

In order to work with a cell— to enter data in it, edit or move it, or perform an action—you **select** the cell so it becomes the active cell. When you want to work with more than one cell at a time—to move or copy them, use them in a **formula**, or perform any group action—you must first select the cells as a **range**. A range can be **contiguous** (where selected cells are adjacent to each other) or **non-contiguous** (where the cells may be in different parts of the worksheet and are not adjacent to each other). As you select a range, you can see the **range reference** in the Name box. A range reference contains the cell address of the top-left cell in the range, a colon (:), and the cell address of the bottom-right cell in the range.

Select a Contiguous Range

1. Click the first cell that you want to include in the range.

2. Drag the mouse to the last cell you want to include in the range.

   When a range is selected, the top-left cell is surrounded by the cell pointer, while the additional cells are selected.

Select a Non-contiguous Range

1. Click the first cell you want to include in the range.

2. Drag the mouse to the last contiguous cell, and then release the mouse button.

3. Press and hold Ctrl, and then click the next cell or drag the pointer over the next group of cells you want in the range.

   To select more, repeat step 3 until all non-contiguous ranges are selected.

Entering Labels on a Worksheet

XL03S-1-1

Labels turn a worksheet full of numbers into a meaningful report by identifying the different types of information it contains. You use labels to describe the data in worksheet cells, columns, and rows. You can enter a number as a label (for example, the year 2004), so that Excel does not use the number in its calculations. To help keep your labels consistent, you can use Excel's **AutoComplete** feature, which automatically completes your entries (excluding numbers, dates, or times) based on previously entered labels.

Enter a Text Label

1. Click the cell where you want to enter a label.

2. Type a label. A label can include uppercase and lowercase letters, spaces, punctuation, and numbers.

3. Press Enter, or click the Enter button on the formula bar.

Enter a Number as a Label

1. Click the cell where you want to enter a number as a label.

2. Type ' (an apostrophe). The apostrophe is a label prefix and does not appear on the worksheet.

3. Type a number value.

4. Press Enter, or click the Enter button on the formula bar.

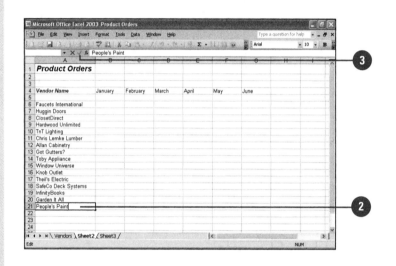

Enter a Label Using AutoComplete

1 Type the first few characters of a label.

If Excel recognizes the entry, AutoComplete completes it.

2 To accept the suggested entry, press Enter or click the Enter button on the formula bar.

3 To reject the suggested completion, simply continue typing.

Did You Know?

Excel doesn't recognize the entry.
The AutoComplete option may not be turned on. To turn on the feature, click the Tools menu, click Options, click the Edit tab, click to select Enable AutoComplete For Cell Values check box, and then click OK.

Long labels might appear truncated.
When you enter a label that is wider than the cell it occupies, the excess text appears to spill into the next cell to the right—unless there is data in the adjacent cell. If that cell contains data, the label will appear truncated—you'll only see the portion of the label that fits in the cell's current width. Click the cell to see its entire contents displayed on the formula bar.

Entering Values on a Worksheet

 Microsoft Office Specialist
Approved Courseware

XL03S-1-1

You can enter values as whole numbers, decimals, percentages, or dates. You can enter values using the numbers on the top row of your keyboard, or by pressing your Num Lock key, the numeric keypad on the right. When you enter a date or the time of day, Excel automatically recognizes these entries (if entered in an acceptable format) as numeric values and changes the cell's format to a default date or time format. You can also change the way values, dates or times of day are shown.

Enter a Value

1 Click the cell where you want to enter a value.

2 Type a value.

3 Press Enter, or click the Enter button on the formula bar.

Enter a Date or Time

1 To enter a date, type the date using a slash (/) or a hyphen (-) between the month, day, and year in a cell or on the formula bar.

To enter a time, type the hour based on a 12-hour clock, followed by a colon (:), followed by the minute, followed by a space, and ending with an "a" or a "p" to denote A.M. or P.M.

2 Press Enter, or click the Enter button on the formula bar.

Did You Know?

You can use the numeric keypad to enter numbers. Make sure NUM appears in the lower-right corner of the status bar. before you begin using the numbers.

Change Date or Time Format

1. Click the cell that contains the date format you want to change.

2. Click the Format menu, and then click Cells.

3. If necessary, click the Number tab.

4. Click Date.

5. Click the date or time format.

6. Click OK.

Did You Know?

You can simplify data entry. Enter values as simply as possible to make data entry quicker. For example, to enter the value "10.00" simply type "10". Use the Cells command on the Format menu to format your cell entries with decimal places, commas, dollar signs, and other formatting attributes.

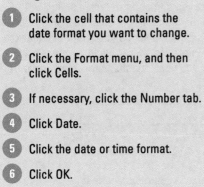

Entering Values Quickly with AutoFill

XL03S-1-1, XL03S-2-3

AutoFill is a feature that automatically fills in data based on the data in adjacent cells. Using the **fill handle**, you can enter data in a series, or you can copy values or formulas to adjacent cells. A single cell entry can result in a repeating value or label, or the results can be a more complex series. You can enter your value or label, and then complete entries such as days of the week, weeks of the year, months of the year, or consecutive numbering.

Enter Repeating Data Using AutoFill

① Select the first cell in the range you want to fill.

② Enter the starting value to be repeated.

③ Position the pointer on the lower-right corner of the selected cell. The pointer changes to the fill handle (a black plus sign).

④ Drag the fill handle over the range in which you want the value repeated.

Create a Complex Series Using AutoFill

① Enter the starting value for the series, and then press Enter.

② Select the first cell in the range you want to fill.

③ Position the pointer on the lower-right corner of the selected cell. The pointer changes to the fill handle (a black plus sign).

④ Drag the fill handle over the range in which you want the value repeated.

Editing Cell Contents

 XL03S-1-1

Even if you plan ahead, you can count on having to make changes on a worksheet. Sometimes it's because you want to correct an error. Other times it's because you want to see how your worksheet results would be affected by different conditions, such as higher sales, fewer units produced, or other variables. You can edit data just as easily as you enter it, using the formula bar or directly editing the active cell.

Edit Cell Contents

1 Double-click the cell you want to edit. The insertion point appears in the cell.

The status bar now displays Edit instead of Ready.

2 If necessary, use the Home, End, and arrow keys to position the insertion point within the cell contents.

3 Use any combination of the Backspace and Delete keys to erase unwanted characters, and then type new characters as needed.

4 Click the Enter button on the formula bar to accept the edit, or click the Esc button to cancel the edit.

Did You Know?

You can change editing options. Click the Tools menu, click Options, click the Edit tab, change the editing options you want, and then click OK.

You can edit cell contents using the formula bar. Click the cell you want to edit, click to place the insertion point on the formula bar, and then edit the cell contents.

Status bar shows Edit

Clearing Cell Contents

You can clear a cell to remove its contents. Clearing a cell does not remove the cell from the worksheet; it just removes from the cell whatever elements you specify: data, comments (also called **cell notes**), or formatting instructions. When clearing a cell, you must specify whether to remove one, two, or all three of these elements from the selected cell or range.

Clear the Contents of a Cell

1. Select the cell or range you want to clear.

2. Right click the cell or range, and then click Clear Contents on the shortcut menu, or press Delete.

Did You Know?

You can find and replace cell contents. Click the cell or cells containing content you want to replace. Click the Edit menu, click Find, and then click the Replace tab for additional options.

Clear Cell Contents, Formatting, and Comments

1. Select the cell or range you want to clear.

2. Click the Edit menu, and then point to Clear.

3. Click All.

Undoing and Redoing an Action

You may realize you've made a mistake shortly after completing an action or a task. The Undo feature lets you "take back" one or more previous actions, including data you entered, edits you made, or commands you selected. For example, if you were to enter a number in a cell, and then decide the number was incorrect, you could undo the entry instead of selecting the data and deleting it. A few moments later, if you decide the number you deleted was correct after all, you could use the Redo feature to restore it to the cell.

Undo an Action

1️⃣ Click the Undo button on the Standard toolbar to undo the last action you completed.

2️⃣ Click the Undo button list arrow to see recent actions that can be undone.

3️⃣ Click an action. Excel reverses the selected action and all actions above it.

Redo an Action

1️⃣ Click the Redo button on the Standard toolbar to restore your last undone action.

2️⃣ Click the Redo button list arrow to see actions that can be restored.

3️⃣ Click the action you want to restore. All actions above it will be restored as well.

Did You Know?

You can display the Redo button. Click the Toolbar Options list arrow, and then click Redo. Once a button is used, it remains on the toolbar.

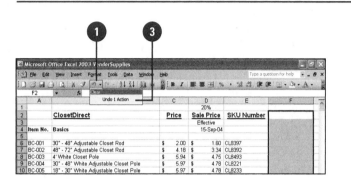

2

Understanding How Excel Pastes Data

If you want to use data that has already been entered on your worksheet, you can cut or copy it, and then paste it in another location. When you cut or copy data, the data is stored in an area of memory called the Windows Clipboard. When pasting a range of cells from the Windows Clipboard, you only need to specify the first cell in the new location. After you select the first cell in the new location and then click the Paste button, Excel automatically places all the selected cells in the correct order. Depending on the number of cells you select before you cut or copy, Excel pastes data in one of the following ways:

◆ **One to one.** A single cell in the Windows Clipboard is pasted to one cell location.

◆ **One to many.** A single cell in the Windows Clipboard is pasted into a selected range of cells.

◆ **Many to one.** Many cells are pasted into a range of cells, but only the first cell is identified. The entire contents of the Windows Clipboard will be pasted starting with the selected cell. Make sure there is enough room for the selection; if not, the selection will copy over any previously occupied cells.

◆ **Many to many.** Many cells are pasted into a range of cells. The entire contents of the Windows Clipboard will be pasted into the selected cells. If the selected range is larger than the selection, the data will be repeated in the extra cells. To turn off the selection marquee and cancel your action, press the Esc key.

A one to one cell ratio.

One cell copied to many cells.

Many cells are copied, but only the first will show.

Many cells paste to other cells.

Storing Cell Contents

Microsoft Office Specialist Approved Courseware

XL03S-5-2

With Office 2003, you can use the **Office Clipboard** to store multiple pieces of information from several different sources in one storage area shared by all Office programs. Unlike the Windows Clipboard, which only stores a single piece of information at a time, the Office Clipboard allows you to copy up to 24 pieces of text or pictures from one or more files. When you copy multiple items, you see the Office Clipboard, showing all the items you stored there. You can paste these pieces of information into any Office program, either individually or all at once.

Copy Data to the Office Clipboard

1. Click the Edit menu, and then click Office Clipboard.

2. Select the data you want to copy

3. Click the Copy button on the Standard toolbar.

   The data is copied into the first empty position on the Clipboard task pane.

4. Click the Close button in the task pane.

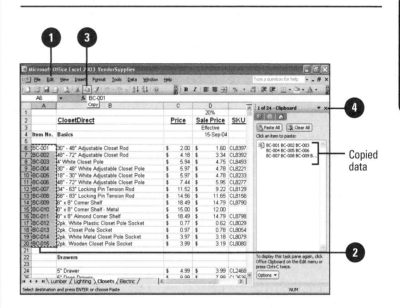

Copied data

Paste Data from the Office Clipboard

1. Click the Edit menu, and then click Office Clipboard.

2. In the Excel worksheet, click the first cell where you want to paste data.

3. Click the Office Clipboard item you want to paste.

4. Click the Close button in the task pane.

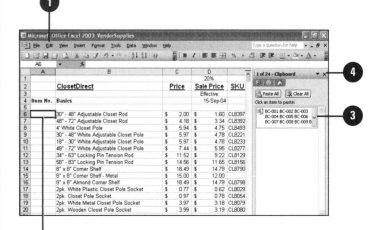

Copying Cell Contents ▶

Microsoft Office Specialist Approved Courseware — XL03S-5-2

You can **copy** and move data on a worksheet from one cell or range to another location on any worksheet in your workbook. When you copy data, a duplicate of the selected cells is placed on the Windows Clipboard. To complete the copy or move, you must **paste** the data stored on the Windows Clipboard in another location. With the Paste Special command, you can control what you want to paste and even perform mathematical operations. To copy or move data without using the Windows Clipboard, you can use a technique called **drag-and-drop**. Drag-and-drop makes it easy to copy or move data short distances on your worksheet.

Copy Data Using the Windows Clipboard

① Select the cell or range that contains the data you want to copy.

② Click the Copy button on the Standard toolbar.

The data in the cells remains in its original location and an outline of the selected cells, called a **marquee**, shows the size of the selection. If you don't want to paste this selection, press Esc to remove the marquee.

③ Click the first cell where you want to paste the data.

④ Click the Paste button on the Standard toolbar.

The data remains on the Clipboard, available for further pasting, until you replace it with another selection.

⑤ If you don't want to paste this selection anywhere else, press Esc to remove the marquee.

Copy Data Using Drag-and-Drop

1. Select the cell or range that contains the data you want to copy.

2. Move the mouse pointer to an edge of the selected cell or range until the pointer changes to an arrowhead.

3. Press and hold the mouse button and Ctrl.

4. Drag the selection to the new location, and then release the mouse button and Ctrl.

Paste Data with Special Results

1. Select the cell or range that contains the data you want to copy.

2. Click the Copy button on the Standard toolbar.

3. Click the first cell where you want to paste the data.

4. Click the Edit menu, and then click Paste Special.

5. Click the option buttons with the paste results and mathematical operations you want.

6. Click OK.

Did You Know?

You can use the Alt key to drag and drop to a different worksheet. Once cells are selected, press and hold Alt, and then drag the selection to the appropriate sheet tab. Release Alt, and then drag the selection to the desired location on the new worksheet.

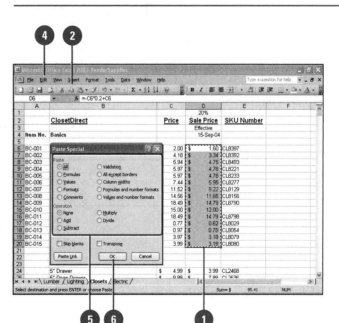

Moving Cell Contents

XL03S-5-2

Unlike copied data, moved data no longer remains in its original location. Perhaps you typed data in a range of cells near the top of a worksheet, but later realized it should appear near the bottom of the sheet. **Moving** data lets you change its location without having to retype it. When you move data, you are cutting the data from its current location and pasting it elsewhere. **Cutting** removes the selected cell or range content from the worksheet and places it on the Windows Clipboard.

Move Data Using the Clipboard

1 Select the cell or range that contains the data you want to move.

2 Click the Cut button on the Standard toolbar.

An outline of the selected cells, called a marquee, shows the size of the selection. If you don't want to paste this selection, press Esc to remove the marquee.

3 Click the top-left cell of the range where you want to paste the data.

4 Click the Paste button on the Standard toolbar.

The marquee disappears. The data is still on the Clipboard and still available for further pasting until you replace it with another selection.

Did You Know?

You can use the Office Clipboard to cut multiple items. When the Clipboard toolbar is displayed, selections you cut can be placed on this clipboard. You can move data to the Clipboard, and then paste it at a later time.

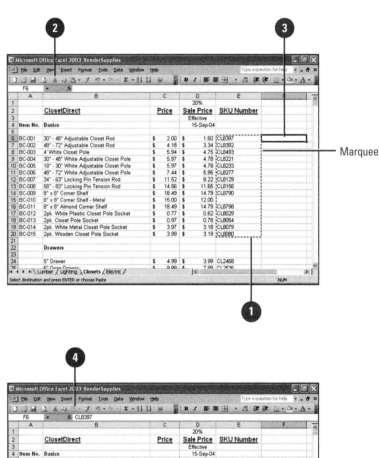

Marquee

Move Data Using Drag-and-Drop

1. Select the cell or range that contains the data you want to move.

2. Move the mouse pointer to an edge of the cell until the pointer changes to an arrowhead.

3. Press and hold the mouse button while dragging the selection to its new location, and then release the mouse button.

Did You Know?

You can reposition the mouse pointer to use drag-and-drop. If the mouse pointer changes to a thick plus sign, reposition the pointer on the edge of the selected range until the pointer changes to an arrowhead.

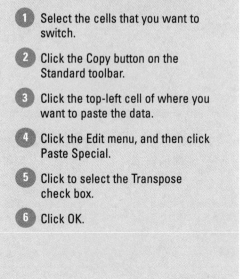

Paste Cells from Rows to Columns or Columns to Rows

1. Select the cells that you want to switch.

2. Click the Copy button on the Standard toolbar.

3. Click the top-left cell of where you want to paste the data.

4. Click the Edit menu, and then click Paste Special.

5. Click to select the Transpose check box.

6. Click OK.

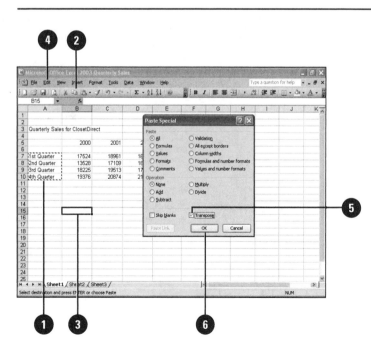

Inserting and Deleting Cell Contents

![Microsoft Office Specialist Approved Courseware] XL03S-5-2

You can **insert** new, blank cells anywhere on the worksheet in order to enter new data or data you forgot to enter earlier. Inserting cells moves the remaining cells in the column or row in the direction of your choice, and Excel adjusts any formulas so they refer to the correct cells. You can also **delete** cells if you find you don't need them; deleting cells shifts the remaining cells to the left or up—just the opposite of inserting cells. When you delete a cell, Excel removes the actual cell from the worksheet.

Insert a Cell

1. Select the cell or cells where you want to insert the new cell(s).

2. Click the Insert menu, and then click Cells.

3. Click the option you want.

   ◆ **Shift Cells Right** to move cells to the right one column.

   ◆ **Shift Cells Down** to move cells down one row.

   ◆ **Entire Row** to move the entire row down one row.

   ◆ **Entire Column** to move entire column over one column.

4. Click OK.

> ### See Also
>
> See "Replace Cell Contents" on page 47 for information on substituting replacement text in a cell.

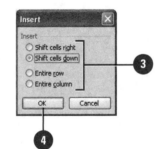

Delete a Cell

1. Select the cell or range you want to delete.

2. Click the Edit menu, and then click Delete.

3. Click the option you want.

   ◆ **Shift Cells Left** to move the remaining cells to the left.

   ◆ **Shift Cells Up** to move the remaining cells up.

   ◆ **Entire Row** to delete the entire row.

   ◆ **Entire Column** to delete the entire column.

4. Click OK.

Did You Know?

There is a difference between deleting a cell and clearing a cell. Deleting a cell is different from clearing a cell: deleting removes the cells from the worksheet; clearing removes only the cell contents, or format, or both.

Finding and Replacing Cell Contents

![Microsoft Office Specialist — Approved Courseware] XL03S-1-2

Find Cell Contents

1. Click at the beginning of the worksheet.

2. Click the Edit menu, and then click Find.

3. Type the text you want to find.

4. Click Find Next until the text you want to locate is highlighted.

    You can click Find Next repeatedly to locate each instance of the cell content.

5. If a message box opens when you reach the end of the worksheet, click OK.

6. Click Close.

The **Find and Replace** commands make it easy to locate or replace specific text or formulas in a document. For example, you might want to find each figure reference in a long report to verify that the proper graphic appears. Or you might want to replace all references to cell A3 in your Excel formulas with cell G3. The Find And Replace dialog boxes vary slightly from one Office program to the next, but the commands work essentially in the same way.

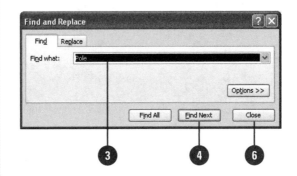

Replace Cell Contents

① Click at the beginning of the worksheet.

② Click the Edit menu, and then click Replace.

③ Type the text you want to search for.

④ Type the text you want to substitute.

⑤ Click Find Next to begin the search, and then select the next instance of the search text.

⑥ Click Replace to substitute the replacement text, or click Replace All to substitute text throughout the entire worksheet.

You can click Find Next to locate the next instance of the cell content without making a replacement.

⑦ If a message box appears when you reach the end of the worksheet, click OK.

⑧ Click Close.

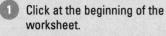

Correcting Cell Contents with AutoCorrect

Excel's **AutoCorrect** feature automatically corrects misspelled words as you type them. AutoCorrect comes with hundreds of text and symbol entries you can edit or remove. Add words and phrases to the AutoCorrect dictionary that you misspell, or add often-typed words and save time by just typing their initials. You could use AutoCorrect to automatically change the initials EPA to Environmental Protection Agency, for example. Use the AutoCorrect Exceptions dialog box to control how Excel handles capital letters.

Add an AutoCorrect Entry

1. Click the Tools menu, and then click AutoCorrect Options.

2. On the AutoCorrect tab, type a misspelled word or an abbreviation.

3. Type the replacement entry.

4. Click Add.

5. Repeat steps 2 through 4 for each entry you want to add.

6. Click OK.

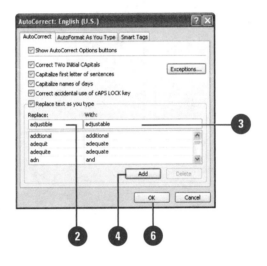

Edit an AutoCorrect Entry

1. Click the Tools menu, and then click AutoCorrect Options.

2. On the AutoCorrect tab, select the AutoCorrect entry you want to change. You can either type the first few letters of the entry to be changed in the Replace box, or scroll to the entry, and then click to select it.

3. Type the replacement entry.

4. Click Replace. If necessary, click Yes to redefine entry.

5. Click OK.

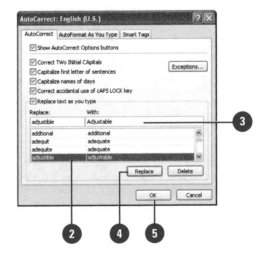

Change AutoCorrect Exceptions

1. Click the Tools menu, and then click AutoCorrect Options.

2. On the AutoCorrect Tab, click Exceptions.

3. Click the First Letter or INitial CAps tab.

   ◆ The First Letter list contains words that end with a (.) but whose following word is never capitalized.

   ◆ The Initial CAps list contains words that have multiple capital letters; adding words to this list means that Excel will not try to correct them.

4. Type the entry you want to add.

5. Click Add, and then click OK.

6. Click OK.

Did You Know?

You can paste data with special exceptions. Click the AutoCorrect Options button, and then choose an option to fit your needs.

Using Smart Tags

Smart Tags help you integrate actions typically performed in other programs directly in Excel. For example, you can insert a financial symbol to get a stock quote, add a person's name and address in a worksheet to the contacts list in Microsoft Outlook, or copy and paste information with added control. Excel analyzes the data you type in a cell and recognizes certain types that it marks with Smart Tags. The types of actions you can take depend on the type of data in the cell with the Smart Tag.

Change Smart Tag Options

1. Click the Tools menu, and then click AutoCorrect options.

2. Click the Smart Tags tab.

3. Select the Label Data With Smart Tags check box.

4. Select the check boxes with the Smart Tags you want.

5. Click the Show Smart Tags As list arrow, and then select a display option.

6. To check the worksheet for new Smart Tags, click Check Workbook.

7. To add more Smart Tags, click More Smart Tags, and then follow the online instructions.

8. Click OK.

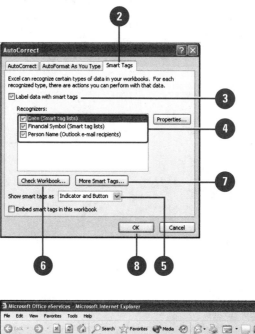

Online resource for Smart Tags

Get a Stock Quote Using a Smart Tag

1. Click a cell where you want to insert a stock quote.

2. Type a recognized financial symbol in capital letters.

3. Click outside the cell, and then point to the purple triangle in the lower-right corner of the cell to display the Smart Tag button. The purple triangle in the corner of a cell indicates a smart tag is available for the cell contents.

4. Click the Smart Tag button, and then click the list arrow next to the button.

5. Click Insert Refreshable Stock Price.

6. Click the On A New Sheet option or the Starting At Cell option , and then click OK.

7. A new worksheet is inserted containing the stock information.

Checking Your Spelling

A worksheet's textual inaccuracies can distract the reader, so it's important that your text be error-free. Excel provides a spelling checker so that you can check the spelling in an entire worksheet. You can even avoid future spelling errors on a worksheet by enabling the AutoCorrect feature to automatically correct words as you type.

Check Spelling

1. Click the Spelling button on the Standard toolbar.

   The Spelling dialog box will open if it comes upon a word it doesn't recognize.

2. If the suggested spelling is unacceptable or you want to use the original word, click Ignore Once or Ignore All.

3. If the suggested spelling is acceptable, click Change or Change All.

4. If you want to add a word to the custom dictionary, click Add To Dictionary.

5. When complete, click OK.

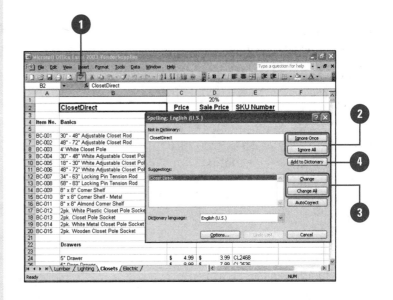

Turn On AutoCorrect

1. Click the Tools menu, and then click AutoCorrect Options.

2. Click the AutoCorrect tab.

3. Click to select the Replace Text As You Type check box.

4. Click OK.

Did You Know?

You can exit our of Spell Checker.
If you want to stop the Spell Checker function at any time, click Cancel.

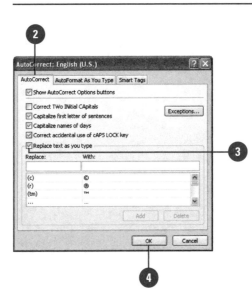

Working with Formulas and Functions

3

Introduction

Once you enter data in a worksheet, you'll want to add formulas to perform calculations. Microsoft Office Excel 2003 can help you get the results you need. Formulas can be very basic entries to more complex ones. The difficulty of the formula depends on the complexity of the result you want from your data. For instance, if you are simply looking to total this months sales, then the formula would add your sales number and provide the result. However, if you were looking to show this months sales, greater than $100.00 with repeat customers, you would take a bit more time to design the formula.

Because Microsoft Excel automatically recalculates formulas, your worksheets remain accurate and up-to-date no matter how often you change the data. Using absolute cell references anchors formulas to a specific cell. Excel provides numerous built-in functions to add to your worksheet calculations. Functions, such as AVERAGE or SUM, allow you to perform a quick formula calculation.

Another way to make your formulas easier to understand is by using name ranges in them. Name ranges—a group of selected cells named as a range—can help you understand your more complicated formulas. It is a lot easier to read a formula that uses name ranges, then to look at the formula and try to decipher it. Excel offers a tool to audit your worksheet. Looking at the "flow" of your formula greatly reduces errors in the calculation. You can see how your formula is built, one level at a time through a series of arrows that point out where the formulas is pulling data from. As you develop your formula, you can make corrections to it.

Creating a Simple Formula

 XL03S-2-3

A **formula** calculates values to return a result. On an Excel worksheet, you can create a formula using values (such as 147 or $10.00), arithmetic operators (shown in the table), and cell references. An Excel formula always begins with the equal sign (=). The equal sign, when entered, automatically formats the cell as a formula entry. By default, only formula results are displayed in a cell, but you can change the view of the worksheet to display formulas instead of results.

Enter a Formula

1. Click the cell where you want to enter a formula.

2. Type = (an equal sign). If you do not begin a formula with an equal sign, Excel will display, not calculate, the information you type.

3. Enter the first **argument**. An argument can be a number or a cell reference.

4. Enter an arithmetic operator.

5. Enter the next argument.

6. Repeat steps 4 and 5 as needed to complete the formula.

7. Click the Enter button on the formula bar, or press Enter.

   Notice that the result of the formula appears in the cell (if you select the cell, the formula itself appears on the formula bar).

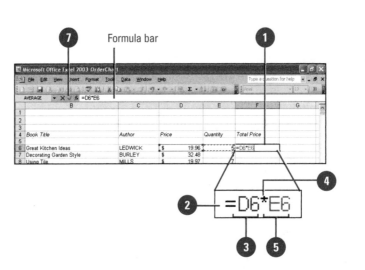

Formula bar

Did You Know?

The best way to start a formula is to have an argument. An argument is the cell references or values in a formula that contribute to the result. Each function uses function-specific arguments, which may include numeric values, text values, cell references, ranges of cells, and so on.

For Your Information

Understanding Order of Precedence

Formulas containing more than one operator follow the order of precedence: exponentiation, multiplication and division, and then addition and subtraction. So, in the formula 5 + 2 * 3, Excel performs multiplication first and addition next for a result of 11. Excel calculates operations within parentheses first. The result of the formula (5 + 2) * 3 is 21.

Display Formulas in Cells

1. Click the Tools menu, and then click Options.

2. Click the View tab.

3. Click to select the Formulas check box.

4. Click OK.

Did You Know?

Pointing to cells reduces errors. When building formulas, pointing to a cell rather than typing its address ensures that the correct cell is referenced.

You can select a cell to enter its address. To avoid careless typing mistakes, click a cell to insert its cell reference in a formula rather than typing its address.

Editing a Formula

Microsoft Office Specialist Approved Courseware — XL03S-2-3

You can edit formulas just as you do other cell contents, using the formula bar or working in the cell. You can select, cut, copy, paste, delete, and format cells containing formulas just as you do cells containing labels or values. Using **AutoFill**, you can quickly copy formulas to adjacent cells. If you need to copy formulas to different parts of a worksheet, use the Office Clipboard.

Edit a Formula Using the Formula Bar

1. Select the cell that contains the formula you want to edit.

2. Press F2 to change to Edit mode.

3. If necessary, use the Home, End, and arrow keys to position the insertion point within the cell contents.

4. Use any combination of Backspace and Delete to erase unwanted characters, and then type new characters as needed.

5. Click the Enter button on the formula bar, or press Enter.

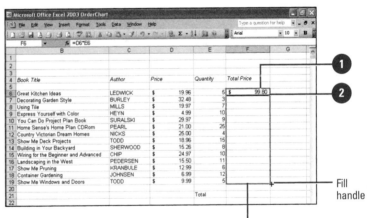

The mode indicator changes to Edit.

Copy a Formula Using AutoFill

1. Select the cell that contains the formula you want to copy.

2. Position the pointer (fill handle) on the lower-right corner of the selected cell.

3. Drag the mouse down until the adjacent cells where you want the formula pasted are selected, and then release the mouse button.

Fill handle

See Also

See "Correcting Formulas" on page 69 for information on correcting errors in a formula.

Copy a Formula Using the Windows Clipboard

1. Select the cell that contains the formula you want to copy.

2. Click the Copy button on the Standard toolbar.

3. Select one or more cells where you want to paste the formula.

4. Click the Paste button on the Standard toolbar.

5. If you don't want to paste this selection anywhere else, press Esc to remove the marquee.

6. Select what type of formatting option you want.

Did You Know?

You can display the Copy button. If the Copy button does not appear on the Standard toolbar, click the Toolbar Options list arrow, and then click the Copy button.

You can use Paste Special to copy only formulas. Select the cells containing the formulas you want to copy, click Copy, click where you want to paste the data, click the Edit menu, click Paste Special, click the Formulas button, and then click OK.

Understanding Cell Referencing

Each cell, the intersection of a column and row on a worksheet, has a unique address, or **cell reference**, based on its column letter and row number. For example, the cell reference for the intersection of column D and row 4 is D4.

Cell References in Formulas

The simplest formula refers to a cell. If you want one cell to contain the same value as another cell, type an equal sign followed by the cell reference, such as =D4. The cell that contains the formula is known as a **dependent cell** because its value depends on the value in another cell. Whenever the cell that the formula refers to changes, the cell that contains the formula also changes.

Depending on your task, you can use either **relative cell references**, which are references to cells relative to the position of the formula, or **absolute cell references**, which are cell references that always refer to cells in a specific location.

Relative Cell References

When you copy and paste or move a formula that uses relative references, the references in the formula change to reflect cells that are in the same relative position to the formula. The formula is the same, but it uses the new cells in its calculation. Relative addressing eliminates the tedium of creating new formulas for each row or column in a worksheet filled with repetitive information.

Absolute Cell References

If you don't want a cell reference to change when you copy a formula, make it an absolute reference by typing a dollar sign ($) before each part of the reference that you don't want to change. You can add a $ before the column letter, the row number, or both. To ensure accuracy and simplify updates, enter constant values (such as tax rates, hourly rates, and so on) in a cell, and then use absolute references to them in formulas.

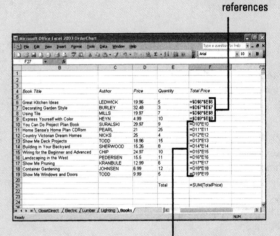

Absolute cell references

Relative cell references

Using Absolute Cell References

Microsoft® Office Specialist Approved Courseware   XL03S-2-3

Use an Absolute Reference

1. Click a cell where you want to enter a formula.

2. Type = (an equal sign) to begin the formula.

3. Select a cell, and then type an arithmetic operator (+, -, *, or /).

4. Select another cell, and then press the F4 key to make that cell reference absolute.

5. If necessary, continue entering the formula.

6. Click the Enter button on the formula bar, or press Enter.

Did You Know?

You can change an absolute reference back to a relative reference. In the cell with the absolute formula, press F4 repeatedly until all the dollar signs are removed from the reference.

When you want a formula to consistently refer to a particular cell, even if you copy or move the formula elsewhere on the worksheet, you need to use an absolute cell reference. An absolute cell reference is a cell address that contains a dollar sign ($) in the row or column coordinate, or both. When you enter a cell reference in a formula, Excel assumes it is a relative reference unless you change it to an absolute reference. If you want part of a formula to remain a relative reference, remove the dollar sign that appears before the column letter or row number.

Even if you move or copy this formula to another location, this cell reference will not change.

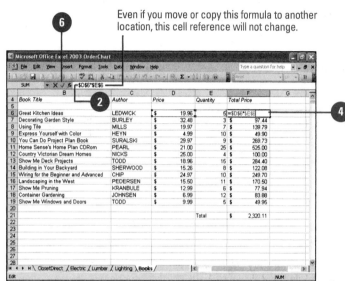

Using Labels for Cell References

Define Label Ranges

1. Select the range containing the row labels you want to reference to cells.

2. Click the Insert menu, point to Name, and then click Label.

   The selected range appears in the Add Label Range box and the Row Labels option is selected.

3. Click Add.

4. Click OK.

Did You Know?

What happens when you zoom in on a label? When you zoom the view of the worksheet to 39 percent or less, Excel adds a blue border around the labels you have created. The blue border does not print.

Many worksheets use labels above columns and to the left of rows. You can use the labels on your worksheet instead of cell addresses to reference cells. You can point to cells to add their labels to a formula. However, before you can point to a cell to use its label, you have to define a **label range**. A label range is the group of row and column labels that you want to use in your formulas. When you define a label range, Excel assigns the row and column labels to the cells.

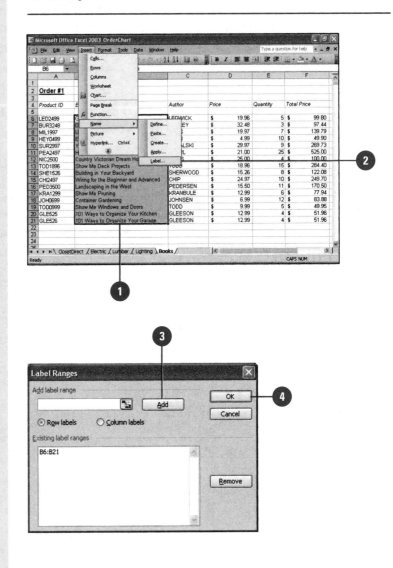

Remove a Label Range

1. Click the Insert menu, point to Name, and then click Label.

2. Click to select the existing label range you want to remove.

3. Click Remove.

4. Click OK.

Did You Know?

What happens when you change a label reference? If you change the name of a reference label, Excel automatically makes the same change to every formula in which the name is used.

You can label names that are relative. When you use a label name in a formula or function, Excel sees it as a relative reference. You can copy the formula to other cells, or use AutoFill to copy it and the reference changes.

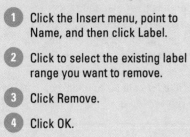

3

Naming Cells and Ranges

To make working with ranges easier, Excel allows you to name them. The name *BookTitle*, for example, is easier to remember than the range reference B6:B21. Named ranges can be used to navigate large worksheets. Named ranges can also be used in formulas instead of typing or pointing to specific cells. If the cell or range you want to name has labels, you can have Excel automatically name the cell or range for you. If you have already entered a cell or range address in a formula or function, you can apply a name to the address instead of re-creating it.

Name a Cell or Range

1. Select the cell or range you want to name.

2. Click the Name box on the formula bar.

3. Type a name for the range. A range name can include uppercase or lowercase letters, numbers, and punctuation, but no spaces. Try to use a simple name that reflects the type of information in the range, such as *BookTitle*.

4. Press Enter. The range name will appear in the Name box whenever you select the range.

Select a Named Cell or Range

1. Click the Name box list arrow on the formula bar.

2. Click the name of the cell or range you want to use.

   The range name appears in the Name box, and all cells included in the range are highlighted on the worksheet.

Let Excel Name a Cell or Range

1. Select the cells, including the column or row header, you want to name.

2. Click the Insert menu, point to Name, and then click Create.

3. Select the check box with the position of the labels in relation to the cells.

   Excel automatically tries to determine the position of the labels, so you might not have to change any options.

4. Click OK.

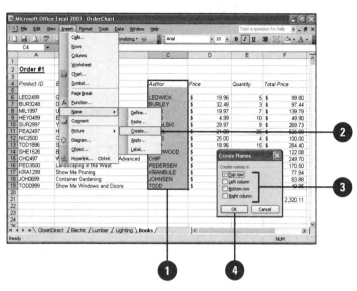

Apply a Name to a Cell or Range Address

1. Select the cells in which you want to apply a name.

2. Click the Insert menu, point to Name, and then click Apply.

3. Click the names you want to apply.

4. Click OK.

Did You Know?

Should I select the Use Row And Column Names option? When you select this option, Excel uses the range row and column headings to refer to the range you've selected (if a cell does not have its own name but is part of a named range).

You can delete a name range. Click the Insert menu, point to Name, click Define, select the range name, and then click Delete.

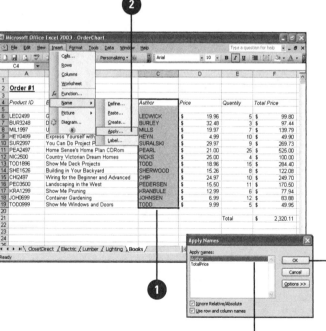

Simplifying a Formula with Ranges

XL03S-2-3, XL03E-1-14

You can simplify formulas by using ranges and range names. For example, if 12 cells on your worksheet contain monthly budget amounts, and you want to multiply each amount by 10%, you can insert one range address in a formula instead of inserting 12 different cell addresses, or you can insert a range name. Using a range name in a formula helps to identify what the formula does; the formula =TotalOrder*0.10, for example, is more meaningful than =SUM(F6:F19)*0.10.

Use a Range in a Formula

1. Put your cursor where you would like the formula. Type an equal sign =SUM(.

2. Click the first cell of the range, and then drag to select the last cell in the range. Excel enters the range address for you.

3. Complete the formula by entering a close parentheses, or another function, and then click the Enter button.

Use a Range Name in a Formula

1. Put your cursor where you would like the formula. Type an equal sign =SUM(.

2. Press F3 to display a list of named ranges.

3. Click the name of the range you want to insert.

4. Click OK.

5. Complete the formula by entering a close parentheses, or another function, and then click the Enter button.

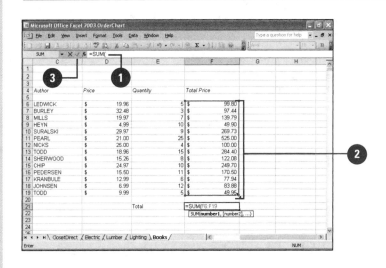

Displaying Calculations with AutoCalculate

You can simplify your work using a feature called **AutoCalculate** when you don't want to insert a formula, but you want to see the results of a simple calculation quickly. Auto-Calculate automatically displays the sum, average, maximum, minimum, or count of the selected values on the status bar. Auto-Calculate results do not appear on the worksheet when printed but are useful for giving you quick answers while you work.

Calculate a Range Automatically

①   Select the range of cells you want to calculate.

The sum of the selected cells appears on the status bar next to SUM=.

②   If you want to change the type of calculation AutoCalculate performs, right-click anywhere on the status bar to open the AutoCalculate sub menu.

③   Click the type of calculation you want.

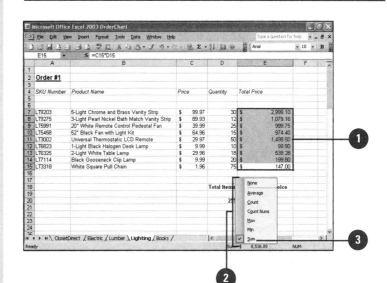

3

Calculating Totals with AutoSum

XL03E-1-1

A range of cells can be easily added using the **AutoSum** button on the Standard toolbar. AutoSum suggests the range to sum, although this range can be changed if it's incorrect. AutoSum looks at all of the data that is consecutively entered, and when it sees an empty cell, that is where the AutoSum stops. Subtotals can be calculated for data ranges using the Tools menu and the Subtotals dialog box. This dialog box lets you select where the subtotals occur, as well as the function type.

Calculate Totals with AutoSum

1. Click the cell where you want to display the calculation.

2. Click the AutoSum button on the Standard toolbar.

3. Click the Enter button on the formula bar, or press Enter.

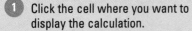

Calculate with Extended AutoSum

1. Click the cell where you want to display the calculation.

2. Click the AutoSum list arrow on the Standard toolbar.

3. Click the function you want to use.

4. Press Enter to accept the range selected.

Calculate Subtotals and Totals

1. Click anywhere within the data to be subtotaled.

2. Click the Data menu, and then click Subtotals.

   If a message box appears, read the message, and then click the appropriate button.

3. Click to select the appropriate check boxes to specify how the data is subtotaled.

4. Click OK.

Did You Know?

You can select additional AutoFill commands. Click the Edit menu, and then click Fill to select additional commands such as Up, Down, Left, Right, Series, or Justify.

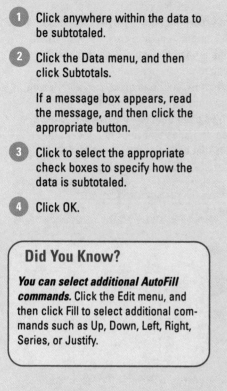

Correcting Calculation Errors

When Excel finds a possible error in a calculation, it displays a green triangle in the upper left corner of the cell. If Excel can't complete a calculation it displays an error message, such as "#DIV/0!". You can use the Error smart tag to help you fix the problem. In a complex worksheet, it can be difficult to understand the relationships between cells and formulas. Auditing tools enable you to clearly determine these relationships. When the Auditing feature is turned on, it uses a series of arrows to show you which cells are part of which formulas. When you use the auditing tools, tracer arrows point out cells that provide data to formulas and the cells that contain formulas that refer to the cells. A box is drawn around the range of cells that provide data to formulas.

Review and Correct Errors

1. Select a cell that contains a green triangle in the upper left corner.

2. Click the Error Smart Tag button.

3. Click one of the troubleshooting options (menu options vary depending on the error).

   ◆ To have Excel fix the error, click one of the available options specific to the error.

   ◆ To find out more about an error, click Help On This Error.

   ◆ To remove the error alert, click Ignore Error.

   ◆ To fix the error manually, click Edit In Formula Bar.

Did You Know?

You can check for errors in the entire worksheet. Click the Tools menu, and then click Error Checking.

You can change error checking options. Click the Tools menu, click Options, click the Error Checking tab, select or clear the options you want to change, and then click OK.

Correcting Formulas

Excel has several tools to help you find and correct problems with formulas. One tool is the **Watch window** and another is the **Error checker**. The Watch window keeps track of cells and their formulas as you make changes to a worksheet. Excel uses an error check in the same way Microsoft Word uses a grammar checker. The Error checker uses certain rules, such as using the wrong argument type, a number stored as text or an empty cell reference, to check for problems in formulas.

Watch Cells and Formulas

1. Select the cells you want to watch.

2. Click the Tools menu, point to Formula Auditing, and then click Show Watch Window.

3. Click the Add Watch button on the Watch Window dialog box.

4. Click Add.

5. Click Close.

Correct Errors

1. Open the worksheet where you want to check for errors.

2. Click the Tools menu, click Options, click the Error Checking tab, select the Enable Background Error Checking check box, select the Rules check boxes in which you want to check, and then click OK.

3. Click the Tools menu, and then click Error Checking. The error check scans the worksheet for errors, generating the Error Checker dialog box every time it encounters an error.

4. Choose a button to correct or ignore the problem.

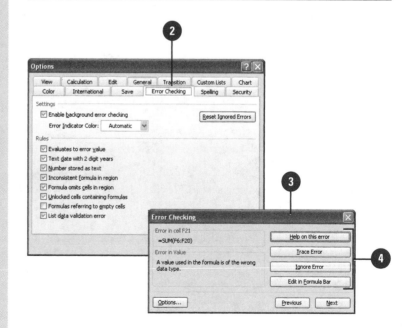

Auyditing a Worksheet

XL03E-1-11

In a complex worksheet, it can be difficult to understand the relationships between cells and formulas. Auditing tools enable you to clearly determine these relationships. When the **Auditing** feature is turned on, it uses a series of arrows to show you which cells are part of which formulas. When you use the auditing tools, **tracer arrows** point out cells that provide data to formulas and the cells that contain formulas that refer to the cells. A box is drawn around the range of cells that provide data to formulas.

Trace Worksheet Relationships

1. Click the Tools menu, point to Formula Auditing, and then click Show Formula Auditing Toolbar.

   ◆ **Trace Precedents** To find cells that provide data to a formula.

   ◆ **Trace Dependents** To find out which formulas refer to a cell.

   ◆ **Trace Error** To locate the problem if a formula displays an error value, such as #DIV/0!.

   ◆ **Remove Precedent Arrows, Remove Dependent Arrows, or Remove All Arrows** To remove precedent and dependent arrows.

2. Click OK to locate the problem.

Did You Know?

You can circle invalid data. To circle invalid data in a formula, click the Circle Invalid Data button on the Formula Auditing toolbar. Click the Clear Validation Circles button to clear the circles.

Formula Auditing Toolbar

Performing Calculations Using Functions

XL03S-2-4

Functions are predesigned formulas that save you the time and trouble of creating commonly used or complex equations. Excel includes hundreds of functions that you can use alone or in combination with other formulas or functions. Functions perform a variety of calculations, from adding, averaging, and counting to more complicated tasks, such as calculating the monthly payment amount of a loan. You can enter a function manually if you know its name and all the required arguments, or you can easily insert a function using the Paste Function feature.

Enter a Function

1. Click the cell where you want to enter the function.

2. Type = (an equal sign), type the name of the function, and then type ((an opening parenthesis). For example, to insert the AVERAGE function, type *=AVERAGE(*.

3. Type the argument or select the cell or range you want to insert in the function.

4. Click the Enter button on the formula bar, or press Enter.

   Excel will automatically add the closing parenthesis to complete the function.

See Also

See "Displaying Calculations with AutoCalculate" on page 65 for information on getting the results of a simple calculation quickly.

Commonly Used Excel Functions

Function	Description	Sample
SUM	Displays the sum of the argument	=SUM(argument)
AVERAGE	Displays the average value in the argument	=AVERAGE(argument)
COUNT	Calculates the number of values in the argument	=COUNT(argument)
PMT	Determines the monthly payment of a loan	=PMT(argument)

Creating Functions

XL03S-2-4

Trying to write a formula that calculates various pieces of data, such as calculating payments for an investment over a period of time at a certain rate, can be difficult and time-consuming. The **Insert Function** feature simplifies the process by organizing Excel's built-in formulas, called functions, into categories so they are easy to find and use. A function defines all the necessary components (also called arguments) you need to produce a specific result; all you have to do is supply the values, cell references, and other variables. You can even combine one or more functions if necessary.

Enter a Function Using Insert Function

1. Click the cell where you want to enter the function.

2. Click the Insert Function button on the Formula bar.

3. Click a function category you want to use.

4. Click a function you want to use.

5. Click OK.

6. Enter the cell addresses in the text boxes. Type them or click the Collapse Dialog button to the right of the text box, select the cell or range using your mouse, and then click the Expand Dialog button.

   In many cases, the Insert Function might try to "guess" which cells you want to include in the function.

7. Click OK.

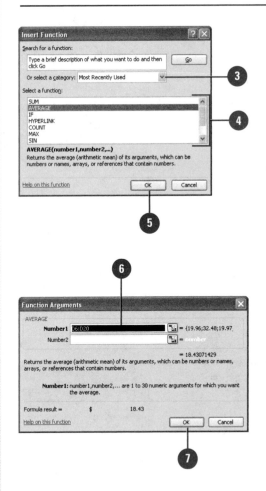

Modifying Worksheets and Workbooks

Introduction

At times, you'll need to reorganize a workbook by adding additional worksheets, moving their appearance order within the workbook, or even deleting an unused or outdated worksheet. You can rename worksheets to better show the theme of your workbook. When using your workbook, there may be times when you'll want to hide certain worksheets due to sensitive or confidential information. You can also freeze the column and row headings to ease viewing a long list of data.

On any worksheet, you can insert and delete cells, rows, and columns. You can adjust column width and row height so that you can structure the worksheet exactly the way you want. It's easy to make changes because Microsoft Office Excel 2003 updates cell references in existing formulas as necessary whenever you modify a worksheet and recalculates formulas automatically to ensure that the results are always up-to-date.

You can create a template to have a consistent worksheet to use each month. Microsoft Excel also comes with a variety of pre-made templates that you can use for your own use. Formatting, formulas and other settings are already set up, so that you can begin working on the task at hand. These templates can be customized to meet your own business or personal needs.

Selecting and Naming a Worksheet

XL03S-3-4, XL03S-5-4

Each new workbook opens with three **worksheets** (or sheets), in which you store and analyze values. You can work in the active, or selected, worksheet. The default worksheet names are Sheet1, Sheet2, and Sheet3, which appear on the sheet tab, like file folder labels. As you create a worksheet, give it a meaningful name to help you remember its contents. The sheet tab size adjusts to fit the name's length. If you work on a project that requires more than three worksheets, add additional sheets to the workbook so all related information is stored in one workbook.

Select a Worksheet

1. If necessary, click a sheet tab scroll button to display other tabs.

2. Click a sheet tab to make it the active worksheet.

3. To select multiple worksheets, press and hold Ctrl as you click other sheet tabs.

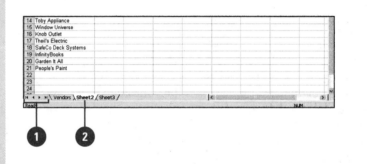

Name a Worksheet

1. Double-click the sheet tab you want to name.

2. Type a new name.

3. Press Enter.

Did You Know?

You can use a short tab name. Because the size of a sheet tab enlarges to accommodate a longer name, using short names means more sheet tabs will be visible.

You can change the color of the sheet tab names. By right-clicking the sheet tab of the worksheet you want, and selecting Select Tab Color from the pop-up menu, you can choose a different color.

Inserting and Deleting a Worksheet

XL03S-5-4

You can add or delete sheets in a workbook. If, for example, you are working on a project that requires more than three worksheets, you can insert additional sheets in one workbook rather than open multiple workbooks. You can insert as many sheets in a workbook as you want. If, on the other hand, you are using only one or two sheets in a workbook, you can delete the unused sheets to save disk space. Before you delete a sheet from a workbook, make sure you don't need the data. You cannot undo the deletion.

Insert a Worksheet

1 Click the sheet tab to the right of where you want to insert the new sheet.

2 Click the Insert menu, and then click Worksheet.

A new worksheet is inserted to the left of the selected worksheet.

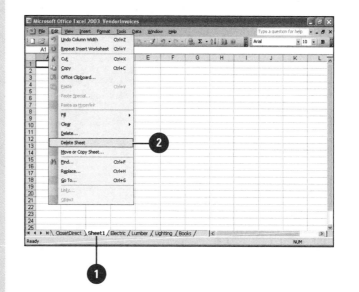

Delete a Worksheet

1 Click the sheet tab of the worksheet you want to delete.

2 Click the Edit menu, and then click Delete Sheet.

Did You Know?

You can hide a worksheet. Click the sheet tab you want to hide, click the Format menu, point to Sheet, and then click Hide. To unhide a worksheet, click the Format menu, point to Sheet, click Unhide, select the worksheet you want to unhide, and then click OK.

4

Moving and Copying a Worksheet

XL03S-5-4

Move a Worksheet Within a Workbook

1 Click the sheet tab of the worksheet you want to move, and then hold down the mouse button.

2 When the mouse pointer changes to a sheet of paper, drag it to the right of the sheet tab where you want to move the worksheet.

3 Release the mouse button.

Did You Know?

You can use the Create A Copy check box to move a worksheet. Clear the Create A Copy check box in the Move Or Copy dialog box to move a worksheet rather than copy it.

You can give your worksheet a different background. Click the tab of the sheet on which you want to insert a background, click the Format menu, point to Sheet, and then click Background. Select the picture you want to use as a background, and then click Insert.

After adding several sheets to a workbook, you might want to reorganize them. You can arrange sheets in chronological order or in order of their importance. You can easily move or copy a sheet within a workbook or to a different open workbook. Copying a worksheet is easier and often more convenient then re-entering similar information on a new sheet. If you are moving or copying a worksheet a short distance, you should use the mouse. For longer distances, you should use the Move Or Copy Sheet command on the Edit menu.

Copy a Worksheet

1. Click the sheet tab of the worksheet you want to copy.

   TIMESAVER *Press and hold the Ctrl key while you drag a sheet name to copy a worksheet.*

2. Click the Edit menu, and then click Move Or Copy Sheet.

3. If you want to copy the sheet to another open workbook, click the To Book list arrow, and then select the name of that workbook. The sheets of the selected workbook appear in the Before Sheet list.

   TROUBLE? *If the workbook you want to copy to does not show up in the To Book drop-down list, you must first open the other workbook.*

4. Click a sheet name in the Before Sheet list. Excel inserts the copy to the left of this sheet.

5. Select the Create A Copy check box.

6. Click OK.

Did You Know?

You can copy or move a sheet to a different workbook. You must first open the other workbook, and then switch back to the workbook of the sheet you want to copy or move.

You can use groups to affect multiple worksheets. Click a sheet tab, press and hold Shift, and click another sheet tab to group worksheets. Right-click a grouped sheet tab, and then click Ungroup Sheet on the shortcut menu.

Hiding and Unhiding Worksheets and Workbooks

XL03S-3-4, XL03S-5-6

Not all worksheets and workbooks should be available to everyone. You can hide sensitive information without deleting it by hiding selected worksheets or workbooks. For example, if you want to share a workbook with others, but it includes confidential employee salaries, you can simply hide a worksheet. Hiding worksheets does not affect calculations in the other worksheets; all data in hidden worksheets is still referenced by formulas as necessary. Hidden worksheets do not appear in a printout either. When you need the data, you can unhide the sensitive information.

Hide or Unhide a Worksheet

◆ **Hide.** Click the sheet tab you want to hide, click the Format menu, point to Sheet, and then click Hide.

◆ **Unhide.** Click the Format menu, point to Sheet, click Unhide, select the worksheet you want to unhide, and then click OK.

Click to hide or unhide a worksheet.

Hide or Unhide a Workbook

◆ **Hide.** Open the workbook you want to hide, click the Window menu, and then click Hide.

◆ **Unhide.** Click the Window menu, click Unhide, select the workbook you want to unhide, and then click OK.

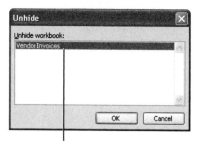

Select a workbook to unhide it.

Selecting a Column or Row

You can select one or more columns or rows in a worksheet in order to apply formatting attributes, insert or delete columns or rows, or perform other group actions. The header buttons above each column and to the left of each row indicate the letter or number of the column or row. You can select multiple columns or rows even if they are non-contiguous—that is, not next to one another in the worksheet.

Select a Column or Row

1. Click the column or row header button of the column or row you want to select.

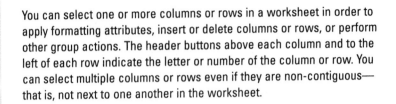

Select Multiple Columns or Rows

1. Drag the mouse over the header buttons of any contiguous columns or rows you want to select.

2. To select non-contiguous columns or rows, press and hold Ctrl while clicking each additional column or row header button.

Did You Know?

You can select the entire worksheet quickly. Click the Select All button located above the row number 1 and the left of column A.

Hiding and Unhiding a Column or Row

XL03S-3-3

Not all the data on a worksheet should be available to everyone. You can hide sensitive information without deleting it by hiding selected columns or rows. For example, if you want to share a worksheet with others, but it includes confidential employee salaries, you can simply hide the salary column. Hiding columns and rows does not affect calculations in a worksheet; all data in hidden columns and rows is still referenced by formulas as necessary. Hidden columns and rows do not appear in a printout either. When you need the data, you can unhide the sensitive information.

Hide a Column or Row

1. Click the column or row header button of the column or row you want to hide. (Drag to select multiple header buttons to hide more than one column or row.)

2. Click the Format menu, point to Column or Row, and then click Hide.

Header button

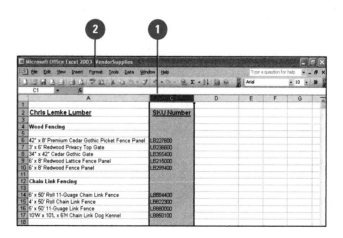

Unhide a Column or Row

1. Drag to select the column or row header buttons on either side of the hidden column or row.

2. Click the Format menu, point to Column or Row, and then click Unhide.

4

Inserting a Column or Row

XL03S-3-3

You can insert blank columns and rows between existing data, without disturbing your worksheet. Excel repositions existing cells to accommodate the new columns and rows and adjusts any existing formulas so that they refer to the correct cells. Formulas containing absolute cell references will need to be adjusted to the new columns or rows. When you insert one or more columns, they insert to the left. When you add one or more rows, they are inserted above the selected row.

Insert a Column or Row

 Click to the right of the location of the new column you want to insert.

To insert a row, click the row immediately below the location of the row you want to insert.

② Click the Insert menu, and then click Columns or Rows.

Insert Multiple Columns or Rows

① Drag to select the column header buttons for the number of columns you want to insert.

To insert multiple rows, drag to select the row header buttons for the number of rows you want to insert.

② Click the Insert menu, and then click Columns or Rows.

Deleting a Column or Row

At some point in time, you may want to remove an entire column or row of data from a worksheet rather than deleting or editing individual cells. You can delete columns and rows just as easily as you insert them. Formulas will need to be checked in your worksheet prior to deleting a row or column, especially when referencing absolute cell addresses. Remaining columns and rows move to the left or up to join the other remaining data.

Delete a Column or Row

1. Select the column header button or row header button that you want to delete.

2. Click the Edit menu, and then click Delete.

See Also

See "Hiding and Unhiding a Column or Row" on page 81 for information on hiding data without deleting it.

Delete Multiple Columns or Rows

1. Select the columns header buttons or rows header buttons that you want to delete.

2. Click the Edit menu, and then click Delete.

Did You Know?

You can re-check your formulas. When deleting columns or rows that are referenced in a formula, it is important to adjust your formula for recalculations.

Adjusting Column Width and Row Height

![Microsoft Office Specialist Approved Courseware] XL03S-3-3

You've entered labels and values, constructed formulas, and even formatted the cells, but now some of your data isn't visible; the value displays as #### in the cell. Also, some larger-sized labels are cut off. You can narrow or widen each column width to fit its contents and adjust your row heights as needed. As you build your worksheet, you can change the default width of some columns or the default height of some rows to accommodate long strings of data or larger font sizes. You can manually adjust column or row size to fit data you have entered, or you can use AutoFit to resize a column or row to the width or height of its largest entry.

Adjust Column Width or Row Height

1. Click the column or row header button for the first column or row you want to adjust.

2. If you want, drag to select more columns or rows.

3. Right-click the selected column(s) or row(s), and then click Column Width or Row Height.

4. Type a new column width or row height in points.

5. Click OK.

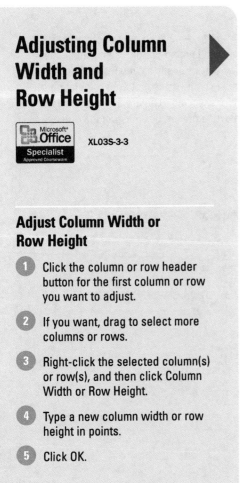

Adjust Column Width or Row Height Using the Mouse

1. Position the mouse pointer on the right edge of the column header button or the bottom edge of the row header button for the column or row you want to change.

2. When the mouse pointer changes to a double-headed arrow, click and drag the pointer to a new width or height.

Change Column Width or Row Height Using AutoFit

1. Position the mouse pointer on the right edge of the column header button or the bottom edge of the row header button for the column or row you want to change.

2. When the mouse pointer changes to a double-headed arrow, double-click the mouse.

Did You Know?

You can correctly position the mouse pointer when adjusting a column's width or height. Position the mouse pointer between the header buttons of the column to be resized and the column to its right. To adjust the height, position the mouse pointer between the header button of the row to be resized and the row below it

What is a point? A point is a measurement unit used to size text and space on a worksheet. One inch equals 72 points.

Freezing a Column or Row

XL03S-5-6

Large worksheets can be difficult to work with, especially on low-resolution or small monitor screens. If you scroll down to see the bottom of the list, you can no longer see the column names at the top of the list. Instead of repeatedly scrolling up and down, you can temporarily set, or **freeze**, those column or row headings so that you can see them no matter where you scroll in the list. When you freeze a row or column, you are actually splitting the screen into one or more **panes** (window sections) and freezing one of the panes. You can split the screen into up to four panes and can freeze up to two of these panes. You can edit the data in a frozen pane just as you do any Excel data, but the cells remain stationary even when you use the scroll bars; only the unfrozen part of the screen scrolls.

Freeze a Column or Row

1. Select the column to the right of the columns you want to freeze, or select the row below the rows you want to freeze.

   To freeze both, click the cell to the right and below of the column and row you want to freeze.

2. Click the Window menu, and then click Freeze Panes.

   ◆ When you freeze a pane horizontally, all the rows **above** the active cell freeze. When you freeze a pane vertically, all the columns to the **left** of the active cell freeze.

   ◆ When you freeze a pane, it has no effect on how a worksheet looks when printed.

Unfreeze a Column or Row

1. Click the Window menu.

2. Click Unfreeze Panes.

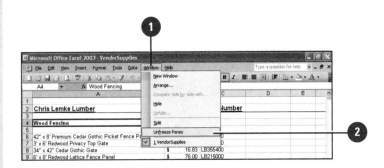

Splitting a Worksheet in Panes

 XL03S-5-6

If you are working on a large worksheet, it can be time consuming and tiring to scroll back and forth between two parts of the worksheet. You can split the worksheet into four panes and two scrollable windows that you can view simultaneously but edit and scroll independently. As you work in two parts of the same worksheet, you can resize the window panes to fit your task. Drag the split bar between the panes to resize the windows. No matter how you display worksheets, Excel's commands and buttons work the same as usual.

Split a Worksheet in Panes

◆ **Split.** Click the Window menu, and then click Split.

◆ **Remove Split.** Click the Window menu, and then click Remove Split.

Did You Know?

You can search for a value or data in a cell, and then replace it with different content. Click the cell or cells containing content you want to replace. Click the Edit menu, click Find, and then click the Replace tab for additional options.

Click to split
the worksheet

Worksheet split
into four panes

Scroll panes
separately.

4

Creating a Template

You can create your own template as easily as you create a worksheet. Like those that come with Excel, custom templates can save you time. Perhaps each month you create an inventory worksheet in which you can enter repetitive information; all that changes is the actual data. By creating your own template, you have a custom form that is ready for completion each time you take inventory.

Create a Template

1 Enter all the necessary information in a new workbook—including formulas, labels, graphics, and formatting.

2 Click the File menu, and then click Save As.

3 Click the Save In list arrow, and then select a location for the template.

To have your new template appear in the Spreadsheet Solutions tab of the New dialog box, select the location C:/Program/Files/ Microsoft Office/Templates/ Spreadsheet Solutions.

4 Type a file name that will clearly identify the purpose of the template.

5 Click the Save As Type list arrow.

6 Click Template.

7 Click Save.

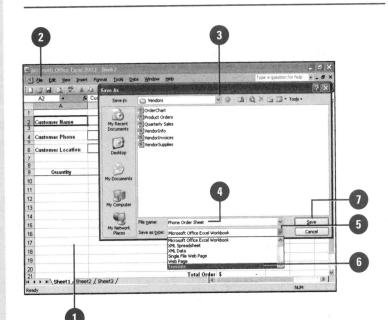

Did You Know?

The difference between macros and templates. Create a macro to make repetitive tasks more efficient; create a template for fill-in-the-blank data whose format rarely changes.

You can test your template as you work. As you create a template, enter fake data in it to make sure the formulas work correctly.

Opening a Template

XL03E-4-4

You may not realize it, but every workbook you create is based on a template. When you start a new workbook without specifying a template, Excel creates a new workbook based on the **default template**, which includes three worksheets and no special formulas, labels, or formatting. When you specify a particular template in the New dialog box, whether it's one supplied by Excel or one you created yourself, Excel starts a new workbook that contains the formulas, labels, graphics, and formatting contained in that template. The template itself does not change when you enter data in the new workbook, because you are working on a new file, not with the template file.

Open a Template

1. Click the Open button on the Standard toolbar.

2. Click the Look In list arrow, and then select the drive and folder that contain the template you want to open.

3. Click the Files Of Type list arrow, and then click Templates.

4. Click the file name of the template you want open.

5. Click Open.

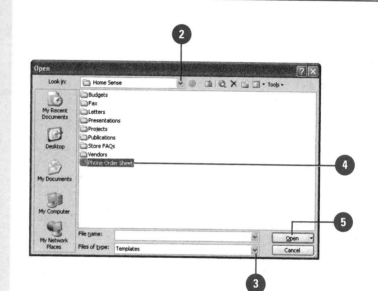

Did You Know?

Changing the default template affects all new workbooks you create. If you decide to make any changes to the template, you must do a File, Save As to ensure that the original template is not adjusted.

You can modify a template. If you want to make changes to an existing template so that all new workbooks incorporate the change, open the actual template—not a copy—and then make your changes. Be sure to save your modified template.

Changing a Template

Microsoft Excel has a selection of premade templates designed for you to use or customize. You can also make changes to the existing templates that you have created. Be aware that as you customize a template, you are changing that template to be the new default. If you don't want to change the original, try a Save As to create a new template from the original.

Change an Excel Template

1. Click the File menu, and then click New.

2. Click On My Computer.

3. Click the Spreadsheet Solutions tab.

4. Click the template you want to change, and then click OK.

5. To change (customize) the template, click the Tools menu, click Protection, and then click Unprotect Sheet.

   You are now able to change the template by inserting graphics, changing labels, values, or formulas, or customizing the template to be company specific.

6. Make the changes you want.

7. Click the File menu, and then click Save As.

8. Select the Save In list arrow, and then choose where you want to save the customized template.

   The file type defaults to template.

9. Type the new file name.

10. Click Save.

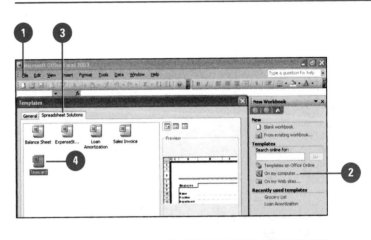

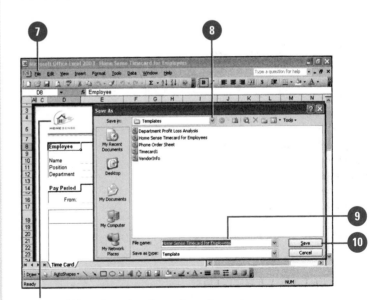

Inserted Home Sense logo for employee timecard

Formatting a Worksheet

Introduction

Microsoft Office Excel 2003 offers several tools for making your worksheets look more attractive and professional. Without formatting, a worksheet can look like a sea of meaningless data. To highlight important information, you can change the appearance of selected numbers and text by adding dollar signs, commas, and other numerical formats or by applying attributes, such as boldface, italics, and underline.

Once you've set up your worksheet, additional changes are available to customize your worksheets look. You can change the default font and font size, or maybe you'd like to adjust the alignment of data in cells. In addition to column, row, or font changes, you can add colors to cells or fonts, and include patterns to cells. You can also add borders around columns of data to help group them visually, or even add some clip art, a company logo, or some pictures.

By using AutoFormats and styles to apply multiple changes, you can speed up the formatting process and ensure a greater degree of consistency among your worksheets. You can use the Find and Replace Formatting feature to find the various formatting attributes and change them.

Formatting Text and Numbers

XL03S-3-1, XL03E-2-1

You can change the appearance of the data in the cells of a worksheet without changing the actual value in the cell. You can format text and numbers with **font attributes**, such as bolding, italics, or underlining, to enhance data to catch the reader's attention. You can also apply **numeric formats** to numbers to better reflect the type of information they represent—dollar amounts, dates, decimals, and so on. For example, you can format a number to display up to 15 decimal places or none at all. If you don't see the number format you need, you can create a custom one.

Format Text Quickly

1. Select a cell or range with the text you want to format.

2. Click one of the buttons on the Formatting toolbar to apply that attribute to the selected range:

   - Bold
   - Italic
   - Underline

3. Click the Font or Font Size list arrow, and then select a font or size.

   You can apply multiple attributes to the range.

Did You Know?

You can remove a numeric format or font attribute quickly. The buttons on the Formatting toolbar are toggle buttons, which means you simply click to turn them on and off. To add or remove a numeric format or a font attribute, select the cell, range, or text, and then click the appropriate button on the Formatting toolbar to turn the format or attribute off.

You can format numbers in international currencies. In the Format Cells dialog box, click the Number tab, click Currency in the Category list, click the Symbol list arrow, and then click an international currency symbol.

Formatting Toolbar Buttons

Button	Name	Example
B	Bold	**Excel**
I	Italic	*Excel*
U	Underline	Excel
$	Currency Style	$5,432.10
%	Percent Style	54.32%
,	Comma Style	5,432.10
+.0 / .00	Increase Decimal	5,432.10 becomes 5,432.100
.00 / +.0	Decrease Decimal	5,432.10 becomes 5,432.1

Format Numbers Quickly

1. Select a cell or range that contains the number(s) you want to format.

2. Click one of the buttons on the Formatting toolbar to apply that attribute to the selected range.

   ◆ Currency Style

   ◆ Percent Style

   ◆ Comma Style

   ◆ Increase Decimal

   ◆ Decrease Decimal

   You can apply multiple attributes to the range.

Format a Number Using the Format Cells Dialog Box

1. Select a cell or range that contains the number(s) you want to format.

2. Click the Format menu, and then click Cells.

3. Click the Number tab.

4. Click to select a category.

5. Select the options you want to apply.

   To create a custom format, click Custom, type the number format code, and then use one of the existing codes as a starting point.

6. Preview your selections in the Sample box.

7. Click OK.

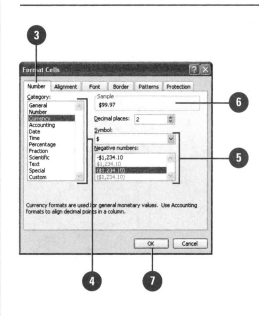

Designing Conditional Formatting

You can make your worksheets more powerful by setting up conditional formatting. **Conditional formatting** lets the value of a cell determine its formatting. For example, you might want this year's sales total to be displayed in red and italics if it's less than last year's total, but in green and bold if it's more. The formatting is applied to the cell values only if the values meet the a condition that you specify. Otherwise, no conditional formatting is applied to the cell values.

Establish a Conditional Format

1. Select a cell or range you want to conditionally format.

2. Click the Format menu, and then click Conditional Formatting.

3. Select the operator and values you want for condition 1.

4. Click the Format button, select the attributes you want applied, and then click OK.

5. Click Add to include additional conditions, and then repeat steps 3 and 4.

6. Click OK.

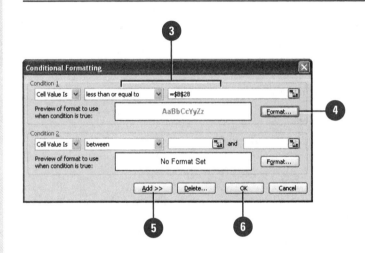

Delete a Conditional Format

1. Click the Format menu, and then click Conditional Formatting.

2. Click Delete.

3. Select the check box for the condition(s) you want to delete.

4. Click OK.

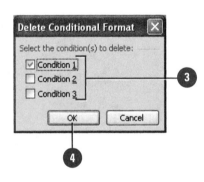

See Also

See "Formatting Data with Auto Format" on page 106 for information on formatting data more efficiently.

Copying Cell Formats

After formatting a cell on a worksheet, you might want to apply those same formatting changes to other cells on the worksheet. For example, you might want each subtotal on your worksheet to be formatted in italic, bold, 12-point Times New Roman, with a dollar sign, commas, and two decimal places. Rather than selecting each subtotal and applying the individual formatting to each cell, you can **paint** (that is, copy) the formatting from one cell to others.

Copy a Cell Format

1. Select a cell or range containing the formatting you want to copy.

2. Click the Format Painter button on the Standard toolbar. If necessary, click the Toolbar Options list arrow to display the button.

3. Drag to select the cell(s) you want to paint. When you release the mouse button, the cells appear with the new formatting.

Did You Know?

You can use the Esc key to cancel format painting. If you change your mind about painting a format, cancel the marquee by pressing Esc.

Changing Fonts

A **font** is a collection of alphanumeric characters that share the same **typeface**, or design, and have similar characteristics. Most fonts are available in a number of styles (such as bold and italic) and sizes. The size of each font character is measured in **points** (a point is approximately 1/72 of an inch). You can use any font that is installed on your computer on a worksheet, but the default is 10-point Arial.

Change Font, Font Style, and Font Size

1. Select a cell or range that contains the font you want to change.

2. Click the Format menu, and then click Cells.

3. Click the Font tab.

4. Select a font.

5. Select a font style.

6. Select a font size.

7. Select any additional formatting effects.

8. Click OK.

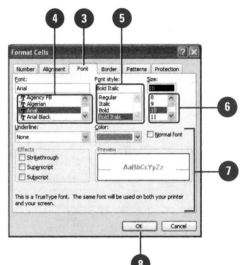

Did You Know?

Each computer has different fonts installed. Users with whom you share files may not have all the fonts you've used in a workbook installed on their computers.

96

Change Font and Font Size Using the Formatting Toolbar

1. Select a cell or range whose font and font size you want to change.

2. Click the Font list arrow on the Formatting toolbar.

3. If necessary, scroll to find the font you want to use, and then click it.

4. Click the Font Size list arrow on the Formatting toolbar. If necessary, click the Toolbar Options list arrow to display the button.

5. If necessary, scroll to find the font size you want to use, and then click it.

Did You Know?

You can tell the difference between a TrueType and printer font. A TrueType (outline) font is a font that uses special software capabilities to print exactly what is seen on the screen. A printer (screen) font is a font that comes only in specified sizes. If you are creating a worksheet for publication, you need to use printer fonts.

You can display font names in their font. Click the Tools menu, click Customize, click the Options tab, and then click to select the List Font Names In Their Font check box.

Changing Data Alignment

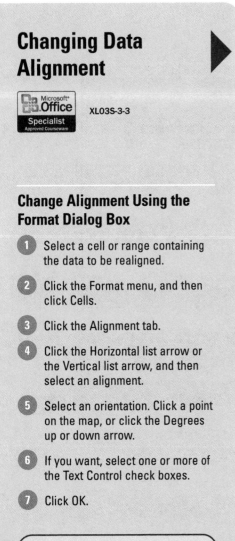

Microsoft® Office Specialist Approved Courseware   XL03S-3-3

When you enter data in a cell, Excel aligns labels on the left edge of the cell and aligns values and formulas on the right edge of the cell. **Horizontal alignment** is the way in which Excel aligns the contents of a cell relative to the left or right edge of the cell; **vertical alignment** is the way in which Excel aligns cell contents relative to the top and bottom of the cell. Excel also provides an option for changing the flow and angle of characters within a cell. The **orientation** of the contents of a cell is expressed in degrees. The default orientation is 0 degrees, in which characters are aligned horizontally within a cell.

Change Alignment Using the Format Dialog Box

1. Select a cell or range containing the data to be realigned.

2. Click the Format menu, and then click Cells.

3. Click the Alignment tab.

4. Click the Horizontal list arrow or the Vertical list arrow, and then select an alignment.

5. Select an orientation. Click a point on the map, or click the Degrees up or down arrow.

6. If you want, select one or more of the Text Control check boxes.

7. Click OK.

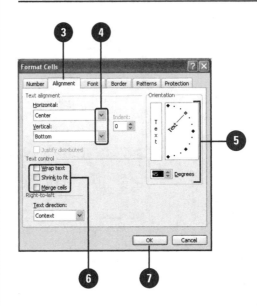

Did You Know?

You can use the Format Cells dialog box to select other alignment options. Many more alignment options are available from the Format Cells dialog box, but for centering across columns and simple left, right, and center alignment, it's easier to use the Formatting toolbar buttons.

Change Alignment Using the Formatting Toolbar

1. Select a cell or range containing the data to be realigned.

2. Click the Align Left, Center, or Align Right button on the Formatting toolbar.

3. To center cell contents across selected columns, click the Merge And Center button on the Formatting toolbar.

See Also

See "Add Color to Worksheet Tabs" on page 108 for information on adding background color or pictures.

Alignment Toolbar Buttons

Button	Name	Description
	Align Left	Aligns cell contents on the left edge of the cell.
	Center	Centers cell contents in the middle of the cell.
	Align Right	Aligns cell contents on the right edge of the cell.
	Merge and Center	Centers cell contents across the columns of a selected range.

5

Controlling Text Flow ▶

The length of a label might not always fit within the width you've chosen for a column. If the cell to the right is empty, text spills over into it, but if that cell contains data, the text will be truncated (that is, cut off). A cell can be formatted so its text automatically wraps to multiple lines; that way, you don't have to widen the column to achieve an attractive effect. For example, you might want the label *Interior Vanity Strips* to fit in a column that is only as wide as *Interior*. Cell contents can also be modified to fit within the available space or can be combined with the contents of other cells.

Control the Flow of Text in a Cell

1. Select a cell or range whose text flow you want to change.

2. Click the Format menu, and then click Cells.

3. Click the Alignment tab.

4. Click to select one or more Text Control check boxes.

   ◆ **Wrap Text** moves the text to multiple lines within a cell.

   ◆ **Shrink To Fit** reduces character size to fit within a cell.

   ◆ **Merge Cells** combines selected cells into a single cell.

5. Click OK.

Changing Data Color

You can change the color of the numbers and text on a worksheet. Strategic use of **font color** can be an effective way of tying similar values together. For instance, on a sales worksheet you might want to display sales in green and returns in red. Or, you may want to highlight column or row headers with colored labels. Either way, using color to highlight numbers and texts makes deciphering your worksheet data easier.

Change Font Color Using the Formatting Toolbar

1 Select a cell or range that contains the text you want to change.

2 Click the Font Color button list arrow on the Formatting toolbar.

3 Click a color.

Did You Know?

The Font Color button on the Formatting toolbar displays the last font color you used. To apply this color to another selection, simply click the button, not the list arrow.

Adding Color and Patterns to Cells

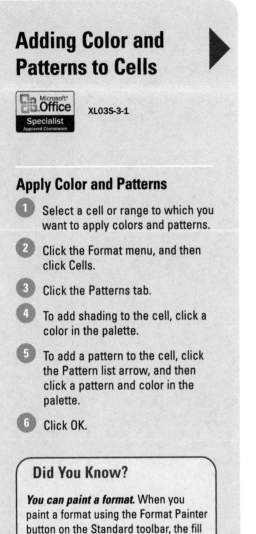

XL03S-3-1

You can **fill** the background of a cell with a color and a pattern to make its data stand out. Fill colors and patterns can also lend consistency to related information on a worksheet. On a sales worksheet, for example, formatting all fourth-quarter sales figures with a blue background and all second-quarter sales with a yellow background would make each group of figures easy to identify. You can use fill colors and patterns in conjunction with text attributes, fonts, and font colors to further enhance the appearance of your worksheet.

Apply Color and Patterns

1 Select a cell or range to which you want to apply colors and patterns.

2 Click the Format menu, and then click Cells.

3 Click the Patterns tab.

4 To add shading to the cell, click a color in the palette.

5 To add a pattern to the cell, click the Pattern list arrow, and then click a pattern and color in the palette.

6 Click OK.

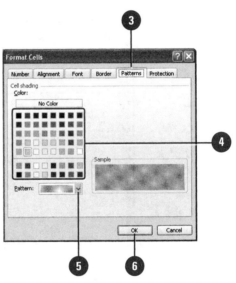

Did You Know?

You can paint a format. When you paint a format using the Format Painter button on the Standard toolbar, the fill colors and patterns get copied too.

Apply Color Using the Formatting Toolbar

① Select a cell or range.

② Click the Fill Color button list arrow on the Formatting toolbar.

If necessary, click the Toolbar Options list arrow to display the button.

③ Click a color.

Did You Know?

You can use the Print Preview button on the Standard toolbar to save time. Preview your worksheet before you print it, especially if you don't have a color printer. Some colors and patterns look great on screen but can make a worksheet difficult to read when printed in black and white.

Adding Borders to Cells

Specialist
Approved Courseware

XL03S-3-1

Apply a Border

1. Select a cell or range to which you want to apply borders.

2. Click the Format menu, and then click Cells.

3. Click the Border tab.

4. Select a line style.

5. Click the Color list arrow, and then click a color for the border.

6. If you want a border on the outside of a cell or range, click Outline. If you want a border between cells, click Inside. If you want to remove a border, click None.

7. To set a custom border, click a Border button, or click the Preview Border box where you want to add a border.

8. Click OK.

The light gray grid that appears on the worksheet helps your eyes move from cell to cell. Although you can print these gridlines, sometimes a different grid pattern better emphasizes your data. For example, you might put a decorative line border around the title, a double-line bottom border below cells with totals, or a thick border between sections of a complicated worksheet. You can add borders of varying colors and widths to any or all sides of a single cell or range.

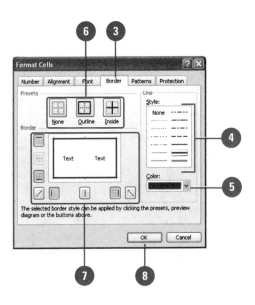

Apply a Border Using the Formatting Toolbar

1 Select a cell or range to which you want to apply a border.

2 Click the Borders list arrow on the Formatting toolbar or the Borders button to select the default border style. If necessary, click the Toolbar Options list arrow to display the button.

3 Select a border from the submenu of available borders. The previous border style you have chosen appears as the default Borders button on the Formatting toolbar.

Did You Know?

You can use the Select All button. To place a border around the entire worksheet, click the Select All button, and then apply the border.

Formatting Data with AutoFormat

Formatting worksheet data can be a lot of fun but also very intensive. To make formatting data more efficient, Excel includes 18 AutoFormats. An **AutoFormat** includes a combination of fill colors and patterns, numeric formats, font attributes, borders, and font colors that are professionally designed to enhance your worksheets. If you don't select any cells before choosing the AutoFormat command, Excel will "guess" which data it should format.

Apply an AutoFormat

1. Select a cell or range to which you want to apply an AutoFormat, or skip this step if you want Excel to "guess" which cells to format.

2. Click the Format menu, and then click AutoFormat.

3. Click an AutoFormat in the list.

4. Click Options.

5. Select one or more Formats To Apply check boxes to turn a feature on or off.

6. Click OK.

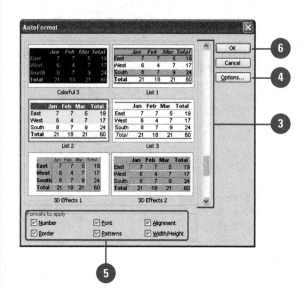

Did You Know?

You can copy cell formats with Format Painter. Select the cell or range whose formatting you want to copy, double-click the Format Painter button on the Standard toolbar, select the cells you want to format, and then click the Format Painter button.

Modifying an AutoFormat

Modify an AutoFormat

① Select a cell or range whose AutoFormat you want to change, or skip this step if you want Excel to "guess" which cells to format.

② Click the Format menu, and then click AutoFormat.

③ Click the AutoFormat you want to modify.

④ Click Options.

⑤ Click to select or clear one or more Formats To Apply check boxes to turn a feature on or off.

⑥ Click OK.

Did You Know?

You can let Excel choose the range to format. If you don't select the cells you want to apply the AutoFormat to, Excel will guess which cells you want formatted.

Excel AutoFormats give any worksheet a professional look, but you may need to modify an AutoFormat to better suit the needs of a particular project. For example, the AutoFormat you applied might be perfect except that the font used should be different—to match the font in the rest of your report. You can control individual elements in an AutoFormat so that not all are applied to the current worksheet. These changes are temporary; you can't permanently alter an AutoFormat.

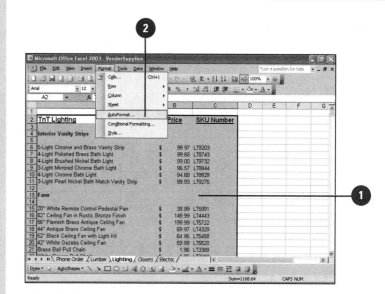

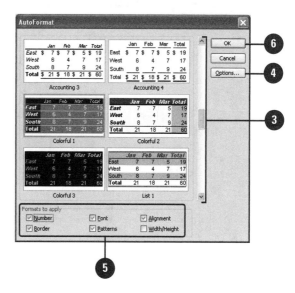

5

Formatting Tabs and Background

![Microsoft Office Specialist Approved Courseware] XL03S-3-4

Add Color to Worksheet Tabs

1. Click the sheet tab you want to color.

2. Click the Format menu, point to Sheet, and then click Tab Color.

3. Click a tab color.

4. Click OK.

Depending on your screen size, the sheet tabs at the bottom of your workbook can be hard to view. You can add color to the sheet tabs to make them more distinguishable. If you want to add artistic style to your workbook or you are creating a Web page from your workbook, you can add a background picture. When you add a background to a worksheet, the background does not print, and it's not included when you save an individual worksheet as a Web page. You need to publish the entire workbook as a Web page to include the background.

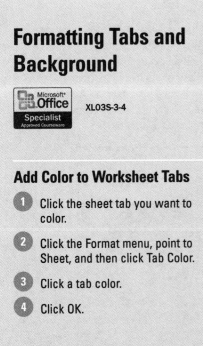

Add or Remove a Background

① Click the sheet tab you want to add a background to.

② Click the Format menu, point to Sheet, and then click Background.

③ Select the folder with the graphic file you want to use.

④ Select the graphic you want.

⑤ Click Insert.

⑥ To remove the background, click the Format menu, point to Sheet, and then click Remove Background.

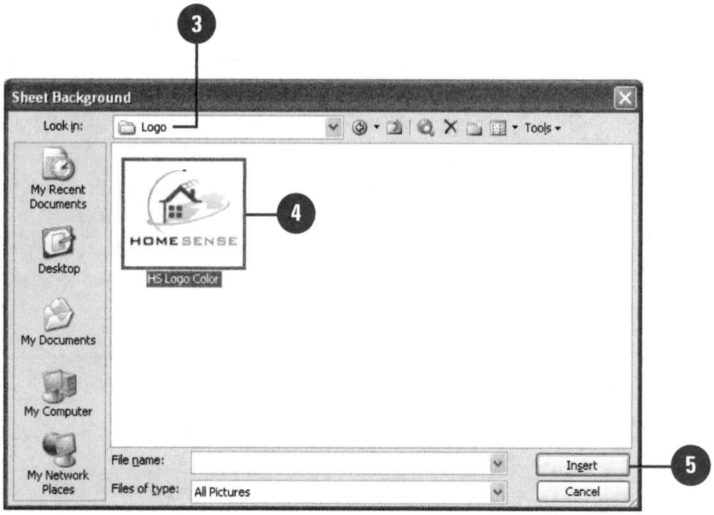

③

Sheet Background

Look in: Logo

My Recent Documents
Desktop
My Documents
My Computer
My Network Places

HOME SENSE

HS Logo Color

④

File name:

Files of type: All Pictures

Insert ⑤

Cancel

5

Creating and Applying Styles

XL03S-3-2

A **style** is a defined collection of formats—font, font size, attributes, numeric formats, and so on—that you can store as a set and later apply to other cells. For example if you always want subtotals to display in blue 14-point Times New Roman, bold, italic, with two decimal places and commas, you can create a style that includes all these formats. If you plan to enter repetitive information, such as a list of dollar amounts in a row or column, it's often easier to apply the desired style to the range before you enter the data. That way you can simple enter each number, and Excel formats it as soon as you press Enter. You can also copy styles from one workbook to another. Once you create a style, it is available to you in every workbook.

Create a New Style

1. Select a cell or range that you want to create a style.

2. Click the Format menu, and then click Style.

3. Type the name of the new style.

4. Clear the check boxes with the options you do not want.

5. Click Modify.

6. Click any of the formatting tabs, and then make additional formatting changes to the style.

7. Click OK.

8. Click OK.

Did You Know?

You can merge a style from another workbook. Click the Format menu, click Style, click Merge, click the workbook that contains the style you want, click OK, and then click OK again.

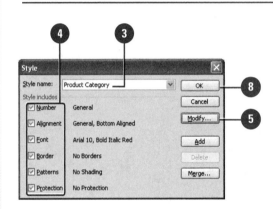

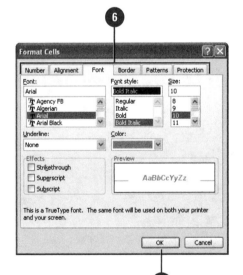

Apply a Style

1. Select a cell or range to which you want to apply a style.

2. Click the Format menu, and then click Style.

3. Click the Style Name list arrow, and then select the style you want to apply.

4. Click OK.

Modifying a Style

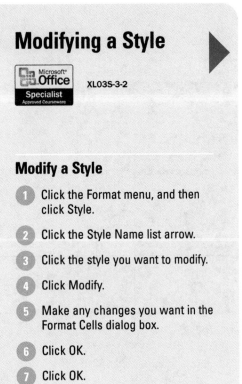

Microsoft® **Office** Specialist
Approved Courseware
XL03S-3-2

Any style—whether it was supplied by Excel or created by you or someone else—can be modified. Suppose you created a style containing fonts and colors your company uses. If those specifications changed, you could modify the style to include the new attributes. If you want to use styles created or modified in another workbook, you can merge the styles into the open workbook. If you no longer use a style, you can delete it from the workbook.

Modify a Style

1. Click the Format menu, and then click Style.

2. Click the Style Name list arrow.

3. Click the style you want to modify.

4. Click Modify.

5. Make any changes you want in the Format Cells dialog box.

6. Click OK.

7. Click OK.

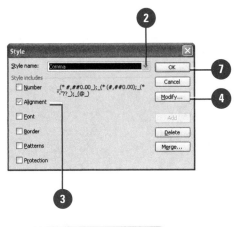

Merge Styles

1. Open the worksheet that contains the styles you want to merge.

2. Click the Format menu, and then click Style.

3. Click Merge.

4. Click the workbook that contains the styles you want to merge with the current workbook.

5. Click OK.

6. Click OK.

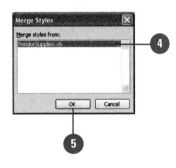

Delete a Style

1. Click the Format menu, and then click Style.

2. Click the Style Name list arrow, and then click the style you want to delete.

3. Click Delete.

4. Click OK.

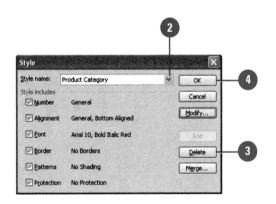

Did You Know?

You can use the Add button to create a new style based on a current style. You never know when you might want to use an original style supplied by Excel. To keep the original style intact, modify the formatting in the Style dialog box as desired, click Add, and then give the modified style a new name.

5

Finding and Replacing Formatting

Specialist
Approved Courseware

XL03S-1-2

Find or Replace Formatting

1 Click the Edit menu, and then click Find or Replace.

2 Enter the word or words you want to find.

3 Click Options to display formatting options. If necessary, click Format, and then click Clear Formatting From Cell to clear previous criteria.

4 Click Format, specify the formatting you want to locate, and then click OK.

5 Click Find Next to find the formatting options you specified.

6 To replace text and formatting, click the Replace tab, and then enter the word or words you want to replace in the Replace With text box.

7 Click the Replace With Format button, specify the formatting you want to replace, and then click OK.

8 Click Find Next to select the next instance of the formatted text or click Replace or Replace All to substitute formatting.

The Find and Replace commands make it easy to locate or replace specific text, numbers, and formatting in a workbook. For example, you might want to replace all the references to cell A6 in your formulas with data contained in cell H2, or you might want to replace bold text with italic text. Or, you may want to change a client name or contact on all of your financial reports. You can be specific in your replacing, by replacing one at a time, or all matches found.

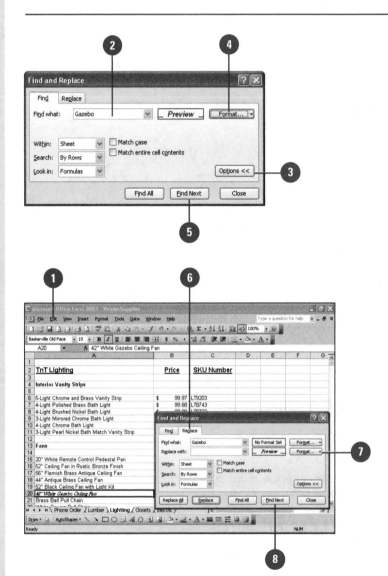

Printing Worksheets and Workbooks

Introduction

When your Microsoft Office Excel 2003 worksheet is completed, you can preview and print its contents. While previewing the worksheet, you might find that rows of data might flow better on one page or the other. You can insert page breaks to control what you print on each page. You can change the orientation of the page from the default of portrait (vertical) to landscape (horizontal). This is helpful when you have wide or multiple columns that would look better on one page. You can also adjust your margins to better fit the worksheet on the page. Previewing a worksheet before printing saves you time and money by not printing unnecessary copies.

After you make layout adjustments you can add headers and footers on the page. Headers are typically a descriptive title about your worksheet or workbook. Footers can include date printed, page numbers, or other company related information. You can add additional elements to your printout by showing gridlines or column letter and row numbers.

To print a worksheet, you can set the print area when you customize worksheet printing or any time when you are working on a worksheet. For example, you might want to print a different range in a worksheet for different people. After you set the print area, you can choose to print your worksheet. The Print dialog box allows you to customize all the options and more, and then you can send your worksheet or entire workbook to the printer.

Inserting Page Breaks

XL03S-5-5, XL03S-5-7

If you want to print a worksheet that is larger than one page, Excel divides it into pages by inserting **automatic page breaks**. These page breaks are based on paper size, margin settings, and scaling options you set. You can change which rows or columns are printed on the page by inserting **horizontal** or **vertical page breaks**. In page break preview, you can view the page breaks and move them by dragging them to a different location on the worksheet.

Insert a Page Break

1. To insert a horizontal page break, click the row where you want to insert a page break.

   To insert a vertical page break, click the column where you want to insert a page break.

2. Click the Insert menu, and then click Page Break.

Preview and Move a Page Break

① Click the View menu, and then click Page Break Preview.

② Drag a page break (a thick blue line) to a new location.

③ When you're done, click the View menu, and then click Normal.

Did You Know?

You can remove a page break. Select the column or row next to the page break, click the Insert menu, and then click Remove Page Break.

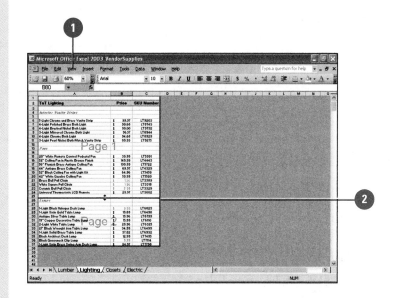

6

Setting Up the Page

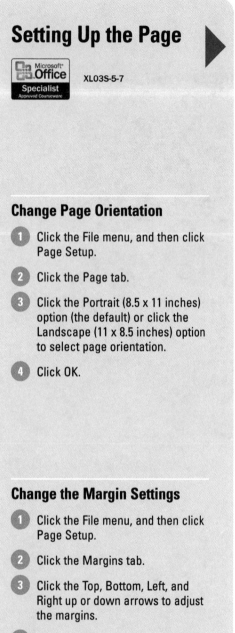

Microsoft®
Office
Specialist
Approved Courseware

XL03S-5-7

You can set up the worksheet page to print just the way you want. With the Page Setup dialog box, you can choose the **page orientation**, which determines whether Excel prints the worksheet data portrait (vertically) or landscape (horizontally). You can also adjust the **print scaling** (to reduce or enlarge the size of printed characters), change the paper size (to match the size of paper in your printer), and resize or realign the left, right, top, and bottom margins (the blank areas along each edge of the paper). Changes made in the Page Setup dialog box are not reflected in the worksheet window. You can see them only when you preview or print the worksheet.

Change Page Orientation

1. Click the File menu, and then click Page Setup.

2. Click the Page tab.

3. Click the Portrait (8.5 x 11 inches) option (the default) or click the Landscape (11 x 8.5 inches) option to select page orientation.

4. Click OK.

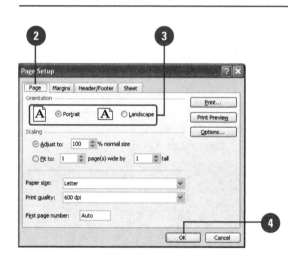

Change the Margin Settings

1. Click the File menu, and then click Page Setup.

2. Click the Margins tab.

3. Click the Top, Bottom, Left, and Right up or down arrows to adjust the margins.

4. Select the Center On Page check boxes to automatically center your data.

5. Click OK.

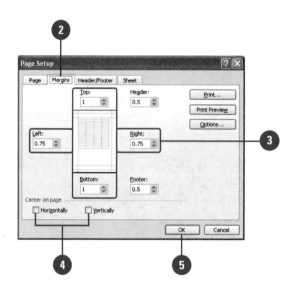

Adding Headers and Footers

XL03S-5-7

Adding a header or footer to a workbook is a convenient way to make your printout easier for readers to follow. Using the Page Setup command, you can add information such as page numbers, the worksheet title, or the current date at the top and bottom of each page or section of a worksheet or workbook. Using the Custom Header and Custom Footer buttons, you can include information such as your computer system's date and time, the name of the workbook and sheet, a graphic, or other custom information.

Change a Header or Footer

1. Click the File menu, and then click Page Setup.

2. Click the Header/Footer tab.

3. If the Header box doesn't contain the information you want, click Custom Header.

4. Type the information in the Left, Center, or Right Section text boxes, or click a button to insert built-in header information. If you don't want a header to appear at all, delete the text and codes in the text boxes.

5. Select the text you want to format, click the Font button, make font changes, and then click OK. Excel will use the default font, Arial, unless you change it.

6. Click OK.

7. If the Footer box doesn't contain the information that you want, click Custom Footer.

8. Type information in the Left, Center, or Right Section text boxes, or click a button to insert the built-in footer information.

9. Click OK.

10. Click OK.

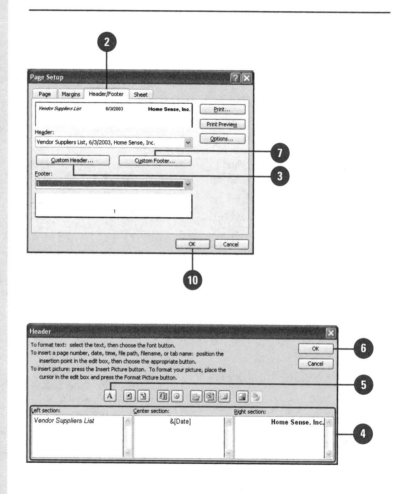

Customizing Worksheet Printing

XL03S-5-7, XL03S-5-8

At some point you'll want to print your worksheet so you can distribute it to others or use it for other purposes. You can print all or part of any worksheet, and you can control the appearance of many features, such as whether gridlines are displayed, whether column letters and row numbers are displayed, or whether to include print titles, columns and rows that are repeated on each page. If you have already set a print area, it will appear in the Print Area box on the Sheet tab of the Page Setup dialog box. You don't need to re-select it.

Print Part of a Worksheet

1. Click the File menu, and then click Page Setup.

2. Click the Sheet tab.

3. Type the range you want to print. Or click the Collapse Dialog button, select the cells you want to print, and then click the Expand Dialog button to restore the dialog box.

4. Click OK.

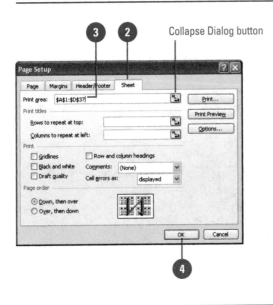

Print Row and Column Titles on Each Page

1. Click the File menu, and then click Page Setup.

2. Click the Sheet tab.

3. Enter the number of the row or the letter of the column that contains the titles. Or click the Collapse Dialog button, select the row or column with the mouse, and then click the Expand Dialog button to restore the dialog box.

4. Click OK.

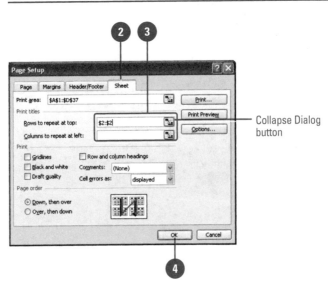

Print Gridlines, Column Letters, and Row Numbers

1. Click the File menu, and then click Page Setup.

2. Click the Sheet tab.

3. Select the Gridlines check box.

4. Select the Row And Column Headings check box.

5. Click OK.

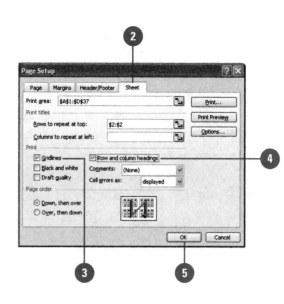

Fit Your Worksheet on a Specific Number of Pages

1. Click the File menu, and then click Page Setup.

2. Click the Page tab.

3. Select a scaling option.

   - ◆ Click the Adjust To option to scale the worksheet using a percentage.

   - ◆ Click the Fit To option to force a worksheet to be printed on a specific number of pages.

4. Click OK.

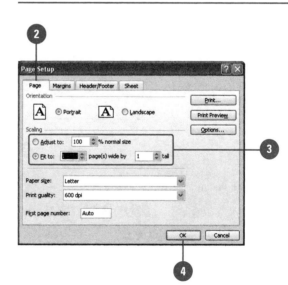

See Also

See "Inserting Page Breaks" on page 116 for information on how to divide a worksheet into different pages

6

Setting the Print Area

 XLO3S-5-7

When you're ready to print your worksheet, you can choose several printing options. The **print area** is the section of your worksheet that Excel prints. You can set the print area when you customize worksheet printing or any time when you are working on a worksheet. For example, you might want to print a different range in a worksheet for different people. In order to use headers and footers, you must first establish, or set, the print area. You can design a specific single cells or a contiguous or non-contiguous range.

Set the Print Area

1. Select the range of cells you want to print.

2. Click the File menu, and then point to Print Area.

3. Click Set Print Area.

Clear the Print Area

1. Click the File menu, and then point to Print Area.

2. Click Clear Print Area.

Did You Know?

You can avoid repeating rows and columns. For best results when printing a multipage worksheet, you'll want to coordinate the print area with specified print titles so that columns or rows are not repeated on a single page.

Previewing a Worksheet

XL03S-5-5

Preview a Worksheet

1. Click the Print Preview button on the Standard toolbar, or click the File menu, and then click Print Preview.

2. Click the Zoom button on the Print Preview toolbar, or position the Zoom pointer anywhere on the worksheet, and then click it to enlarge a specific area of the page.

3. If you do not want to print from Print Preview, click the Close button to return to the worksheet.

4. If you want to print from Print Preview, click the Print button on the Print Preview toolbar.

5. Click OK.

Did You Know?

You can preview your work from the Print dialog box. In the Print dialog box, click Preview. After previewing, you can click the Print button on the Print Preview toolbar to print the worksheet or click the Close button to return to your worksheet.

Before printing, you should verify that the page looks the way you want. You save time, money, and paper by avoiding duplicate printing. **Print Preview** shows you the exact placement of your data on each printed page. You can view all or part of your worksheet as it will appear when you print it. The Print Preview toolbar makes it easy to zoom in and out to view data more comfortably, set margins and other page options, preview page breaks, and print.

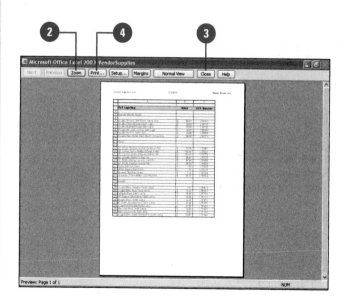

6

Printing a Worksheet and Workbook

XL03S-5-8

When you're ready to print your worksheet, you can choose several printing options. You can print all or part of any worksheet and control the appearance of many features, such as whether gridlines are displayed, whether column letters and row numbers are displayed, and whether to include print titles, which are the columns and rows that repeat on each page. You can print a copy of your worksheet quickly to review it by clicking the Print button on the Standard or Print Preview toolbar. You can also use the Print dialog box to specify several print options, such as choosing a new printer, selecting the number of pages in the worksheet you want printed, and specifying the number of copies.

Print All or Part of a Worksheet

1. Click the File menu, and then click Print.

2. If necessary, click the Name list arrow, and then click the printer you want to use.

3. Select whether you want to print the entire document or only the pages you specify.

4. Select whether you want to print the selected text or objects, the selected worksheets, or all the worksheets in the workbook with data.

5. Click the Number Of Copies up or down arrow to specify the number of copies you want.

6. Click OK.

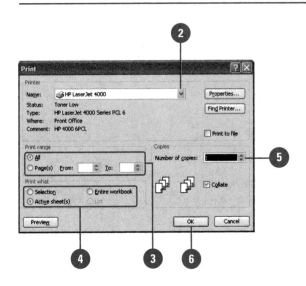

Did You Know?

You can change printer properties. Click the File menu, click Print, and then click Properties to change general printer properties for paper size and orientation, graphics, and fonts.

Inserting Graphics and Related Material

Introduction

Some data on your worksheet might be better displayed using colorful graphic images that come with Microsoft Office Excel 2003, or you create in a separate graphics program. Graphic images can serve to reinforce a corporate identity or illustrate subject matter in a worksheet.

Microsoft Office Excel 2003 has many features to help you enhance your worksheets. The Office Clipboard can hold up to 24 images or groupings of selected text to use as you enhance your worksheet. Additional research and language tools are available to build up the content of your worksheet. You can insert pictures from a digital camera or the Clip Art gallery. You can also insert a sound clip and even a motion clip to help fine tune your worksheet.

When adding images, it might become necessary to adjust the pictures by changing their contrast, making them brighter, changing their coloring, and cropping. WordArt is a creative tool that can really add eye catching details to your worksheet. Used for titles or other areas to call out, WordArt can be colored and stylized to match your workbooks overall them.

You can also include organization charts and diagrams in your worksheets. You can set up an organization chart to have various styles such as color, formatted text, and different chart boxes to name a few. Use diagrams as part of your overall workbook to include some graphical details about workflows, procedures, or other conceptual ideas.

Working with the Clipboard

The Office Clipboard is available from within any Office program and holds up to 24 pieces of copied information, any or all of which you can paste to a new location. As you cut or copy information, Office collects it in the Office Clipboard. You can use the Office Clipboard task pane to manage the information and use it in documents. The Office Clipboard allows you to collect multiple items and paste them quickly. When you paste an item, the Paste Options button appears below it. When you click the button, a menu appears with options to specify how Excel pastes the information. The available options differ depending on the content you are pasting.

Paste Items from the Office Clipboard

1 Click the Edit menu, and then click Office Clipboard.

TIMESAVER *Press Ctrl+C twice to access the Office Clipboard.*

2 Click where you want to insert the text.

3 Click any icon on the Clipboard task pane to paste that selection. If there is more than one selection, you can paste all the selections at once, by clicking Paste All.

4 When you're done, click the Close button on the task pane.

Did You Know?

You can turn on or off paste options. Click the Tools menu, click Options, click the Edit tab, select or clear the Show Paste Options Buttons check box, and then click OK.

You can paste information in a different format. Select the object or text, click the Copy button on the Standard toolbar, click to indicate where you want to paste the object, click the Edit menu, click Paste Special, click the object type you want, and then click OK.

Delete Items from the Office Clipboard

1. Click the Edit menu, and then click Office Clipboard.

2. Click the list arrow of the item you want to paste, and then click Delete.

3. To erase all items in the Office Clipboard, click Clear All.

4. When you're done, click the Close button on the task pane.

Change Clipboard Options

1. Click the Edit menu, and then click Office Clipboard.

2. Click Options, and then click any of the following options. (A check mark turns the feature on):

    ◆ Show Office Clipboard Automatically

    ◆ Show Office Clipboard When Ctrl+C Pressed Twice

    ◆ Collect Without Showing Office Clipboard

    ◆ Show Office Clipboard Icon On Taskbar

    ◆ Show Status Near Taskbar When Copying

3. When you're done, click the Close button on the task pane.

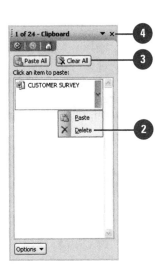

7

Inserting Research Material

 XL03S-1-3

With the Research task pane, you can find research material and incorporate it into your worksheet quickly and easily. The Research task pane allows you to access informational services and insert the material right into your worksheet without leaving your Excel. The Research task pane can help you access dictionaries, thesauruses, research sites, language translations, stock quotes, and company information. You can also add and remove the services from the Research task pane.

Locate and Insert Research Material

1. Click the Tools menu, and then click Research.

2. Type the topic you want to research.

3. Click the Reference list arrow, and then select a reference source, or select All Reference Books.

4. Click the Start Searching button.

5. Copy and paste the material into your Office document.

6. When you're done, click the Close button on the task pane.

Use the Thesaurus

1. Press and hold the Alt key, and then click the cell with the word which you want to find a synonym.

2. Point to the word you want to use.

3. Click the list arrow, and then click Insert.

4. When you're done, click the Close button on the task pane.

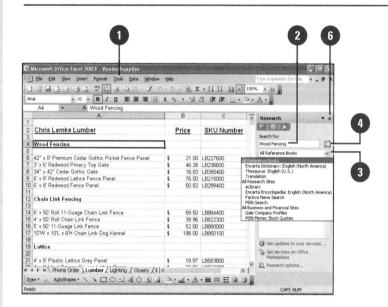

Translate a Word

1. Click the Tools menu, and then click Research.

2. Type the word you want to translate.

3. Click the Reference list arrow, and then click Translation.

4. Select the language you want the word translated to.

5. Copy and paste the translated word into your Office document.

6. When you're done, click the Close button on the task pane.

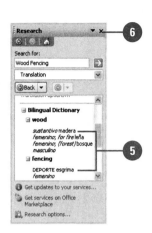

Change Research Options

1. Click the Tools menu, and then click Research.

2. Click Research Options.

3. Do one or more of the following:

    ◆ **Services.** To activate or remove research services.

    ◆ **Add Services.** To add research services.

    ◆ **Update/Remove.** To update or remove a service provider.

    ◆ **Parental Controls.** To turn on parental controls.

4. Click OK.

5. When you're done, click the Close button on the task pane.

Inserting and Deleting Pictures

XL03S-1-4

You can add pictures to a worksheet. Your company might have a logo that it includes on all worksheets. Or you might want to use **clip art**, copyright-free graphics, on your worksheet for a special presentation. In Excel, a **picture** is any graphic object that you insert as a single unit. You can also insert pictures that you've created in a drawing program or scanned in and saved as a file, or you can insert clip art provided with Microsoft Office or that you've acquired separately. After you insert a graphic object, you can easily delete it if it does not serve your purposes.

Insert Clip Art from the Clip Gallery

1. Select the cell or range where you want to insert a picture.

2. Click the Insert menu, point to Picture, and then click Clip Art.

3. Type one or more keywords on which to search, and then click the Go button.

4. If necessary, scroll through the collection in the list.

5. To quickly insert clip art, double-click a picture in the task pane.

6. When you're done, click the Close button on the task pane.

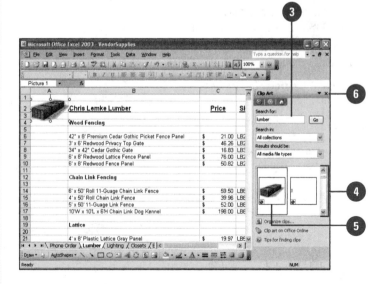

Insert a Picture from an Existing File

① Click the cell or range where you want the picture to appear.

② Click the Insert menu, point to Picture, and then click From File.

③ Click the Look In list arrow, select the drive and folder with the picture, and then click the file you want to insert.

④ If you want, click the Views button list arrow, and then select Preview to view the picture.

⑤ Click Insert.

Delete a Picture

① Click the object to display its handles.

② Press Delete.

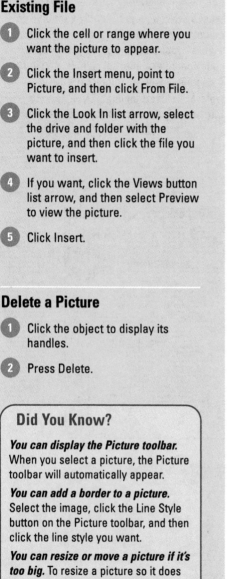

Selection handles

Did You Know?

You can display the Picture toolbar. When you select a picture, the Picture toolbar will automatically appear.

You can add a border to a picture. Select the image, click the Line Style button on the Picture toolbar, and then click the line style you want.

You can resize or move a picture if it's too big. To resize a picture so it does not obscure existing data, drag the handle to reduce or enlarge the picture. To move the picture, point to an edge, but not to a handle, and then drag the picture to a new location.

Inserting Media Clips

You can insert sounds or motion clips into a workbook by accessing them using the Clip Gallery. A **motion clip** is an animated picture—also known as an animated GIF—frequently used in Web pages. To play a motion clip, you need to view your workbook or worksheet as a Web page. When you insert a sound, a small icon appears representing the sound file. To play sounds other than your computer's internal sounds, you need a sound card and speakers. You can also insert images from a Twain-compatible scanner or digital camera. To insert an image, you need to connect the scanner or digital camera to your computer and install the Twain device software.

Insert a Clip Gallery Sound or Motion Clip

1. Click the Insert menu, point to Picture, and then click Clip Art.

2. Click the Results Should Be list arrow, and then make sure the Movies and/or Sounds check boxes are selected.

3. Click Go.

4. Click the media you want to insert.

5. To play a sound, double-click the sound icon.

   To play a motion clip, save your workbook or worksheet as a Web page, and then view it in a Web browser.

6. When you're done, click the Close button on the task pane.

Did You Know?

You can preview a motion clip. To see how a motion clip will appear, click the File menu, and then click Web Page Preview.

Insert a Picture from a Scanner or Camera

1. Set up the image in the scanning device or digital camera.

2. Click the Insert menu, point to Picture, and then click From Scanner Or Camera.

3. Click the Device list arrow, and then select the device connected to your computer.

4. Select the resolution (the visual quality of the image).

5. Select or clear the Add Pictures To Clip Organizer check box.

6. To use default settings, click Insert.

7. To specify your own settings to scan a picture or capture and select a camera image, click Custom Insert, and then follow the device instructions.

Did You Know?

You can connect to the Web for access to additional clip art. Click the Clip Art On Office Online button to open your Web browser and connect to a clip art Web site to download files.

You can display clip art categories. Click the All Categories button on the Insert Clip Art task pane.

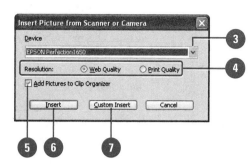

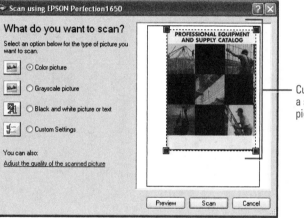

Customizing a scanned picture

Modifying Pictures

 XL03E-2-3

Once you have inserted clip art and other objects into your presentation, you can adapt them to meet your needs. Perhaps the clip is too small to be effective, or you don't quite like the colors it uses. Like any object, you can resize or move the clip art. You can also control the images colors, brightness, and contrast using the Picture toolbar. You can use these same methods with bitmapped pictures. To further modify a picture, you change its color to default colors (automatic), grayscale, black and white, or washout, also known as watermark.

Change Contrast

1 Click the picture whose contrast you want to increase or decrease.

2 Choose the contrast you want.

◆ Click the More Contrast button on the Picture toolbar to increase color intensity, resulting in less gray.

◆ Click the Less Contrast button on the Picture toolbar to decrease color intensity, resulting in more gray.

Change Brightness

1 Click the picture whose brightness you want to increase or decrease.

2 Choose the image brightness you want.

◆ Click the More Brightness button on the Picture toolbar to lighten the object colors by adding more white.

◆ Click the Less Brightness button on the Picture toolbar to darken the object colors by adding more black.

Choose a Color Type

1. Click the image whose color you want to change.

2. Click the Color button on the Picture toolbar.

3. Click one of the Image Control options.

   ◆ Automatic (default coloring)

   ◆ Grayscale (whites, blacks, and grays)

   ◆ Black & White

   ◆ Washout (whites and very light colors)

Restore Original Settings

1. Click the picture whose settings you want to restore.

2. Click the Reset Picture button on the Picture toolbar.

Did You Know?

You can set an image color to transparent. Select the image, and then click the Set Transparent Color button on the Picture toolbar.

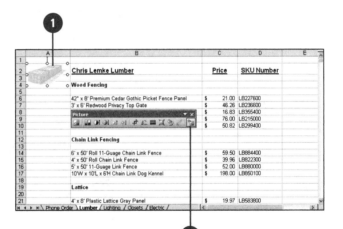

Cropping Pictures

XL03E-2-3

You can crop clip art to isolate just one portion of the picture. Because clip art uses vector image technology, you can **crop**, or cut out, even the smallest part of it and then enlarge it, and the clip art will still be recognizable. You can also crop bitmapped pictures; but if you enlarge the area you cropped, you lose picture detail. You can crop an image by hand using the Crop button on the Picture toolbar.

Crop a Picture

1. Click the image you want to crop.

2. Click the Crop button on the Picture toolbar.

3. Drag the sizing handles until the borders surround the area you want to crop.

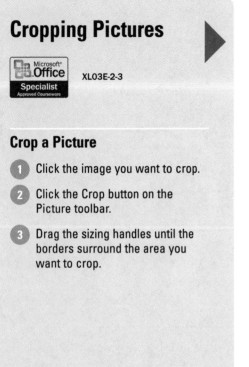

Redisplay a Cropped Picture

1. Click the picture you want to restore.

2. Click the Crop button on the Picture toolbar.

3. Drag the sizing handles to reveal the areas that were originally cropped.

4. Click outside the image when you are finished.

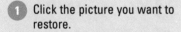

Stylizing Text with WordArt

WordArt is a Microsoft program you can use to stylize specific text on your worksheet. WordArt provides a wide variety of text styles pre-designed with dynamic patterns and effects; all you have to do is choose a style, and then type in the text. For example, if you don't have a logo for your company, you can easily create one using WordArt. You can easily move or resize a WordArt object, even though it might contain many components.

Create WordArt

1. Click the Insert menu, point to Picture, and then click WordArt.

2. Click a WordArt style.

3. Click OK.

4. Type the text you want in the Edit WordArt Text dialog box.

5. If you want, use the font, font size, bold, or italics buttons to format the text.

6. Click OK.

   Move the WordArt image to the desired spot.

7. If you want, use the WordArt toolbar buttons to make additional modifications.

8. To deselect the WordArt, click anywhere on the worksheet, or press Esc.

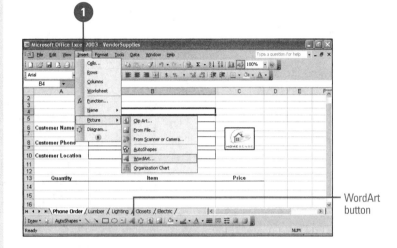

WordArt button

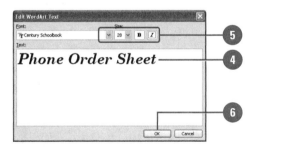

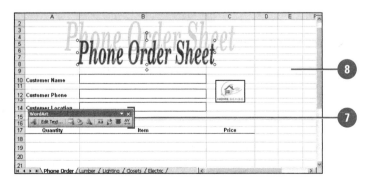

Editing WordArt Text ▶

With WordArt, in addition to applying one of the preformatted styles, you can create your own style. You can shape text into a variety of shapes, curves, styles, and color patterns. When you select a WordArt object to edit the text, the WordArt toolbar opens. This toolbar contains tools for coloring, rotating, and shaping your text. You can also format a WordArt object using the tools that are available in the Format dialog box, including positioning and sizing your WordArt. Once you are finished, either click anywhere on the worksheet or click the Close button to close the WordArt toolbar.

Change the Shape of WordArt Text

① Click the WordArt object.

② Click the WordArt Shape button on the WordArt toolbar.

③ Click the shape you want to apply to the text.

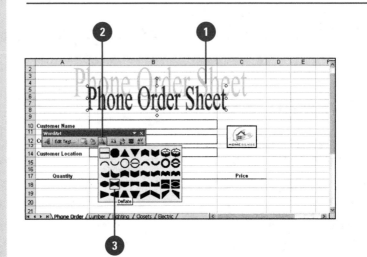

Rotate WordArt Text

① Click the WordArt object.

② Click the Free Rotate handle on the WordArt object.

③ Rotate the WordArt object in any direction.

④ Click a blank area of the worksheet to deselect the WordArt object.

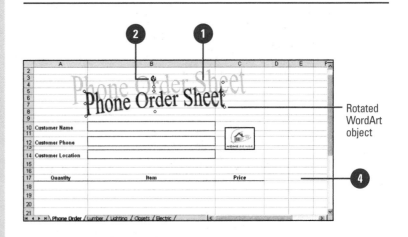

Rotated WordArt object

Color WordArt Text

1. Click the WordArt object.

2. Click the Format WordArt button on the WordArt toolbar.

3. Click the Colors And Lines tab.

4. Click the Fill Color list arrow, and then select a color or fill effect.

5. Click OK.

6. Click a blank area of the worksheet to deselect the WordArt object.

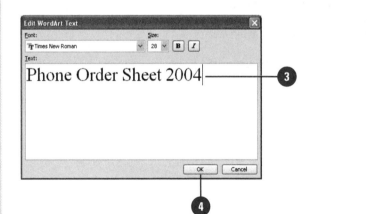

Edit or Format WordArt Text

1. Click the WordArt object.

2. Click the Edit Text button on the WordArt toolbar.

3. Click in the text box to position the insertion point, and then edit or format the text.

4. Click OK.

5. Click a blank area of the worksheet to deselect the WordArt object.

Applying WordArt Text Effects

You can apply a number of text effects to your WordArt objects to change letter heights, justification, and spacing. The effect of some of the adjustments you make will be more pronounced for certain WordArt styles than for others. Some of these effects will make the text unreadable for certain styles, so apply them carefully. Other effects—such as making uppercase and lower-case characters the same height—add an interesting dimension to the text.

Make All Letters the Same Height

1. Click the WordArt object.

2. Click the WordArt Same Letter Heights button on the WordArt toolbar.

3. Click a blank area of the worksheet to deselect the WordArt object.

Did You Know?

You can format WordArt text vertically. Click the WordArt object, click the WordArt Vertical Text button on the WordArt toolbar. When you're done, click a blank area of the worksheet to deselect it.

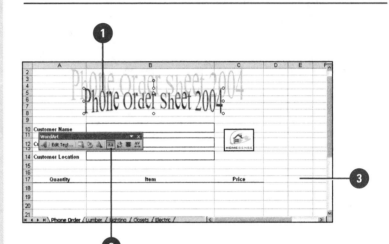

Align WordArt

1. Click the WordArt object.

2. Click the WordArt Alignment button on the WordArt toolbar.

3. Click an alignment button.

4. Click a blank area of the worksheet to deselect the WordArt object.

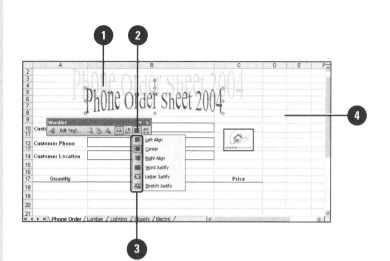

Adjust Character Spacing

1. Click the WordArt object.

2. Click the WordArt Character Spacing button on the WordArt toolbar.

3. Click a spacing setting button, or click Custom and type a custom percentage.

4. Click to select or clear the Kern Character Pairs option to adjust the space between characters.

5. Click a blank area of the worksheet to deselect the WordArt object.

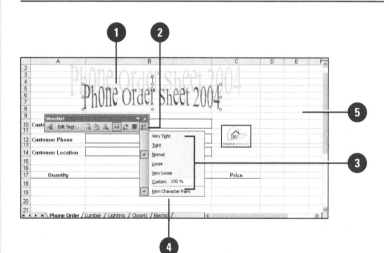

Did You Know?

You can print a sample of your WordArt document. The look of a WordArt object on your screen may differ from the printed output, especially if you do not have access to a color printer. Print a sample to make sure you like the final result.

Inserting an Organization Chart

An **organization chart**, also known as an **org chart**, shows the personnel structure in an organization. You can include an organization chart on a worksheet using **Microsoft Organization Chart**. Microsoft Organization Chart provides chart structures; all you have to do is type names in the appropriate places. Each chart box is identified by its position in the chart. Managers, for example, are at the top, while subordinates are below, co-workers to the sides, and so on.

Create an Organization Chart

1 Click the Insert menu, click Picture, and then click Organization Chart.

2 Click an org chart box, and then type replacement text.

3 To add subordinates or co-workers, click the Insert Shape toolbar button, and then click the box which contains the individual to whom the subordinate or co-worker reports.

4 To change groups of employees, click the Layout button, and then make a selection.

5 Click anywhere outside of the organization chart to return to the worksheet.

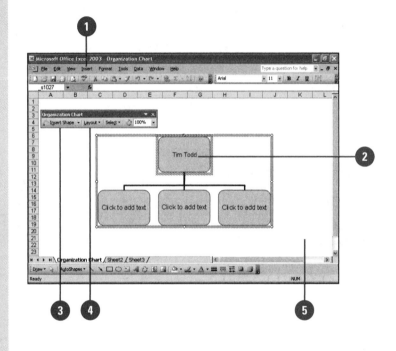

Use the Style Gallery

1 Click an existing organization chart.

2 Click the Autoformat button on the Organization Chart toolbar.

3 Click a style from the Organization Chart Style Gallery dialog box.

4 Click OK.

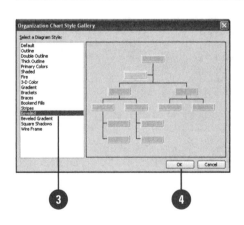

Type Text in a Chart Box

1. Click an existing organization chart.

2. Click a chart box in which you want to type text. (After you start Microsoft Organization Chart, the first chart box is selected for you, and you can just start typing.)

3. Click to place the insertion point, and then type the text you want.

4. To continue on the next line, press Enter and then type the text you want.

5. When you are finished, click outside the chart box.

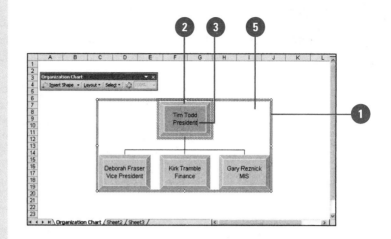

Did You Know?

You can change chart text alignment. Select the chart box(es) you want to change, click the Format menu, click AutoShape, click the Alignment tab, select the alignment options you want, and then click OK.

See Also

See "Modifying an Organization Chart" on page 144 for information on changing an organization chart layout.

Modifying an Organization Chart

In most companies, personnel and corporate structures change often. You can modify an existing organization chart whenever changes occur at your company. These modifications are done in Microsoft Organization Chart. Chart boxes exist in relation to each other. For example, if you want to add a Subordinate chart box, you must select the chart box to which it will be attached. The buttons on the toolbar show the relationship between the different chart boxes you can add. When you add a Subordinate, it is automatically placed below the selected chart box. You can, however, display the chart box levels in a different structure, and you can customize the organization chart's appearance using the formatting options.

Add a Chart Box

1. Click an existing organization chart.

2. Click the Insert Shape button on the Organization Chart toolbar, and then click the chart box type that you want to add.

3. Click the chart box to which you want to attach the new chart box.

4. Enter the information for the box you just added.

5. When you are finished, click outside the chart box.

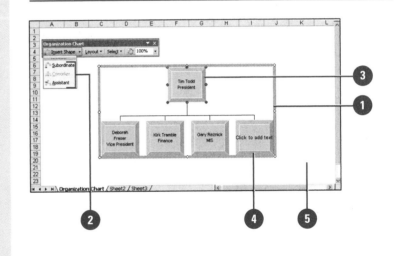

Change the Organization Chart Layout

1. Click an existing organization chart.

2. Click the Layout button on the Organization Chart toolbar, and then click the layout type that you want to add.

3. Click the Layout button.

4. Click the button with the organization chart style you want.

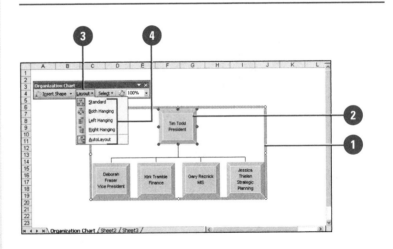

Rearrange a Chart Box

1 Click an existing organization chart.

2 Select the chart box you want to move.

3 Drag the chart box over an existing chart box.

The chart box appears below the existing chart box.

4 Release the mouse button to reposition the chart box.

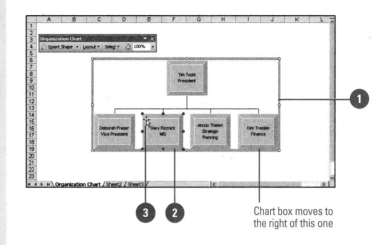

Chart box moves to the right of this one

Format a Chart Box

1 Click an existing organization chart.

2 Select the chart box(es) you want to format.

3 Use the buttons (Fill Color, Line Color, Font Color, Line Style, Dash Style, Shadow Style, or 3-D Style) on the Drawing toolbar to format the chart box(es).

TROUBLE? *Some pre-defined chart styles do not allow to format some parts of a chart box.*

Did You Know?

You can quickly delete a chart box. Click the chart box, and then press Delete.

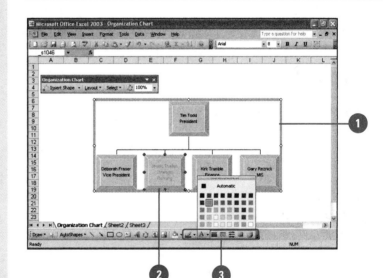

Creating a Diagram

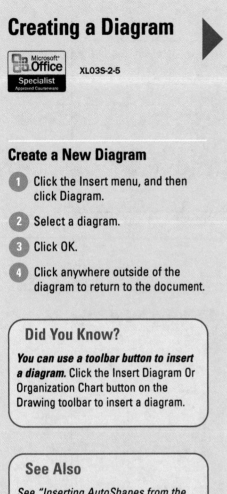

Microsoft® Office Specialist Approved Courseware

XL03S-2-5

A **diagram** is a collection of shapes that illustrates conceptual material. Excel 2003 offers a variety of built-in diagrams from which to choose, including pyramid, cycle, radial, and Venn diagrams as well as organization charts. Using built-in diagrams makes it easy to create and modify charts without having to create them from scratch. You can customize different parts of the diagram the same way you modify the shapes you create using the Drawing toolbar.

Create a New Diagram

1. Click the Insert menu, and then click Diagram.

2. Select a diagram.

3. Click OK.

4. Click anywhere outside of the diagram to return to the document.

Did You Know?

You can use a toolbar button to insert a diagram. Click the Insert Diagram Or Organization Chart button on the Drawing toolbar to insert a diagram.

See Also

See *"Inserting AutoShapes from the Clip Gallery"* on page 154 for information on inserting objects.

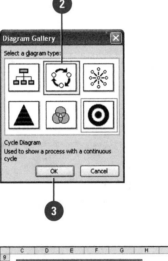

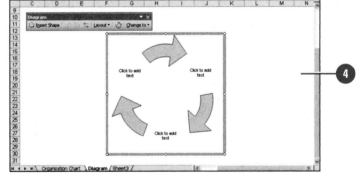

Modify a Diagram

1. Select the diagram you want to modify.

2. Select the diagram element you want to modify.

3. Use the Diagram toolbar to format the diagram. You may be asked to turn on AutoFormat.

   ◆ Click the Insert Shape button to insert a shape. You can use the Delete key to remove a shape.

   ◆ Click the Move Shape Forward, Move Shape Backward, or Reverse Diagram buttons to move shapes around.

   ◆ Click the Layout button to change the diagram size.

   ◆ Click AutoFormat button to change formats.

   ◆ Click Change To to select a different diagram.

4. Click the placeholder "Click to add text," and then type to add text.

5. Click anywhere outside of the diagram to return to the document.

See Also

See "Moving and Resizing an Object" on page 156 for information on formatting objects.

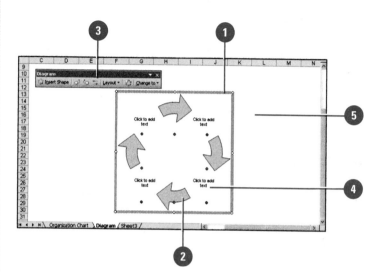

7

Formatting a Diagram

Microsoft® Office
Specialist
Approved Courseware

XL03E-2-4

After you create a diagram, you can use the AutoFormat button on the Diagram toolbar to format the diagram with the Diagram Style Gallery. The Diagram Style Gallery comes with 10 preset styles, such as Outline, Double Outline, Shaded, Fire, 3-D Color, and Square Shadows to name a few. The preset styles make it quick and easy to format a diagram with a professional look.

Format a Diagram

1 Select the diagram you want to modify.

2 Click the AutoFormat button on the Diagram toolbar.

3 Click a diagram style.

4 Click OK.

5 Click anywhere outside of the diagram to return to the document.

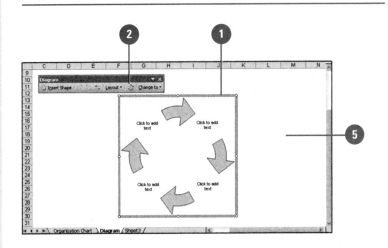

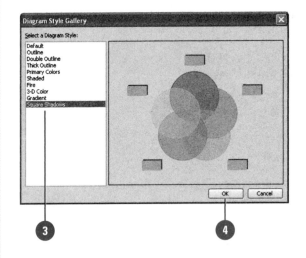

Drawing and Modifying Objects

Introduction

When you need to add pictures to a spreadsheet, Microsoft Office Excel 2003 makes it easy to get the job done. You can choose from a set of predesigned shapes, or you can use tools that allow you to draw and edit your own shapes and forms. Excel's drawing tools control how you place objects on your worksheet.

Drawing objects can be classified into three categories: lines, AutoShapes, and freeforms. Lines connect two points, AutoShapes are preset objects, such as stars, circles, or block arrows, and if you want to construct a new shape, you can draw a freeform shape. Once you have created a drawing object, you can manipulate it in many ways, such as moving and resizing the object, rotating and flipping the object, or by applying color and shadows to it. Additionally, you can take your object to a whole new level by adding a 3-D element to it. Excel also provides formatting commands that allow you precise control over your drawing object's appearance.

When working with objects in your worksheet, you might find it necessary to re-align or distribute the objects. You can group them so that when you move the objects, they become one large cluster. You can also change your view so that the objects are marked with a placeholder on your worksheet.

Drawing Lines and Arrows

The most basic drawing objects you create on your worksheets are lines and arrows. Excel includes several tools for this purpose. The Line tool creates line segments. The Drawing toolbar's Line Style and Dash Style tools let you determine the type of line used in any drawing object—solid, dashed, or a combination of solid and dashed lines. The Arrow tool lets you create arrows to emphasize key features of your worksheet.

Draw a Straight Line

① Click the Line button on the Drawing toolbar.

② Drag the pointer to draw a line on your worksheet.

③ Release the mouse button when the line is the length you want.

The endpoints of the line are where you started and finished dragging.

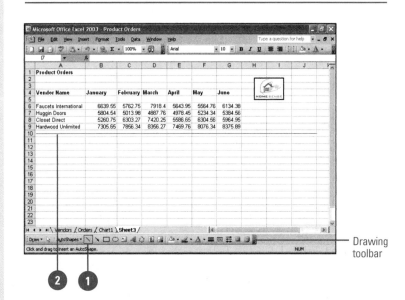

Drawing toolbar

Edit a Line

① Click the line you want to edit.

② Click the Line Style button on the Drawing toolbar to select a line thickness.

③ Click the Dash Style button on the Drawing toolbar to select a dash style.

④ Click the Line Color button on the Drawing toolbar to select a line color.

⑤ Drag the sizing handle at either end to a new location to change the size or angle of the line.

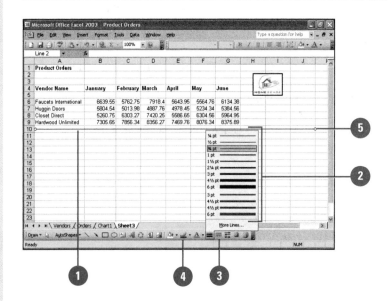

Draw and Edit an Arrow

1. Click the Arrow button on the Drawing toolbar.

2. Drag the pointer from the base of the arrow to the arrow's point.

3. Release the mouse button when the arrow is the length and angle you want.

4. Click the Arrow Style button on the Drawing toolbar.

5. Click the arrow type you want to use, or click More Arrows.

6. If you clicked More Arrows, modify the arrow type in the Format AutoShape dialog box as necessary.

7. Click OK.

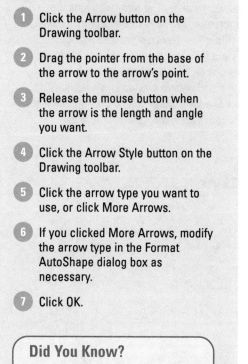

> ### Did You Know?
>
> **You can display the Drawing toolbar.**
> If the Drawing toolbar is not visible, click the View menu, point to Toolbars, and then click Drawing.

Drawing AutoShapes

You can choose from many different AutoShapes, ranging from hearts to lightening bolts, to draw on your worksheets. The two most common AutoShapes, the oval and the rectangle, are available directly on the Drawing toolbar. The rest of the AutoShapes are organized into categories that you can view and select from the AutoShapes button on the Drawing toolbar. Once you have placed an AutoShape on a worksheet, you can resize it using the sizing handles (small white circles). Many AutoShapes have an **adjustment handle**, a small yellow diamond located near a resize handle, which you can drag to alter the shape of the AutoShape.

Draw an Oval or Rectangle

① Click the Oval or Rectangle button on the Drawing toolbar.

② Drag over the worksheet where you want to place the oval or rectangle. Press and hold Shift as you drag to draw a circle or square.

③ Release the mouse button when the object is the shape you want.

The shape you drew takes on the line color and fill color defined by the presentation's color scheme.

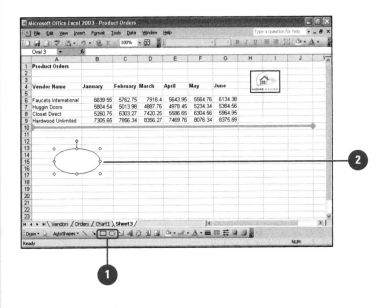

Draw an AutoShape

① Click the AutoShapes button on the Drawing toolbar, and then point to the AutoShape category you want to use.

② Click the symbol you want.

③ Drag the pointer across the worksheet until the drawing object is the shape and size that you want.

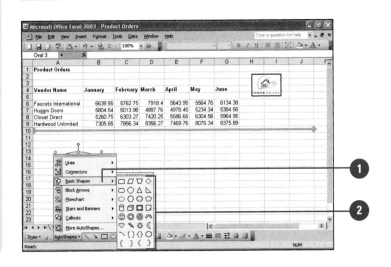

Adjust an AutoShape

1. Click the AutoShape you want to adjust.

2. Click the adjustment handle (yellow diamond), and then drag the handle to alter the form of the AutoShape.

Did You Know?

You can replace an AutoShape.
Replace one AutoShape with another, while retaining the size, color, and orientation of the AutoShape. Click the AutoShape you want replace, click Draw on the Drawing toolbar, point to Change AutoShape, and then select the new AutoShape you want.

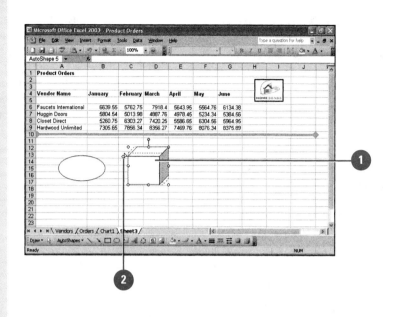

Resize an AutoShape

1. Click the AutoShape you want to resize.

2. Click one of the sizing handles (white circles), and then drag the handle to change the size of the AutoShape.

See Also

See "Resize an Embedded Chart" on page 179 for information on resizing objects.

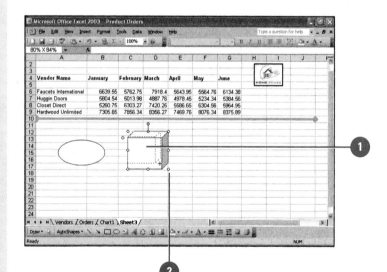

Inserting AutoShapes from the Clip Gallery

In addition to drawing AutoShapes, you can insert AutoShapes, such as computers and furniture, from the Clip Art Gallery. These AutoShapes are called **clips**. The Clip Art Gallery gives you a miniature of each clip. You can drag the clip onto your worksheet or click the clip to select other options, such as previewing the clip or searching for similar clips. After you insert a AutoShape, you can add text to it. You can format the text in an AutoShape in the same way you format text in a word processing program.

Insert an AutoShape from the Clip Gallery

1. Click the AutoShapes button on the Drawing toolbar, and then click More AutoShapes.

2. If necessary, use the scroll arrows to display more AutoShapes.

3. Click the shape you want onto your worksheet.

4. When you're done, click the Close button on the task pane.

Did You Know?

You can quickly delete an AutoShape. Click the AutoShape to select it, and then press Delete.

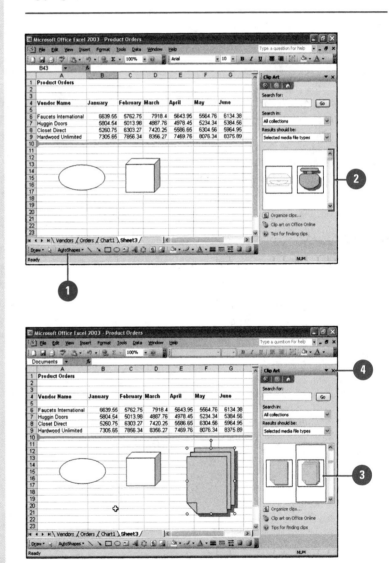

Find Similar AutoShapes in the Clip Gallery

1. Click the AutoShapes button on the Drawing toolbar, and then click More AutoShapes.

2. Point to the AutoShape in which you want to find a similar one.

3. Click the list arrow, and then click Find Similar Style.

   The similar AutoShape styles appear in the results box.

4. When you're done, click the Close button on the task pane.

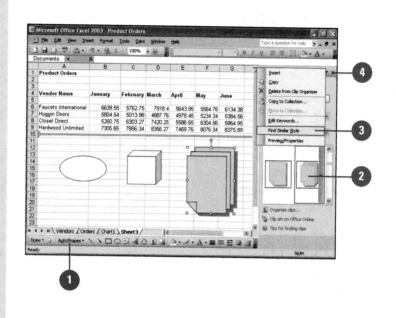

Add Text to an AutoShape

1. Click the AutoShape you want to add text.

2. Type the text you want.

Did You Know?

You can edit text in an AutoShape. Click the AutoShape to select it, click the text in the AutoShape to place the insertion point, and then edit the text.

You can align text in an AutoShape. Click the AutoShape to select it, click the Format menu, click AutoShape, click the Alignment tab, select an alignment option, and then click OK.

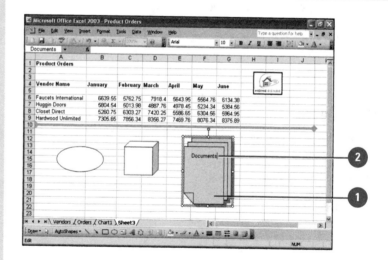

Moving and Resizing an Object

After you create a drawing object, you might need to change its size or move it to a different worksheet location. Although you can move and resize objects using the mouse, if you want more precise control over the object's size and position, use the AutoShape command on the Format menu to exactly specify the location and size of the drawing object. You can use the Nudge command to move drawing objects in tiny increments, up, down, left, or right.

Move an Object

1. Position the pointer over the object you want to move. (The pointer changes to a four-headed arrow.)

2. Drag the object to a new location on the worksheet. Make sure you aren't dragging a sizing handle or adjustment handle.

   If you are working with a freeform and you are in Edit Points mode, drag the interior of the object, not the border, or you will end up resizing or reshaping the object, not moving it.

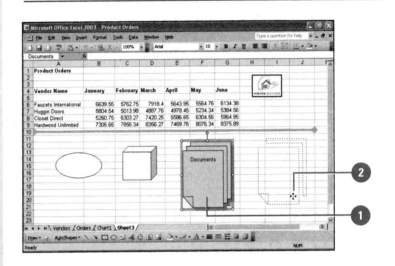

Nudge an Object

1. Click the object you want to nudge.

2. Click Draw on the Drawing toolbar, point to Nudge, and then click Up, Down, Left, or Right.

Did You Know?

You can nudge a selected object using the keyboard. Once selected, an object can be nudged by pressing any of the arrow keys.

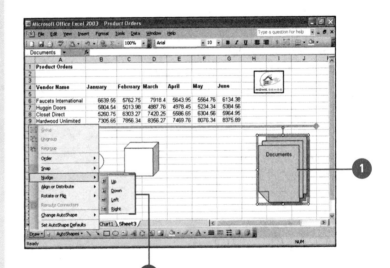

Resize a Drawing Object with the Mouse

1. Click the object to be resized.

2. Drag one of the sizing handles.

   ◆ To resize the object in the vertical or horizontal direction, drag a sizing handle on the side of the selection box.

   ◆ To resize the object in both the vertical and horizontal directions, drag a sizing handle on the corner of the selection box.

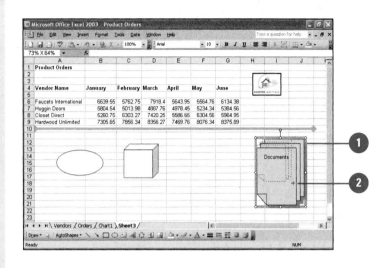

Resize an Object Precisely

1. Click the object to be resized.

2. Click the Format menu, and then click AutoShape.

3. Click the Size tab, and then adjust the height and width.

4. Click OK.

Did You Know?

You can retain the proportions of the object you're resizing. Press and hold Shift as you drag the object to the new size.

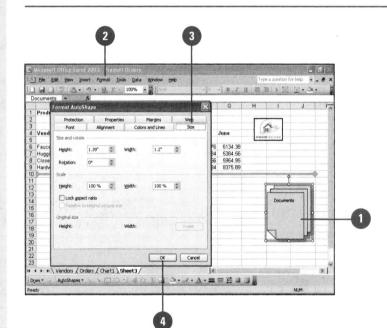

Rotating and Flipping an Object

You can change the orientation of a drawing object by rotating or flipping it. For example, if you want to create a mirror image of your object, you can flip it. To turn an object on its side, you can rotate it 90 degrees. Rotating and flipping tools work with drawing and text objects. Excel provides several different ways to rotate an object. You can use the rotate commands on the Drawing menu, the green rotate handle at the top of an AutoShape object, or the Format AutoShape dialog box to rotate an object. However, you can not rotate or flip chart objects.

Rotate an Object to Any Angle

1. Click the object you want to rotate.

2. Click the Draw button on the Drawing toolbar, point to Rotate Or Flip, and then click Free Rotate.

3. Drag a handle to rotate the object.

4. Click outside the object to set the rotation.

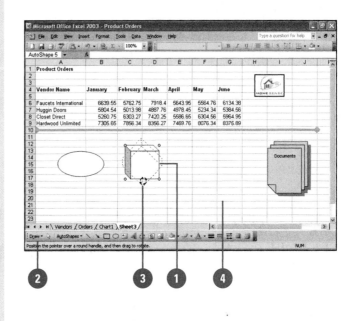

Rotate or Flip a Object Using Preset Increments

1. Click the object you want to rotate.

2. Click the Draw button on the Drawing toolbar.

3. Point to Rotate Or Flip, and then click one of the rotate or flip commands.

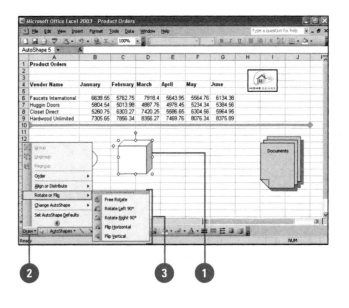

Rotate a Drawing Object Around a Fixed Point

1. Click the object you want to rotate.

2. Click the Draw button on the Drawing toolbar, point to Rotate or Flip, and then click Free Rotate.

3. Click the rotate handle opposite the point you want to rotate, and then press and hold Ctrl as you rotate the object.

4. Click outside the object to set the rotation.

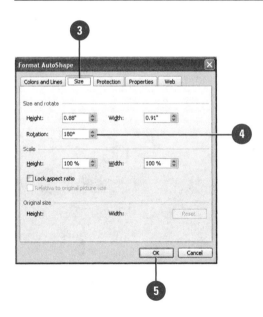

Rotate a Object Precisely

1. Click the object you want to rotate.

2. Click the Format menu, and then click AutoShape.

3. Click the Size tab.

4. Enter the angle of rotation.

5. Click OK.

Choosing Object Colors

When you create a closed drawing object, you can choose the fill color and the line color. When you create a drawing object, it uses a default color. You can change the fill and line color settings for drawing objects using the same color tools you use to change a text color. You can use fill effects as well, including gradients, patterns, and even clip art pictures.

Change a Drawing Object's Fill Color

1 Click the object whose fill color you want to change.

2 Click the Fill Color button list arrow on the Drawing toolbar.

3 Select the fill color or fill effect you want.

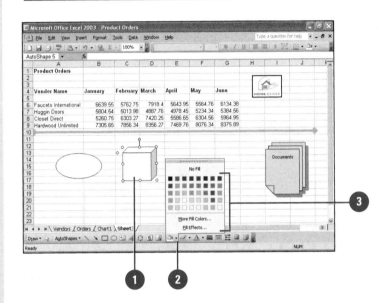

Change Colors and Lines in the Format AutoShape Dialog Box

1 Click the object you want to modify.

2 Click the Format menu, and then click AutoShape.

3 Click the Colors and Lines tab.

4 Select the Fill, Line, and Arrows format options you want.

5 Click OK.

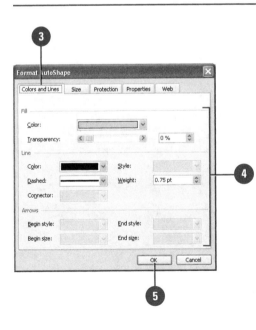

Create a Line Pattern

1. Click the line you want to modify.

2. Click the Line Color button list arrow on the Drawing toolbar, and then click Patterned Lines.

3. Click the Foreground list arrow, and then select the color you want as a foreground.

4. Click the Background list arrow, and then select the color you want as a background.

5. Click the pattern you want.

6. Click OK.

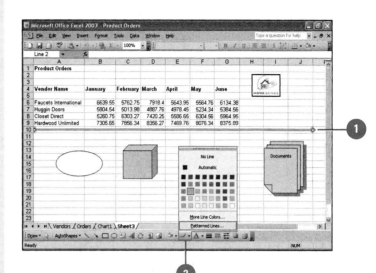

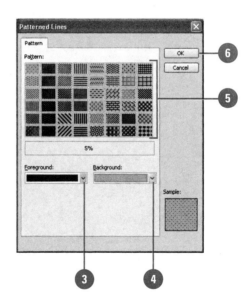

Adding Object Shadows

You can give objects on your worksheet the illusion of depth by adding shadows. Excel provides several preset shadowing options, or you can create your own by specifying the location and color of the shadow. If the shadow is falling on another object in your worksheet, you can create a semi-transparent shadow that blends the color of the shadow with the color of the object underneath it.

Use a Preset Shadow

1 Click the object to which you want to add a preset shadow.

2 Click the Shadow Style button on the Drawing toolbar.

3 Click one of the 20 preset shadow styles.

See Also

See "Add a Drop Shadow to a Text Annotation" on page 188 for information on shadows.

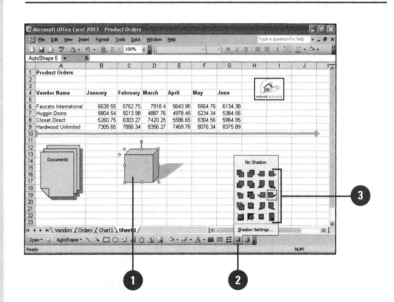

Change the Location of a Shadow

1 Click the object that has the shadow you want to change.

2 Click the Shadow Style button on the Drawing toolbar, and then click Shadow Settings.

3 Click an effects button on the Shadow Settings toolbar.

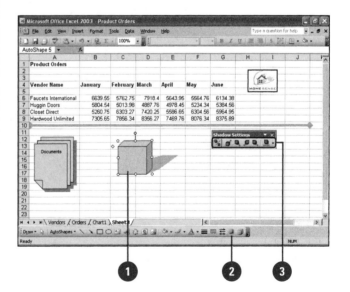

Change the Color of a Shadow

1 Click the object that has the shadow you want to change.

2 Click the Shadow Style button on the Drawing toolbar, and then click Shadow Settings.

3 Click the Shadow Color button list arrow on the Shadow Settings toolbar, and then click a new color.

Did You Know?

You can turn a shadow on and off.
Click the Shadow Style button on the Drawing toolbar, and then click Shadow Settings. Click the Shadow On/Off button on the Shadow Settings toolbar.

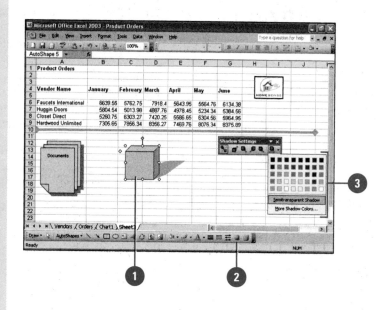

8

Creating a 3-D Object

You can add the illusion of depth to your worksheets by giving your drawings a three-dimensional appearance using the 3-D tool. Although not all objects can be turned into 3-D objects, most AutoShapes can. You can create a 3-D effect using one of the 20 preset 3-D styles, or you can use the 3-D tools to customize your own 3-D style. You can control several elements using the customization tools, including the angle at which the 3-D object is tilted and rotated, the depth of the object, and the direction of light falling upon the object.

Apply a Preset 3-D Style

1. Click the object you want to apply a preset 3-D style.

2. Click the 3-D Style button on the Drawing toolbar.

3. Click one of the 20 preset 3-D styles.

Did You Know?

You can set a surface for a 3-D object. On the 3-D Settings toolbar, click the Surface button, and then click the surface (Wire Frame, Matte, Plastic, or Metal) you want.

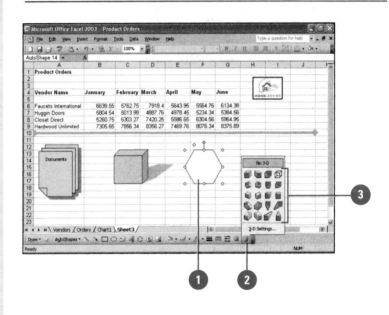

Spin a 3-D Object

1. Click the 3-D object you want to spin.

2. Click the 3-D Style button on the Drawing toolbar, and then click 3-D Settings.

3. Click the spin setting button you want on the 3-D Settings toolbar.

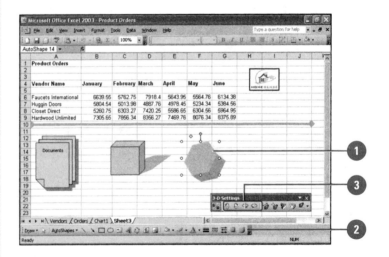

Set Lighting for a 3-D Object

1. Click the 3-D object.

2. Click the 3-D Style button on the Drawing toolbar, and then click 3-D Settings.

3. Click the Lighting button.

4. Click the spotlight, and then click Bright, Normal, or Dim to create the effect you want.

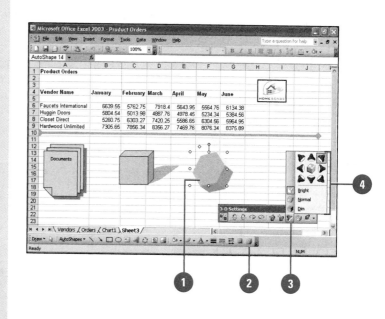

Set Depth for a 3-D Object

1. Click the 3-D object.

2. Click the 3-D Style button on the Drawing toolbar, and then click 3-D Settings.

3. Click the Depth button.

4. Click the size of the depth in points, or enter the exact number of points you want in the Custom box.

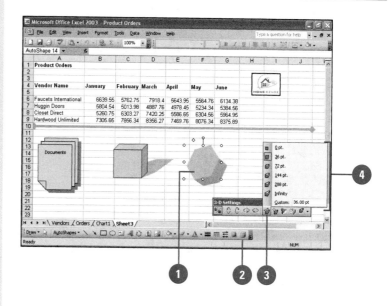

Did You Know?

You can set direction for a 3-D object. On the 3-D Settings toolbar, click the Direction button, and then click the direction you want. You can also change the direction to show the object with a perspective or parallel point of view.

Aligning and Distributing Objects

Often when you work with three similar or identical objects, they look best when aligned in relation to each other. For example, you can align three objects so the tops of all three objects match along an invisible line. Sometimes your task will not be alignment but distributing objects evenly across a space. Excel includes commands to distribute your items horizontally and vertically. You can specify whether you want the distribution to occur in the currently occupied space or across the entire worksheet.

Align Objects

1. Press Shift, and then click the objects that you want to align.

2. Click the Draw button on the Drawing toolbar, and then point to Align Or Distribute.

3. Click the alignment option you want.

   ◆ **Align Left.** Lines up the left edges of the selected objects.

   ◆ **Align Center.** Lines up the centers of the selected objects.

   ◆ **Align Right.** Lines up the right edges of the selected objects.

   ◆ **Align Top.** Lines up the top edges of the selected objects.

   ◆ **Align Middle.** Lines up horizontally the middles of the selected objects.

   ◆ **Align Bottom.** Lines up the bottom edges of the selected objects.

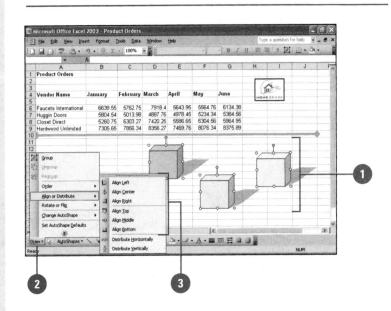

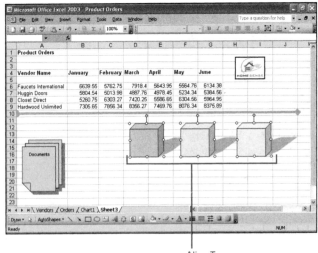

Align Top

Distribute Objects

1. Press Shift, and then click the objects that you want to distribute.

2. Click the Draw button on the Drawing toolbar, and then point to Align Or Distribute.

3. Click the distribution option you want.

    ◆ **Distribute Horizontally.** Distributes the objects evenly horizontally.

    ◆ **Distribute Vertically.** Distributes the objects evenly vertically.

Did You Know?

You can open the Drawing toolbar. If the Drawing toolbar is not open, click the View menu, point to Toolbars, and then click Drawing.

You can snap an object to a shape or grid. When you drag an object, you can have Excel snap the object you're dragging to another object or an invisible grid on the worksheet. Click the Draw button on the Drawing toolbar, point to Snap, and then click To Grid or To Shape.

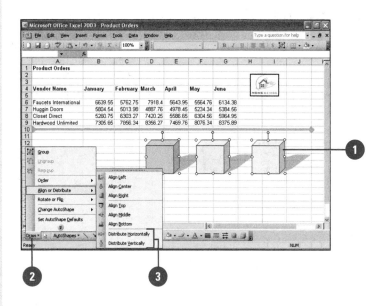

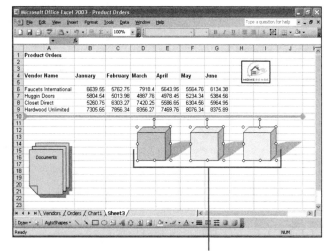

Distribute Horizontally

Arranging and Grouping Objects

When a worksheet contains multiple objects, you might need to consider how they interact with each other. If the objects overlap, the most recently created drawing will be placed on top of older drawings, but you can change how the stack of objects is ordered. If you have created a collection of objects that work together, you might want to group them to create a new drawing object that you can move, resize, or copy as a single unit.

Change the Order of Objects

1. Click the drawing object you want to place.

2. Click the Draw button on the Drawing toolbar, and then point to Order.

3. Click the stacking option you want.

   ◆ Click Bring To Front or Send To Back to move the drawing to the top or bottom of the stack.

   ◆ Click Bring Forward or Bring Backward to move a drawing up or back one location in the stack.

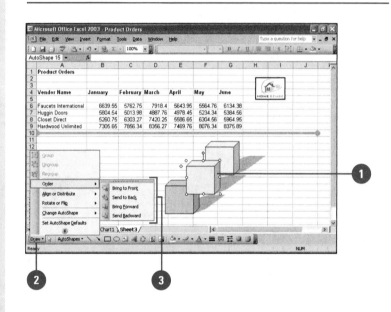

Group Objects Together

1. Press Shift while you click to select the drawing objects you want to group together.

2. Click the Draw button on the Drawing toolbar.

3. Click Group.

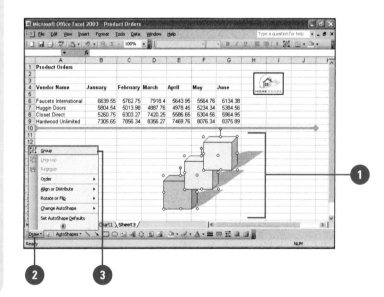

Ungroup an Object

1. Select the object you want to ungroup.

2. Click the Draw button on the Drawing toolbar.

3. Click Ungroup.

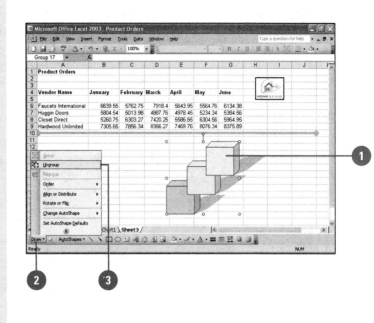

Regroup an Object

1. Click one or more of the objects in the original group.

2. Click the Draw button on the Drawing toolbar.

3. Click Regroup.

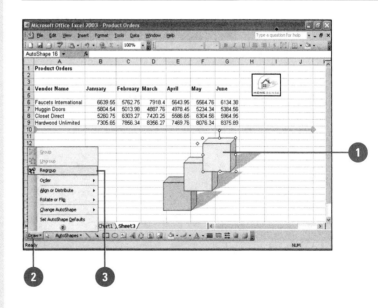

Changing Object View Settings

After drawing or inserting different types of objects on your worksheet, you might find it difficult to work with the information on the worksheet. You can change view settings in Excel to show or hide objects on your worksheets. You can also show objects as **placeholders**. A placeholder is an empty box that takes the place of the object.

Change View Settings for Objects

1. Click the Tools menu, and then click Options.

2. Click the View tab.

3. Click the view setting options you want.

4. Click OK.

Creating and Modifying Charts

9

Introduction

When you're ready to share data with others, a worksheet might not be the most effective way to present the information. A page full of numbers, even if formatted attractively, can be hard to understand and perhaps a little boring. Microsoft Office Excel 2003 makes it easy to create and modify charts so that you can effectively present your information. A **chart**, also called a graph, is a visual representation of selected data in your worksheet.

A well-designed chart draws the reader's attention to important data by illustrating trends and highlighting significant relationships between numbers. Excel generates charts based on data you select; the Chart Wizard makes it easy to select the best chart type, design elements, and formatting enhancements for any type of information.

Once you create a chart, you might find you want to change your chart type to see how your data displays in a different style. You can move and resize your chart, and you can even draw on your chart to highlight achievements. Other formatting elements are available to assure a well designed chart.

Understanding Chart Terminology

Title
Optional text that identifies the purpose of a chart

Handles
Small black boxes that appear around the perimeter of a selected object, indicating that you can move, resize, copy, or delete the object

Data Marker
A chart object, such as a circle, dot, or square, that denotes a data point

Y-axis
The vertical axis of a chart - by default, a value axis

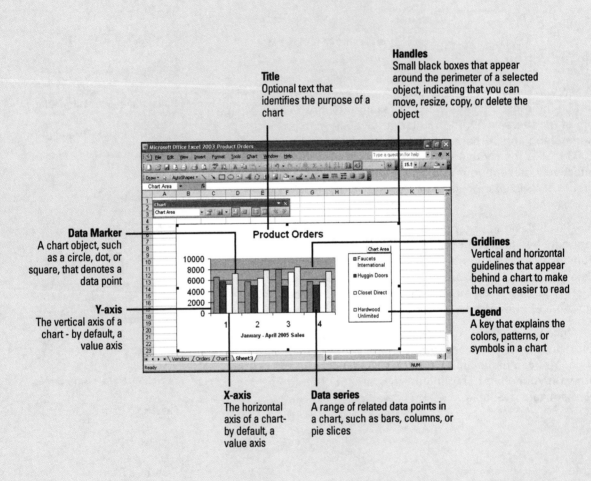

Gridlines
Vertical and horizontal guidelines that appear behind a chart to make the chart easier to read

Legend
A key that explains the colors, patterns, or symbols in a chart

X-axis
The horizontal axis of a chart - by default, a value axis

Data series
A range of related data points in a chart, such as bars, columns, or pie slices

Choosing the Right Type of Chart

When you create a chart in Excel, you can choose from a variety of chart types. Each type interprets data in a slightly different way. For example, a pie chart is great for comparing parts of a whole, such as regional percentages of a sales total, while a column chart is better for showing how different sales regions performed throughout a year. Although there is some overlap, each chart type is best suited for conveying a different type of information.

When you generate a chart, you need to evaluate whether the chart type suits the data being plotted, and whether the formatting choices clarify or overshadow the information. Sometimes a colorful 3-D chart is just what you need to draw attention to an important shift; other times, special visual effects might be a distraction.

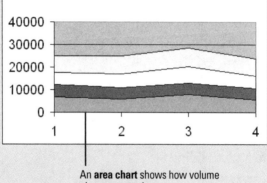
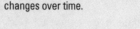

An **area chart** shows how volume changes over time.

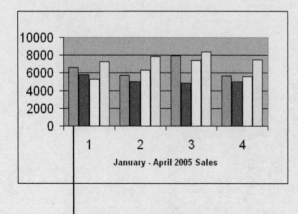

A **bar chart** contains data having different scales.

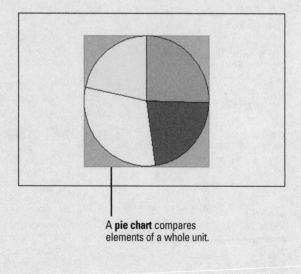

A **pie chart** compares elements of a whole unit.

Creating a Chart

A **chart** provides a visual, graphical representation of numerical data. Whether you turn numbers into a bar, line, pie, surface, or bubble chart, patterns become more apparent. For example, the trend of annual rising profits becomes powerful in a line chart. A second line showing diminishing annual expenses creates an instant map of the success of your business. **Titles** on the chart, horizontal (x-axis), and vertical (y-axis) identify the data. A legend connects the colors and patterns in a chart with the data they represent. **Gridlines** are horizontal and vertical lines to help the reader determine data values in a chart. Excel simplifies the chart-making process with the **Chart Wizard**, a series of dialog boxes that leads you through all the steps to create an effective chart on a new or an existing worksheet. When you choose to place the chart on an existing sheet, rather than on a new sheet, the chart is called an **embedded object**. You can then resize or move it just as you would any graphic object.

Create a Chart Using the Chart Wizard

1 Select the data range you want to chart.

Make sure you include the data you want to chart and the column and row labels in the range. The Chart Wizard expects to find this information and incorporates it in your chart.

2 Click the Chart Wizard button on the Standard toolbar.

To move backward or forward in the Chart Wizard, click Back or Forward. You can click Finish at any time.

3 Click a chart type.

4 Click a chart sub-type.

5 Click the Press And Hold To View Sample button to preview your selection.

6 Click Next to continue.

7 Verify the data range, and then select to plot the data series in rows or in columns.

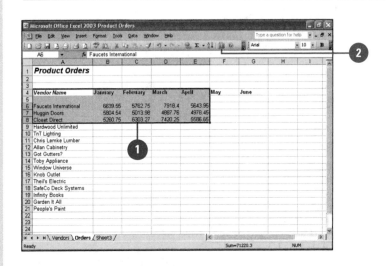

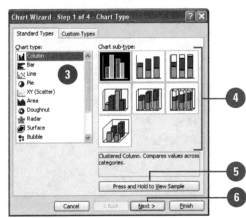

8 Click Next to continue.

9 Click a chart options tab.

◆ **Titles tab.** Type titles for the chart, x-axis, and y-axis in the appropriate text boxes.

◆ **Axes tab**. Select the axes you want to display for the data.

◆ **Gridlines tab**. Select the type of gridlines you want for the x-axis and y-axis.

◆ **Legend tab**. Select options to display a legend and its location.

◆ **Data Labels tab**. Select the labels you want for the data.

◆ **Data Table tab**. Click to add a table to the chart.

10 Preview the options, and then click Next to continue.

11 Select to place the chart on a new sheet or as an embedded object.

12 Click Finish.

13 Drag the chart to a new location if necessary.

Did You Know?

The difference between major and minor gridlines. Major gridlines occur at each value on an axis; minor gridlines occur between values on an axis. Use gridlines sparingly and only when they improve the chart's readability.

You can change chart options. You can revise titles, gridlines, and legends at anytime. Select the chart, click the Chart menu, click Chart Options, click the appropriate tab, select or change options, and then click OK.

Chart title

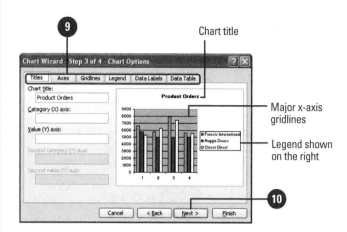

Major x-axis gridlines

Legend shown on the right

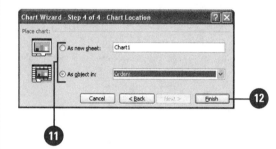

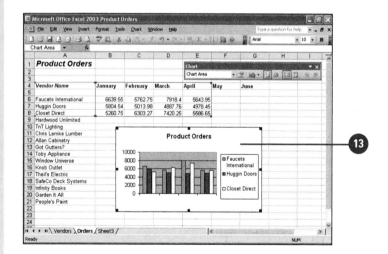

9

Creating and Modifying Charts   **175**

Editing a Chart

Editing a chart means altering any of its features, from data selection to formatting elements. You might want to use more effective colors or patterns in a data series, for example. To change a chart's type or any element within it, you must select the chart or element. When a chart is selected, handles are displayed around the window's perimeter, and the Chart toolbar is displayed: all buttons on this toolbar function when the chart is selected. As the figure below illustrates, you can point to any object or area on a chart to see what it is called.

When you select an object, its name appears in the Chart Objects list box on the Chart toolbar, and you can then edit it.

Editing a chart has no effect on the data used to create it. You don't need to worry about updating a chart if you change worksheet data because Excel automatically does it for you. The only chart element you might need to edit is a data range. If you decide you want to plot more or less data in a range, you can select the data series on the worksheet, as shown in the figure below, and then drag the outline to include the range you want in the chart.

Point to any chart object to see
what type of object it is.

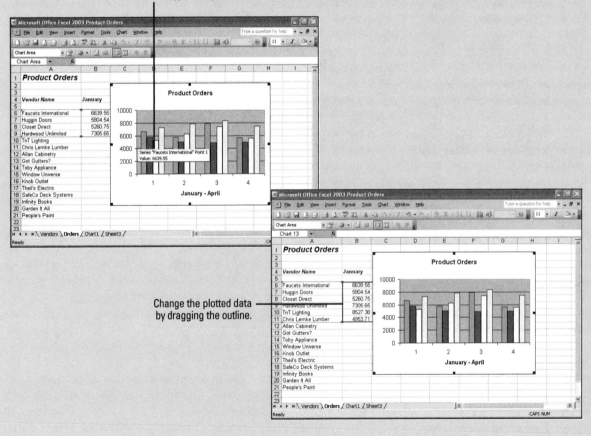

Change the plotted data
by dragging the outline.

176

Selecting and Editing a Chart Object

XL03S-2-5

When you edit a chart, you alter its features, which can include selecting data or formatting elements. For example, you might want to use different colors or patterns in a data series. To change the type of chart or any element in it, you must first select the chart or element. When you select a chart, handles (small black squares) display around the window's perimeter, and the Chart toolbar displays on screen (docked or floating). When you select a chart, all of the buttons on this toolbar become active. You can use the ScreenTip feature to display the data value and the name of any object or area on a chart. When you select an object in a chart, the name of the object appears in the Chart Objects list box on the Chart toolbar, which indicates that you can now edit the object. Editing a chart does not affect the data used to create it. You don't need to worry about updating a chart if you change data in the worksheet because Excel automatically updates the chart. You can change the data range at any time. If you want to plot more or less data in a range, you can select the data series on the worksheet and then drag the range to the chart.

Select and Edit a Chart Object

1. Select a chart. The Chart toolbar appears.

2. Position the mouse pointer over a chart object, and then click the object to select it.

3. To edit the object, double-click it, make changes, and then click OK.

4. Click another area of the chart, or press Esc to deselect a chart object.

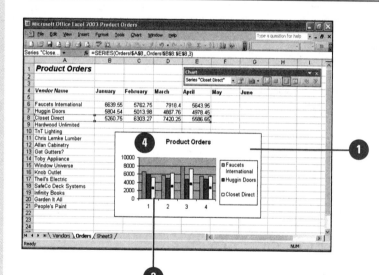

Did You Know?

You can use the Chart toolbar to select chart elements. Select a chart element by clicking the Chart Objects list arrow on the Chart toolbar. Once an element is selected, double-click it to open a corresponding Format dialog box.

Changing a Chart Type

Excel's default chart type is the column chart, although there are many other types from which to choose. A column chart might adequately display your data, while a pie chart is great at providing you with a general overview. Experiment with a variety of chart types to find the one that shows your data in the most effective way.

Change a Chart Type Quickly

1. Select the chart you want to change.

2. Click the Chart Type button list arrow on the Chart toolbar.

3. Select a chart type. Excel changes the chart type when you release the mouse button.

Did You Know?

You can move and resize a chart. Drag the selected chart from its center to a new location. Drag a resize handle to enlarge or shrink the chart's size.

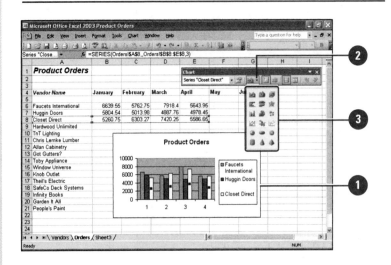

Moving and Resizing a Chart

XL03S-2-5

You can move or resize an embedded chart after you select it. If you've created a chart as a new sheet instead of an embedded object on an existing worksheet, the chart's size and location are fixed by the sheet's margins. You can change the margins to resize or reposition the chart. You can also move your embedded chart off the original worksheet and onto another worksheet. When resizing a chart downward, be sure to watch out for legends and axis titles.

Move an Embedded Chart

1. Select a chart you want to move.

2. Position the mouse pointer over a blank area of the chart, and then drag the pointer to move the outline of the chart to a new location.

3. Release the mouse button.

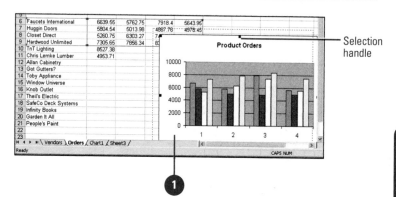

Selection handle

Resize an Embedded Chart

1. Select a chart you want to resize.

2. Position the mouse pointer over one of the handles.

3. Drag the handle to the new chart size.

4. Release the mouse button.

Did You Know?

You can avoid clicking a chart's handle. Clicking and dragging a chart's handle resizes the chart. If you accidentally resize a chart, press Ctrl+Z to undo the change.

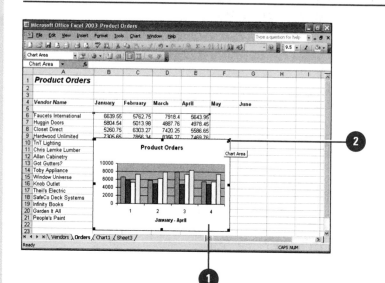

Pulling Out a Pie Slice ▶

A pie chart is an effective and easily understood chart type for comparing parts that make up a whole entity, such as departmental percentages of a company budget. You can call attention to individual pie slices that are particularly significant by moving them away from the other pieces, or **exploding** the pie. Not only will this make a visual impact, it will also restate the values you are graphing.

Explode a Single Pie Slice

1. Select a pie chart.

2. Double-click to select the pie slice you want to explode.

3. Drag the slice away from the pie.

4. Release the mouse button.

Did You Know?

You can select a pie slice to make it stand out. Because a pie chart has only one data series, clicking any slice selects the entire data series. Click a second time to select a specific slice.

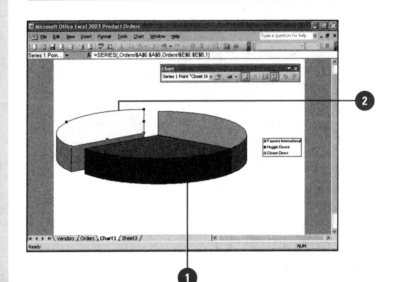

Explode an Entire Pie

1. Select a pie chart.

2. Drag all pie slices away from the center of the pie.

3. Release the mouse button.

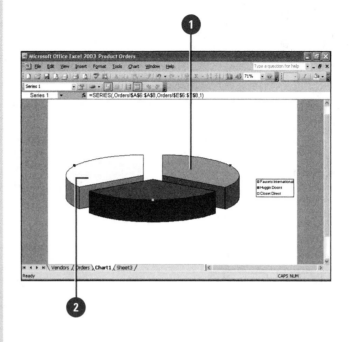

Undo a Pie Explosion

1. Select a pie chart.

2. Drag a slice toward the center of the pie.

3. Release the mouse button.

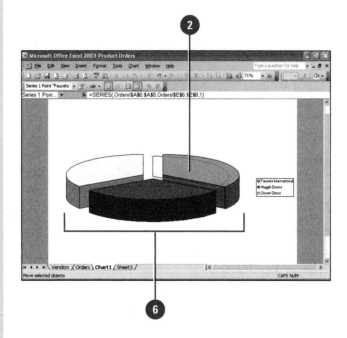

Adding and Deleting a Data Series

Many components make up a chart. Each range of data that comprises a bar, column, or pie slice is called a **data series**; each value in a data series is called a **data point**. The data series is defined when you select a range on a worksheet and then open the Chart Wizard. But what if you want to add a data series once a chart is complete? Using Excel, you can add a data series by using the mouse, the Chart menu, or the Chart Wizard. As you create and modify more charts, you might also find it necessary to delete or change the order of one or more data series. You can delete a data series without re-creating the chart.

Add a Data Series Quickly

1. Select the range that contains the data series you want to add to your chart.

2. Drag the range into the existing chart.

3. Release the mouse button to display the chart with the added data series.

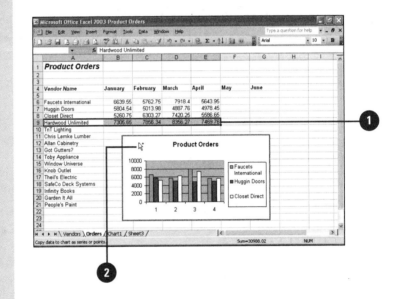

Delete a Data Series

1. Select the chart that contains the data series you want to delete.

2. Click any data point in the data series to select the series in the chart and the worksheet.

   To delete one data point but keep the rest of the series in the chart, click the data point twice.

3. Press Delete.

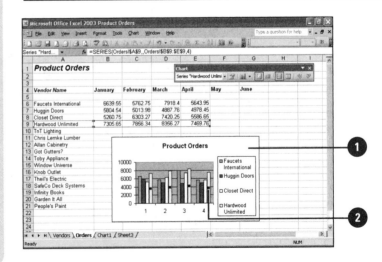

Change a Data Series

1. Select the chart that contains the data series you want to change.

2. Click the Chart menu, and then click Source Data.

3. Click the Series tab.

4. Click the series name you want to change.

5. Click the Name or Values Collapse Dialog button to change the name or value, make the change, and then click the Expand Dialog button.

6. Click OK.

Change Data Series Order

1. Select the chart and the data series you want to change.

2. Click the Format menu, and then click Selected Data Series.

3. Click the Series Order tab.

4. Click the series you want to reorder.

5. Click Move Up or Move Down.

6. Click OK.

Did You Know?

You can add a trendline. A trendline helps you analyze problems of prediction. Select the chart to which you want to add a trendline, click the Chart menu, click Add Trendline, select a trend type, select a series, and then click OK.

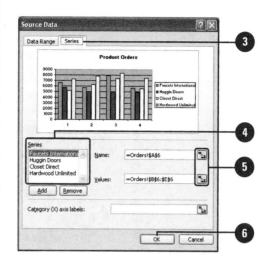

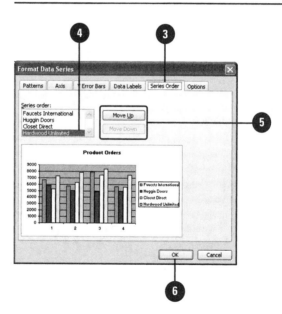

Enhancing a Data Series

XL03E-2-4

Change a Data Series Color or Pattern

① Click any data point in a data series to select it.

② Double-click a data point in the selected data series.

③ Click the Patterns tab.

④ Click a color in the Area palette. The selected color displays in the Sample box.

⑤ If you want to add effects, such as textures, patterns, gradients, or pictures, click the Fill Effects button.

⑥ Click the Gradient, Texture, or Pattern tab to change the qualities of the data series color.

⑦ When you're done, click OK.

⑧ Click OK if you're satisfied with the results shown in the Sample box, or select different options.

Did You Know?

You can format a chart object quickly. Double-clicking an object opens a corresponding Format dialog box, which you can use to change the object's attributes. Depending on which objects are selected, your formatting options will vary.

When you initially use the Chart Wizard, Excel automatically selects the colors that it will use to represent each data series. You can change one or all of the default colors. You may want more dynamic colors—adding patterns and texture to further enhance a data series. Or, perhaps you'll be printing your charts in black and white and you want to ensure the readability of each data series. You can also insert a picture in a chart so that its image occupies a bar or column.

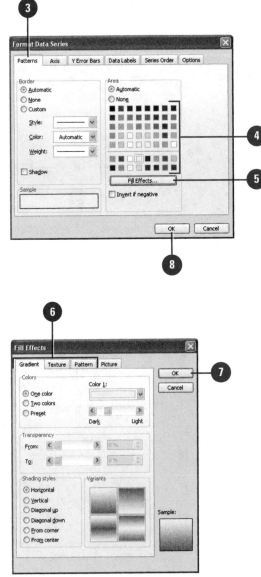

Add a Picture to a Data Series

1. Select a data series.

2. Double-click a data point in the selected series.

3. Click Fill Effects.

4. Click the Picture tab.

5. Click Select Picture.

6. Locate and select the graphics file.

7. Click OK.

   If you want the data point to contain one copy of the image stretched to fill it, click the Stretch option; or if you want the data point to contain many copies of the image, click the Stack option.

8. Click OK.

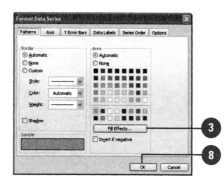

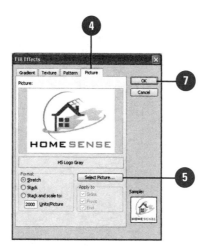

Delete a Picture from a Data Series

1. Select a data series.

2. Double-click a data point in the selected series.

3. Select a Color Area.

4. Select a Border.

5. Click OK.

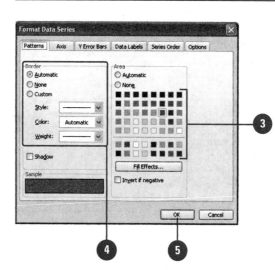

Enhancing a Chart

Add **chart objects**, such as titles, legends, and text annotations to a chart to enhance its appearance and increase its overall effectiveness. A **chart title** identifies the primary purpose of the chart; a title for each axis further clarifies the data that is plotted. Titles can be more than one line and can be formatted just like other worksheet text. You can also add a **text annotation**, additional text not attached to a specific axis or data point, to call attention to a trend or some other area of interest. A **legend** helps the reader connect the colors and patterns in a chart with the data they represent.

Add a Title

1. Select a chart to which you want to add a title or titles.

2. Click the Chart menu, and then click Chart Options.

3. Click the Titles tab.

4. Type the text you want for the title of the chart.

5. To add a title for the x-axis, press Tab, and then type the text.

6. To add a title for the y-axis, press Tab, and then type the text.

7. If you want a second line for the x- or y-axis, press Tab to move to the Second Category or Second Value box, and then type the title text.

8. Preview the title(s) you are adding.

9. Click OK.

Did You Know?

You can resize the text box to create a multiple-line title. Select the text box, and then drag a resize handle. Click in the text, and then type in the text box.

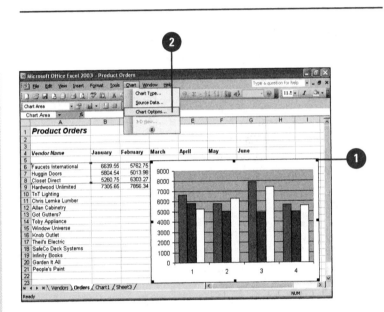

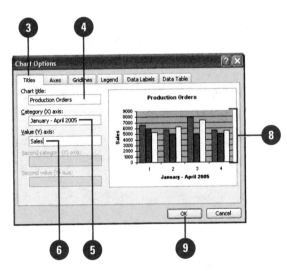

Add or Delete a Legend

1. Select the chart to which you want to add or delete a legend.

2. Click the Legend button on the Chart toolbar. You can drag the legend to move it to a new location.

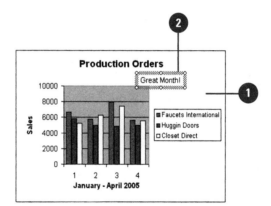

Add a Text Annotation

1. Select a chart to which you want to add a text annotation.

2. Type the text for the annotation, and then press Enter. A text box containing your text appears within the chart area.

3. Position the mouse pointer over the text box until the pointer changes shape.

4. Drag the selected text box to a new location.

5. Press Esc to deselect the text box.

Did You Know?

You can customize your legend. Legend text is derived from the data series plotted within a chart. You can rename an item within a legend by changing the text in the data series.

9

Drawing on a Chart

Once titles and text have been added and the chart fine-tuned, you might want to accentuate information in a chart using tools on the Drawing toolbar. For example, a drop shadow adds dimension to a chart's title; an arrow shows a connection between annotated text and specific data in your chart.

Add a Drop Shadow to a Text Annotation

1. Select a chart that contains a text annotation you want to enhance.

2. Select the text annotation in the chart.

3. Click the Shadow Style button on the Drawing toolbar.

4. Select a shadow based on the effect you want. Experiment until you find the one you want.

Did You Know?

You can use the Shift key to draw straight lines. Press and hold Shift while you drag the pointer to create a vertical, horizontal, or diagonal arrow.

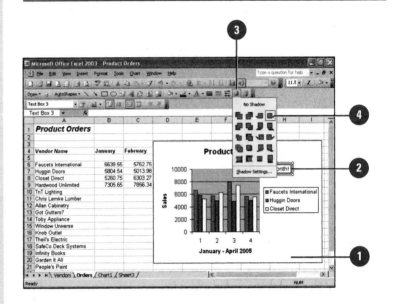

Add a Drop Shadow to a Chart Title

1. Select the chart.

2. Double-click the title.

3. Click the Patterns tab.

4. Click to select the Shadow check box.

5. Click OK.

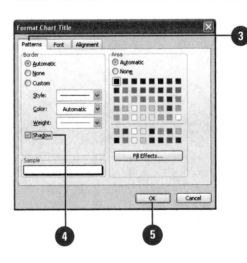

Draw an Arrow on a Chart

① Select the chart.

② If necessary, click the Drawing button on the Standard toolbar to display the Drawing toolbar.

③ Click the Arrow button on the Drawing toolbar.

④ Click and drag the pointer from the base object to another object. The arrowhead appears at the point of the second object.

Click anywhere in the worksheet to deselect the arrow.

Did You Know?

You can use the Drawing toolbar to modify the arrow object. Click the Line Style, Dash Style, or Arrow Style button on the Drawing toolbar to modify the arrow object.

Arrow-drawing techniques. When you draw an arrow, the arrowhead appears at the conclusion (or end) of the line.

See Also

See "Draw a Straight Line" on page 150 for information on arrows and lines.

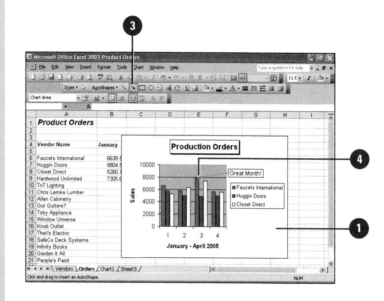

Arrow inserted

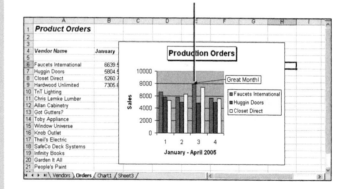

9

Formatting Chart Elements

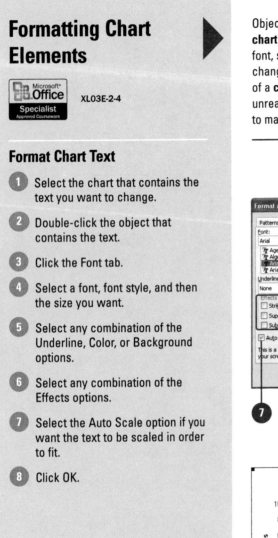

Format Chart Text

1 Select the chart that contains the text you want to change.

2 Double-click the object that contains the text.

3 Click the Font tab.

4 Select a font, font style, and then the size you want.

5 Select any combination of the Underline, Color, or Background options.

6 Select any combination of the Effects options.

7 Select the Auto Scale option if you want the text to be scaled in order to fit.

8 Click OK.

Objects such as annotated text, data labels, and titles are referred to as **chart text**. To make chart text more readable, you can change the text font, style, and size. You might decide to increase your chart title, or change the labels of your x- and y-axis. You can also change the format of a **chart axis**. For example, if axis labels or scales are too long and unreadable, you might want to reduce the font size or change the scale to make the labels fit better in a small space.

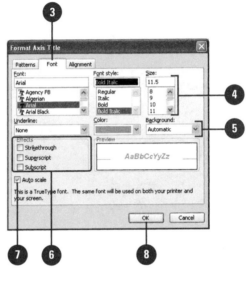

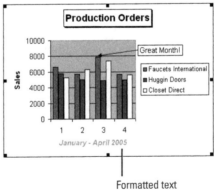

Formatted text

Format a Chart Axis

1. Select the chart that contains the axis you want to change.

2. Double-click the axis you want to format.

3. Click the Scale tab.

4. Select the scale and display units you want.

5. If you need to change the number format, click the Number tab.

6. Click OK.

Did You Know?

You can change chart text alignment.
Double-click the text you want to change, click the Alignment tab, change the orientation, and then click OK.

You can change chart axis patterns.
Double-click the axis you want to change, click the Patterns tab, change the line style, major or minor tick mark type, and labels, and then click OK.

Chart axis

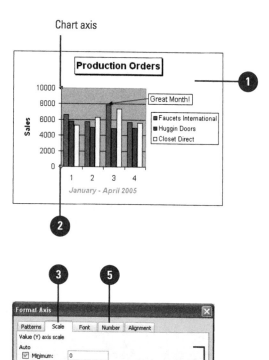

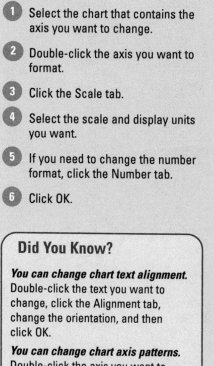

9

Adding Chart Gridlines

You can change chart options to add gridlines to a chart. **Gridlines** are horizontal and vertical lines you can add to help the reader determine data point values in a chart. There are two types of gridlines: major and minor. Major gridlines occur at each value on an axis, while minor gridlines occur between values on an axis. Use gridlines sparingly and only when they improve the readability of a chart.

Add Gridlines

1. Select a chart to which you want to add gridlines.

2. Click the Chart menu, and then click Chart Options.

3. Click the Gridlines tab.

4. Select the type of gridlines you want for the x-axis (vertical) and y-axis (horizontal).

5. Click OK.

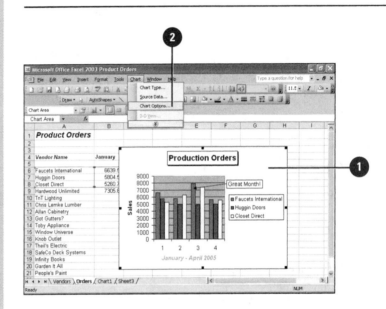

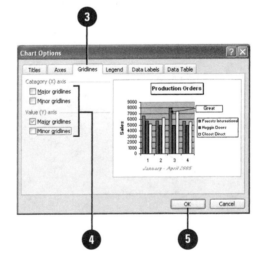

Analyzing Worksheet Data

Introduction

In addition to using a worksheet to calculate values, you can also use it to manage and analyze a list of information, also called a **database**. For example, you can create an inventory list, a school grade book, or a customer database. You can enter data directly in a worksheet, or you can use a **Data Form**, which is an on-screen data entry tool, that resembles a paper form. A Data Form lets you easily enter data by filling in blank text boxes. Data entry in a list is further enhanced by features such as a pick list to ensure restricted field entry, and adding data validation rules which will restrict the entry of data into certain fields. If you want to make sure that an order isn't placed for an out of stock item, you can restrict that item's code from entry onto an order form.

Once you've entered your records into the database, you can use the Data Form to display certain records. Instead of scrolling through a long list of data to find a record, you can find it with the Data Form's criteria feature. Once the record is found, you can make your changes to it or delete it. You can also find records in your database that match a certain criteria, such as all clients in a certain zip code, or all students who have an average of B or higher. Sorting data in your list can be accomplished a few ways: one with the sort ascending or descending buttons, the other by using Excel's AutoFilter option. By typing in a set field to sort by, you can pull all the records in your list that contain a matching field.

PivotTables are also available to pull your data together for easier viewing and reporting. The PivotChart Wizard walks you through setting up a PivotTable. Excel has some designed reports that contain layout formatting to give that extra touch to your reports.

Understanding Lists

A **database** is a collection of related records.
Examples of databases are an address book,
a list of customers or products, and a telephone directory. In Excel, a database is referred
to as a **list**.

Record
One set of related fields, such as all the fields
pertaining to one customer or product. In a
worksheet, each row represents a unique record.

Field name
The title of a field.
In an Excel list,
the first row
contains the
names of each
field. Each field
name can have
up to 255
characters,
including
uppercase and
lowercase letters
and spaces.

List range
The block of
cells that
contains some
or all of the list
you want to
analyze. The
list range
cannot occupy
more than one
worksheet.

	A	B	C	D	E	F	G
2	Vendor Name	Contact Name	Address	City	State	Zip Code	Phone Nu
4	Faucets International	Deanne Reinig	901 Riverton Way	Mammoth	MI	95463	(724) 555-8
5	Huggin Doors	Joe Huggins	1111 Acton Road	Mystic	SD	48297	(604) 555-1
6	ClosetDirect	Debbie Higuera	3126 Bank Avenue	Diamond	NV	86120	(835) 555-4
7	Hardwood Unlimited	Trina Halama	548 Dustin Street	Winnett	CA	93883	(831) 555-2
8	TnT Lighting	Peggy Keating	926 Black Iron Trail	Tabriz	WA	60025	(406) 555-2
9	Chris Lemke Lumber	Taeko Lemke	1074 Oregon Trail	Merced	CA	95887	(707) 555-2
10	Allan Cabinetry	Lynn Allan	22 Katie Way	Paradise Knoll	CA	93991	(936) 555-0
11	Got Gutters?	Joey Cramer	4 Wheeler Road	Jess	MN	67288	(319) 555-0
12	Toby Appliance	Ty Hale	2003 Main Street	Trey	TX	34039	(350) 555-9
13	Window Universe	Teresa Hull	321 Sixth Street West	Trevor	CA	97554	(924) 555-7
14	Knob Outlet	Noelle Sorenson	747 Briar Place	Crossroads	FL	83726	(753) 555-1
15	Theil's Electric	Rob Theil	52003 Skip Trail	Clyde	MT	59203	(499) 555-2
16	SafeCo Deck Systems	Judy Mudge	400 Stirling Heights	Carlton	NV	88122	(451) 555-0
17	Infinity Books	Jan Besel	2 Carneige Road	Riverside	NJ	39293	(202) 555-8
18	Garden It All	Doris Eleine	15381 Sleepy Hollow Road	Earl	MS	29873	(631) 555-2
19	People's Paint	Eva Zasomovich	15149 Sewing Street	Five Canyons	RI	62837	(361) 555-9

Field
One piece of information, such as customer's last name or an item's
code number. On a worksheet, each cell represents a field.

Creating a List

![Microsoft Office Specialist Approved Courseware] XL03E-1-5

To create a list in Excel, you can enter data on worksheet cells, just as you do on any other worksheet data, but the placement of the field names and list range must follow these rules: (1) Enter field names in a single row that is the first row in the list (2) Enter each record in a single row (3) Do not include any blank rows within the list range (4) Do not use more than one worksheet for a single list range. You can enter data directly in the list or in a data form, a dialog box in which you can view, change, add, or delete records in a list. Don't worry about entering records in any particular order; Excel tools can organize an existing list alphabetically, by date, or in almost any order you can imagine.

Create a List

1. Open a blank worksheet, or use a worksheet that has enough empty columns and rows for your list.

2. Enter a label for each field in adjacent columns across the first row of the list.

3. Enter field information for each record in its own row; start with the row directly below the field names.

4. Select the range of cells for the list.

5. Click the Data menu, point to List, and then click Create List.

6. Click OK.

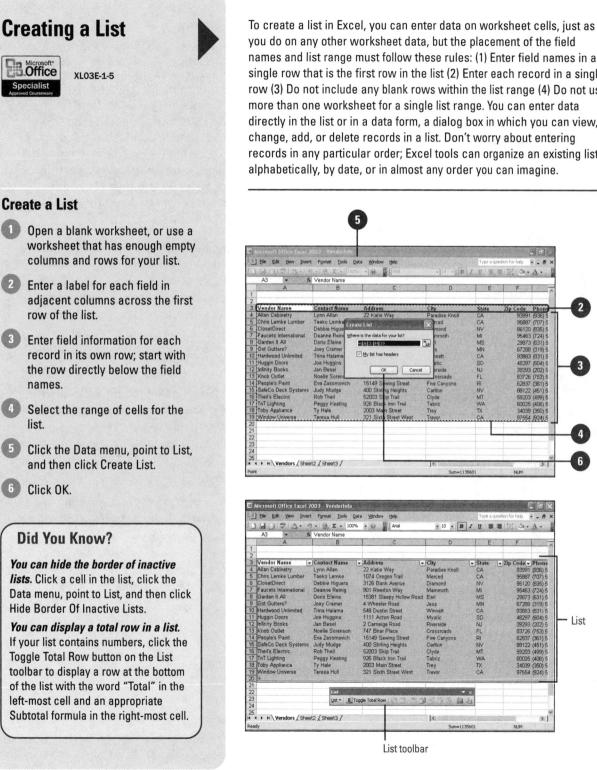

Did You Know?

You can hide the border of inactive lists. Click a cell in the list, click the Data menu, point to List, and then click Hide Border Of Inactive Lists.

You can display a total row in a list. If your list contains numbers, click the Toggle Total Row button on the List toolbar to display a row at the bottom of the list with the word "Total" in the left-most cell and an appropriate Subtotal formula in the right-most cell.

List toolbar

Understanding a Data Form

If you prefer entering information in a pre-designed form to typing and tabbing on a worksheet, you'll appreciate the Data Form feature. A **Data Form** is a dialog box that contains field names from your list range and text boxes you fill in to enter the data. Excel automatically generates a Data Form based on the field names you assign when you create a list.

You can use the Data Form to enter repetitive information one record at a time. You can also use the Data Form to move around in a list and to search for specific data.

When you select a list range and open the Data Form, the form displays a field name and text boxes for all fields in the list. Data for the currently selected record appears in the text boxes (if the list already contains data). In a Data Form, you can enter new data in the text boxes of a blank record, edit data in existing records (although you cannot change field names), navigate to different records, and search for selected records:

♦ Click the New button to enter a new record.

♦ Click the Delete button to remove an existing record.

♦ Click the Restore button to undo the previous action.

♦ Click the Find Prev button to locate the closest previous record matching the criteria.

♦ Click the Find Next button to locate the closest record matching the criteria.

♦ Click the Criteria button to display the Data Form with all fields blank. Enter the field items you want to find.

♦ Click the Close button to close the Data Form and return to the worksheet.

Adding Records Using a Data Form

A **Data Form** provides an optional method of entering information in a list. Once field names are entered, you can access a Data Form using the Data menu. You don't even need to select the list range first; as long as the active cell is somewhere within the list range when the Data Form is opened, Excel will automatically locate the list. As you add new records to the form, the list range is constantly updated with the new rows, and Excel automatically enlarges the list range to include them.

Add to a List Using a Data Form

1. Click any cell within the list range. If you have not entered any records for the list yet, click one of the field names.

2. Click the Data menu, and then click Form.

3. Click New.

4. Type each field entry in the appropriate text box.

   Click in each field or press Tab to move from field to field.

5. Click Close.

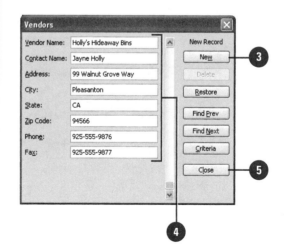

Managing Records Using a Data Form

You can use a Data Form to display, edit, or delete selected records in a list. To display only selected records in the Data Form, you can specify the **search criteria**—the information a record must contain—in the Data Form, and Excel uses that criteria to find and display matching records. Although the Data Form shows only the records that match your criteria, the other records still exist in the list. If more than one record matches your criteria, you can use the Data Form buttons to move through the records, editing or deleting them.

Display Selected Records

1. Click anywhere within the list range.

2. Click the Data menu, and then click Form.

3. Click Criteria.

4. Type the information you want matching records to contain.

5. Click Find Prev or Find Next to advance to a matching record.

6. Repeat step 5 until Excel beeps or all records have been viewed.

7. Click Close.

Edit a Record

1. Click anywhere within the list range.

2. Click the Data menu, and then click Form.

3. Find a record that requires modification.

4. Click to position the insertion point in the field to edit, and then use Backspace and Delete to modify the text.

5. Click Close.

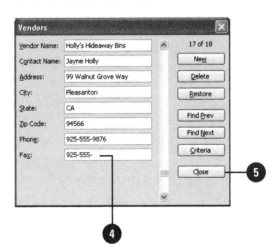

Delete a Record

1. Click anywhere within the list range.

2. Click the Data menu, and then click Form.

3. Click Criteria.

4. Type the information you want matching records to contain. You can fill in one or more fields.

5. Click Find Prev or Find Next to advance to a matching record.

6. Click Delete.

7. Click OK in the warning dialog box.

8. Click Close.

Did You Know?

You can return to the complete list of records. Click the Form button to return to the initial Data Form.

You can use wildcards to find data in a list quickly. The wildcard "?" stands for any single character, while "*" stands for many characters. R?N might find RAN or RUN while R*N might find RUN, RAN, RUIN, or RATION.

You can use the search option and not worry about case sensitivity. By default, the criteria on which Excel searches is not case-sensitive.

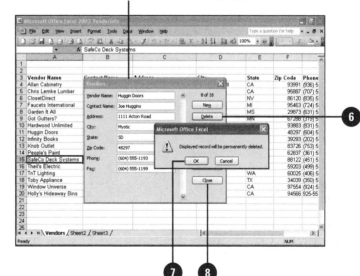

Found record with matched criteria.

10

Sorting Data in a List ▶

XL03S-2-2

After you enter records in a list, you can reorganize the information by sorting the records. For example, you might want to sort records in a client list alphabetically by last name or numerically by their last invoice date. **Ascending order** lists records from A to Z, earliest to latest, or lowest to highest. **Descending order** lists records from Z to A, latest to earliest, or highest to lowest. You can sort the entire list or use **AutoFilter** to select the part of the list you want to display in the column. You can also sort a list based on one or more **sort fields**— fields you select to sort the list. A sort, for example, might be the telephone directory numerically by area code and then alphabetically by last name.

Sort Data Quickly

1. Click the field name by which you want to sort.

2. Click the Sort Ascending or the Sort Descending button on the Standard toolbar.

Did You Know?

You can sort data in rows. If the data you want to sort is listed across a row instead of down a column, click Options in the Sort dialog box, and then click the Sort Left To Right option.

Display Parts of a List

1. Click in the list range.

2. Click the Data menu, point to Filter, and then click AutoFilter.

3. Click the list arrow of the field you want to use.

4. Select the item that the records must match to be displayed.

5. To redisplay all records in the list, click the Data menu, point to Filter, and then click Show All.

6. To remove the field list arrows, click the Data menu, point to Filter, and then click AutoFilter.

Sort a List Using More Than One Field

1. Click anywhere within the list range.

2. Click the Data menu, and then click Sort.

3. Click the Sort By list arrow, and then click the field on which the sort is based (the *primary sort field*).

4. Click the Ascending or Descending option.

5. Click the top Then By list arrow, select a second sort field, and then click Ascending or Descending.

6. If you want, click the lower Then By list arrow, select a third sort field, and then click Ascending or Descending.

7. If available, click the Header Row option to *exclude* the field names (in the first row) from the sort, or click the No Header Row option to *include* the field names (in the first row) in the sort.

   The header row is the first row in your list that contains the column names or field labels.

8. Click OK.

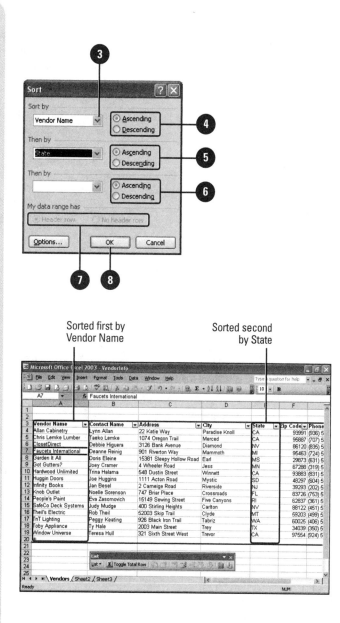

Sorted first by Vendor Name

Sorted second by State

Displaying Parts of a List with AutoFilter

Display Specific Records Using AutoFilter

1. Click anywhere within the list range.

2. Click the Data menu, point to Filter, and then click AutoFilter.

3. Click the list arrow of the field for which you want to specify search criteria.

4. Select the item that records must match in order to be included in the list.

5. Repeat steps 3 and 4, as necessary, to filter out more records using additional fields.

6. Click the Data menu, point to Filter, and then click AutoFilter to turn off AutoFilter and redisplay all records in the list.

Did You Know?

You can speed up your work with the Top 10 list. AutoFilter offers a Top 10 command in the list of every field. Click this command to quickly create a filter for the top or bottom 10 items in a list.

Working with a list that contains numerous records can be difficult—unless you can narrow your view of the list when necessary. For example, rather than looking through an entire inventory list, you might want to see records that come from one distributor. The **AutoFilter** feature creates a list of the items found in each field. You select the items that you want to display in the column (that is, the records that meet certain criteria). Then you can work with a limited number of records.

Filtered records

Creating Custom Searches

There are many times you'll want to search for records that meet multiple criteria. For example, you might want to see out-of-stock records of those orders purchased from a particular distributor. Using the AutoFilter feature and the Custom command, you can create complex searches. You can use **logical operators** to measure whether an item in a record qualifies as a match with the selected criteria. You can also use the **logical conditions AND** and **OR** to join multiple criteria within a single search. The result of any search is either true or false; if a field matches the criteria, the result is true. The OR condition requires that only one criterion be true in order for a record to qualify. The AND condition, on the other hand, requires that both criteria in the statement be true in order for the record to qualify.

Create a Custom Search Using AutoFilter

1. Click anywhere within the list range.

2. Click the Data menu, point to Filter, and then click AutoFilter to enable the command (a check mark appears).

3. Click the list arrow next to the first field you want to include in the search.

4. Click Custom.

5. Click the Field list arrow (on the left), and then select a logical operator.

6. Click the list arrow (on the right), and then select a field choice.

7. If you want, click the And or Or option.

8. If you want, click the list arrow (on the left), and then select a logical operator.

9. If you want, click the list arrow (on the right), and then select a field choice.

10. Click OK.

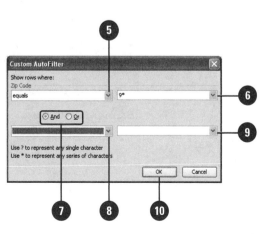

10

Entering Data in a List

XL03E-1-5

Entering data in a list—whether you use the Data Form or the worksheet—can be tedious and repetitive. You can enter data using the PickList or List AutoFill feature to make the job easier. **PickList** is activated once you have entered at least one record in the list; it uses your previous entries to save you the trouble of typing repetitive information. PickList displays previous entries made in the current field in a list format. **List AutoFill** automatically extends the list's formatting and formulas to adjacent cells. As data is added to a list, AutoFill looks at the preceding cells to determine what formatting and formulas should be extended.

Enter Data in a List Using Pick From Drop-Down List

1. Right-click the cell in which you want to use PickList, and then click Pick From Drop-Down List.

2. Click a selection in the list.

3. Press Enter or Tab to accept the entry, or press Esc to cancel the entry.

Working with Lists

Microsoft Office Specialist — Approved Courseware

XL03E-1-5

After you create a list, you can sort the entries, add new entries, and display totals. You can insert rows anywhere in a list or add rows at the bottom of the list. The last row of the list is a blank row with a blue asterisk (*) inside the left-most cell. You can type a new entry in the list directly into the last row. When the list is inactive, the asterisk does not appear in the list, and the list border shifts up to the bottom of the last row of data. If you no longer need the data in list form, you can convert the list back to normal Excel data.

Insert a Row in a List

1. Click a cell in the list where you want to insert a row.

2. Click the List button on the List toolbar, point to Insert, and then click Row.

See Also

See "Insert a Column or Row" on page 82 for information on inserting a row.

Convert a List to a Range

1. Click a cell in the list.

2. Click the List button on the List toolbar, and then click Convert To Range.

3. Click OK.

Analyzing Data Using a PivotTable

XL03E-1-8

When you want to summarize information in a lengthy list using complex criteria, use the **PivotTable** to simplify your task. Without the PivotTable, you would have to manually count or create a formula to calculate which records met certain criteria, and then create a table to display that information. Once you determine what fields and criteria you want to use to summarize the data and how you want the resulting table to look, the Pivot Table and PivotChart Wizard does the rest.

Create a PivotTable Report

1. Click any cell within the list range.

2. Click the Data menu, and then click PivotTable And PivotChart Report.

3. If using the list range, click the Microsoft Office Excel List Or Database option.

4. Click the PivotTable option, and then click Next.

5. If the range does not include the correct data, click the Collapse Dialog button. Drag the pointer over the list range, including the field names, to select a new range, and then click the Expand Dialog button.

6. Click Next to continue.

7. Click the New Worksheet option to place the PivotTable report.

8. Click Finish.

9. Drag fields from the Field List to areas on the PivotTable Report.

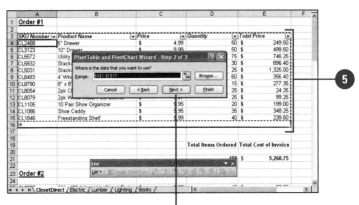

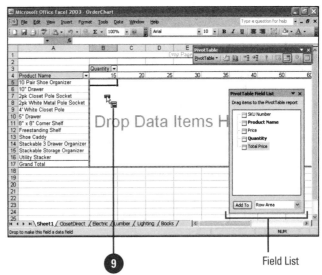

Field List

206

Updating a PivotTable and PivotChart

You can quickly update a PivotTable report using the PivotTable toolbar, which appears whenever a PivotTable is active. This saves you from having to recreate a PivotTable every time you add new data to a list. When you do want to add new data, Excel makes it easy by allowing you to drag data fields to and from a PivotTable or PivotChart.

Update a PivotTable Report

1. Make any necessary change(s) in the worksheet where your list range resides.

2. If necessary, select a different worksheet, and then click any cell in the PivotTable Report.

3. Click the Refresh Data button on the PivotTable toolbar, or click the PivotTable drop-down arrow on the PivotTable toolbar, and then click Refresh Data.

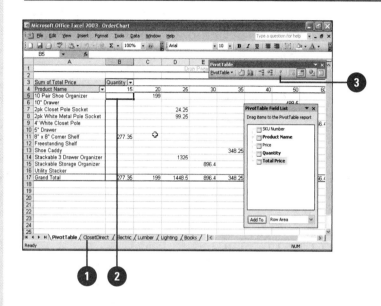

Add or Remove a Field in a PivotTable or PivotChart Report

1. Position the pointer over the field that you want to add to or remove from the PivotTable.

2. Drag the field on the PivotTable to add the field or drag it off the PivotTable to remove the field.

Did You Know?

You can hide and display fields on the PivotTable toolbar. Click the Hide Fields button on the PivotTable toolbar. Click the button again to display the PivotTable fields.

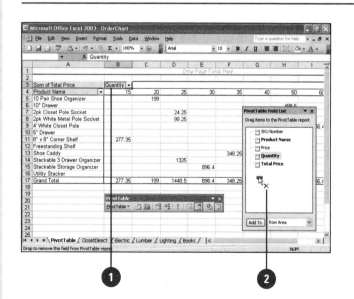

10

Modifying a PivotTable and PivotChart

You can modify PivotTable or PivotChart reports. With Excel's AutoFormat feature, you can quickly format a PivotTable to create professional looking reports. You can also change field settings to format a number or show the data in a different form. The field settings include functions such as Sum, Count, Average, Max, and Min. If you want to set different scenarios, you can also hide fields while you change field settings.

AutoFormat a PivotTable Report

1. Click any field in the PivotTable report.

2. Click the Format Report button on the PivotTable toolbar.

3. Click the AutoFormat style you want.

4. Click OK.

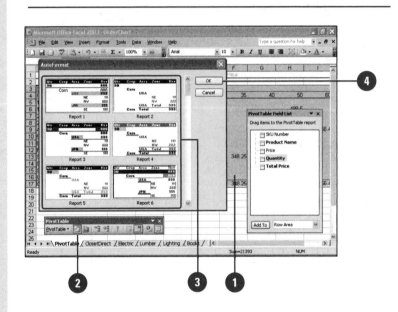

Change Field Settings in a PivotTable or PivotChart Report

1. Select the field you want to change.

2. Click the Field Settings button on the PivotTable toolbar.

3. Make the necessary changes to the field.

4. Click OK.

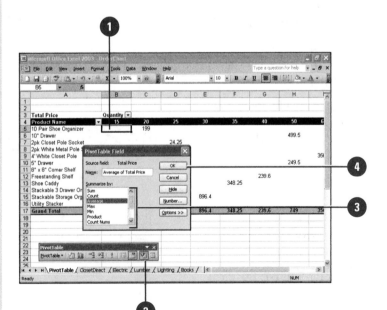

Create a PivotTable Report from an Existing PivotTable or PivotChart

1. Open the worksheet containing the PivotTable.

2. Click the Data menu, and then click PivotTable And PivotChart Report.

3. Click the Another PivotTable Report Or PivotChart Report option.

4. Click the PivotTable option.

5. Click Next to continue.

6. Click the name of the report associated with the PivotChart.

7. Click Next to continue.

8. Click a location option for the new PivotTable.

9. If you want, click Layout or Options to change the way the PivotTable looks or functions, and then click OK.

10. Click Finish.

11. Drag fields from the Field List to areas on the PivotTable Report.

Did You Know?

You can change the layout of a PivotTable. Click a field in the PivotTable, click the PivotTable Wizard button on the PivotTable toolbar, click Layout, make the changes you want, click OK, and then click Finish.

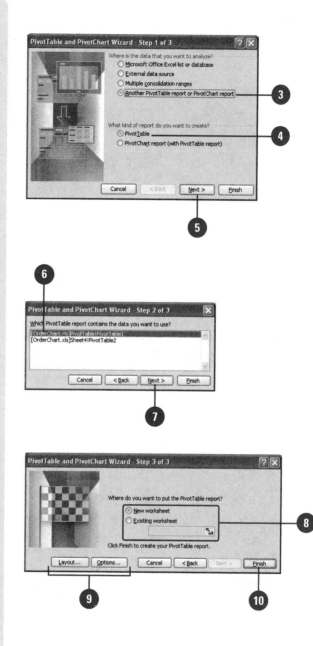

Charting a PivotTable

Data summarized in a PivotTable is an ideal candidate for a chart, since the table itself represents an overwhelming amount of data. A chart of a PivotTable is called a **PivotChart**. Once you select data within the PivotTable, you can chart it like any other worksheet data using the Chart Wizard. If you don't have a PivotTable, you can create a PivotChart and a PivotTable at the same time.

Create a PivotChart Report from a PivotTable Report

1. Click any data field in the PivotTable.

2. Click the Chart Wizard button on the PivotTable or Standard toolbar.

   The PivotChart is created on a new worksheet.

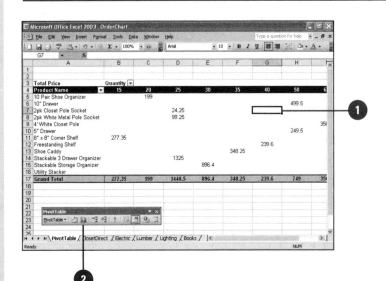

Modify a PivotChart Report

1. Click the worksheet tab with the PivotChart you want to modify.

2. Click the Chart Wizard button on the PivotTable or Standard toolbar.

3. Make selections from each of the four Chart Wizard dialog boxes.

4. Click Finish.

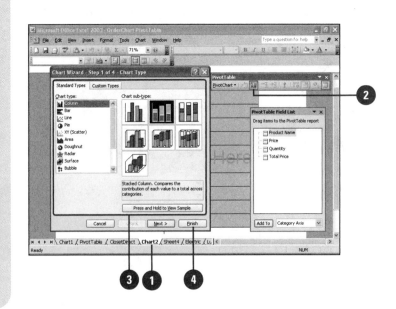

Create a PivotChart Report with a PivotTable Report

1. Click any cell within the list range.

2. Click the Data menu, and then click PivotTable And PivotChart Report.

3. If using the list range, click the Microsoft Excel List Or Database option.

4. Click the PivotChart Report (With PivotTable Report) option.

5. Click Next to continue.

6. If the range does not include the correct data, click the Collapse Dialog button, drag the pointer over the list range, including the field names, to select a new range, and then click the Expand Dialog button.

7. Click Next to continue.

8. Click the desired location of the new PivotTable.

9. Click Finish.

10. Drag the data and fields you want from the PivotTable toolbar to the different area of the PivotChart.

    The PivotTable is created as you create the PivotChart.

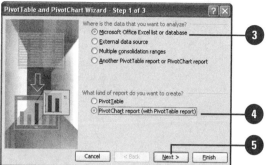

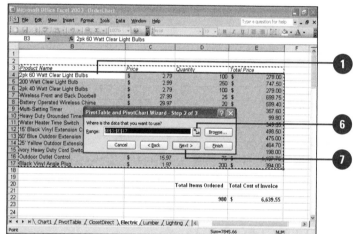

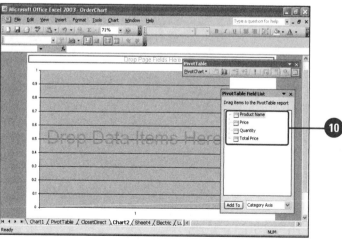

10

Creating Groups and Outlines

XL03E-1-3

Create an Outline or Group

1. Organize data in a hierarchical fashion—place summary rows below detail rows and summary columns to the right of detail columns.

2. Select the data that you want to outline.

3. To create an outline, click the Data menu, point to Group And Outline, and then click Auto Outline.

4. To create a group, click the Data menu, point to Group And Outline, and then click Group. Click the Rows or Columns option, and then click OK.

Work an Outline or Group

1. Click a plus sign (+) to expand an outline level; click a minus sign (-) to collapse an outline level.

Did You Know?

You can ungroup outline data. Select the data group, click the Data menu, point to Group And Outline, click Ungroup, click the Rows or Columns option, and then click OK.

You can clear an outline. Select the outline, click the Data menu, point to Group And Outline, and then click Clear Outline.

A sales report that displays daily, weekly, and monthly totals in a hierarchical format, such as an outline, helps your reader to sift through and interpret the pertinent information. In outline format, a single item can have several topics or levels of information within it. An **outline** in Excel indicates multiple layers of content by displaying a plus sign (+) on its left side. A minus sign (-) indicates that the item has no contents, is fully expanded, or both.

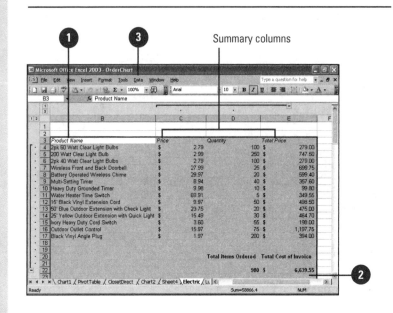

Summary columns

Click numbers to display specific levels.

Sublevels are indented and no longer display a plus sign.

Using Database Functions in a List

Microsoft Office Specialist
Approved Courseware

XL03E-1-10

If you need to perform calculations in a list, you can use database functions in Excel. For example, you can use the function DAVERAGE or DSUM in a list to average or add the values in a column that match certain criteria. Each function uses three arguments (pieces of data) as shown in the following definition: =DSUM (database, field, criteria). Database is the range of cells in the list; field is the columns you want to use; and criteria is the range cells with the conditions. There are other database functions available, such as DCOUNT, DPRODUCT, DMAX, DMIN, and DSTDEV. Each function uses the same arguments.

Use the DSUM or DAVERAGE Function

1️⃣ Create a data range in which the left-most column contains a unique value in each row.

2️⃣ Click the cell you want to place the function.

3️⃣ Type the function you want.

=DSUM(*database,field,criteria*) or **=DAVERAGE**(*database,field,criteria*)

4️⃣ Press Enter.

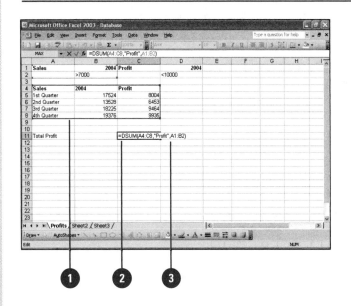

Adding Data Validation to a Worksheet

![Microsoft Office Specialist Approved Courseware] XL03E-1-4

Worksheet cells can be adjusted so that only certain values can be entered. Controlling how data is entered decreases errors and makes a worksheet more reliable. You might, for example, want it to be possible to enter only specific dates in a range of cells. You can use **logical operators** (such as equal, not equal to, less than, or greater than) to set validation rules. When invalid entries are made, a message—developed and written by you—appears indicating that the entry is in violation of the validation rules. The rule set will not allow data to flow into the cell.

Create Validation Rules

1. Select the range you want covered in the validation rules.

2. Click the Data menu, and then click Validation.

3. Click the Settings tab.

4. Click the Allow list arrow, and then select a value type.

5. Click the Data list arrow, and then select a logical operator.

6. Enter values or use the Collapse Dialog button to select a range for the minimum and maximum criteria.

7. Click the Input Message tab.

8. Type a title and the input message that should be displayed when invalid entries are made.

9. Click OK.

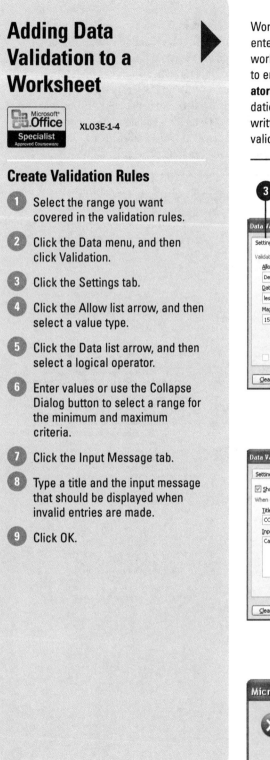

214

Building More Powerful Worksheets

Introduction

If your worksheet or workbook needs to go beyond simple calculations, Microsoft Office Excel 2003 offers several tools to help you create more specialized projects. With Excel, you can perform "what if" analysis using several different methods to get the results you want.

You can customize Excel by automating frequently performed tasks and keystrokes using macros. A macro records a series of tasks and keystrokes so you don't have to repeat them each time. Once a macro is recorded, you can run it, make modifications to it, add comments so other users will understand its purpose, and test it to make sure it runs correctly. Excel also includes a variety of add-ins—programs that provide added functionality—to increase your efficiency. Some of these supplemental programs are useful to almost anyone using Excel. Others, such as the Analysis ToolPak, add customized features, functions, or commands specific to use in financial, statistical, and other highly specialized fields. The purpose of each of these customization features is the same—to make Excel even easier to use and to enable you to accomplish more with less effort.

Microsoft Office includes a free trial for Information Rights Management (IRM) software that allows you to restrict access to your workbooks. This software, coupled with the password protection feature in Excel, can greatly increase the amount of protection needed for some of your more sensitive worksheets and workbooks. Digital signatures and file encryption go the extra mile in making sure that your data is not tampered with, nor seen by unauthorized users.

Loading and Unloading Add-Ins

XL03E-1-7

To increase your efficiency, Excel includes a variety of **add-ins**—programs that are included with Excel but not essential to its functionality. Some of these supplemental programs are useful to almost anyone using Excel. Others, such as the Analysis ToolPak, add customized features, functions, or commands for use in financial, statistical, engineering or other highly specialized fields. Before you can use an Excel add-in, you need to load it first. The first time you load an add-in, you may need to install it using the Office 2003 CD. When you load an add-in, the feature may also add a command to a menu. You can load one or more add-ins. If you no longer need an add-in, you should unload it to save memory and reduce the number of commands on the Tools or Data menu. When you unload an add-in, you also need to restart Excel to remove an add-in command from a menu.

Load or Unload Add-Ins

1. Click the Tools menu, and then click Add-Ins.

2. If the add-in you want to use is not listed, click Browse, and then locate the add-in you want.

3. To load an add-in, select the check box next to the add-in you want to load, or to unloaded an add-in, clear the check box.

4. Click OK.

5. Either follow the setup instructions to load the add-in, or and click Yes to restart Excel to remove the add-in from the menu.

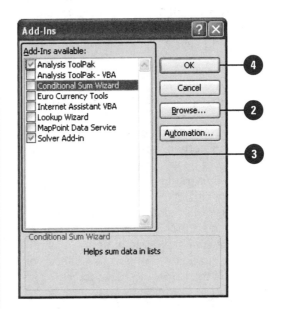

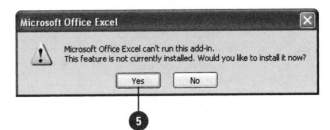

Using Data Analysis Tools

 XL03E-1-7

Excel provides a collection of statistical functions and macros to analyze data in the **Analysis ToolPak**. The Analysis Toolpak is an add-in program, which may need to be loaded using the Add-In command on the Tools menu. The tools can be used for a variety of scientific and engineering purposes and for general statistical analysis. You provide the data, and the tools use the appropriate functions to determine the result. To use these tools effectively, you need to be familiar with the area of statistics or engineering that you want to develop an analysis for. You can view a list of all the tools in the Data Analysis dialog box. For additional information about each tool, see the online Help.

Use Data Analysis Tools

1 Click the Tools menu, and then click Data Analysis.

2 Click the analysis tool you want to use.

3 Click OK.

4 Select or enter the input range (a single row or column). You can use the Collapse Dialog box button to select a range and the Expand Dialog box to return.

5 Select or enter the output range. You can use the Collapse Dialog box button to select a range and the Expand Dialog box to return.

6 Specify any additional tool specific options you want.

7 Click OK.

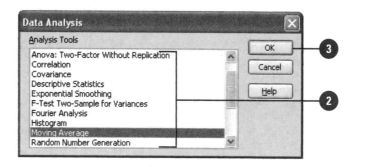

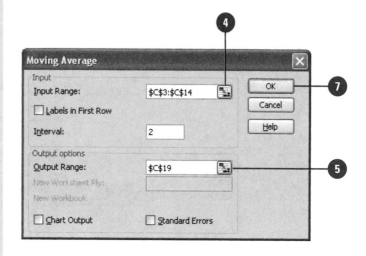

11

Looking at
Alternatives
with Data Tables

XL03E-1-7

You can look to see a range of possible values for your formulas. Data tables provide a shortcut by calculating all of the values in one operation. A **data table** is a range of cells that shows the results of substituting different values in one or more formulas. For example, you can compare loan payments for different interest rates. There are two types of data tables: one-input and two-input. With a **one-input table**, you enter different values for one variable and see the effect on one or more formulas. With a **two-input table**, you enter values for two variables and see the effect on one formula.

Create a One-Input Data Table

1 Enter the formula you want to use.

If the input values are listed down a column, specify the new formula in a blank cell to the right of an existing formula in the top row of the table. If the input values are listed across a row, enter the new formula in a blank cell below an existing formula in the first column of the table.

2 Select the data table, including the column or row that contains the new formula.

3 Click the Data menu, and then click Table.

4 Enter the input cell.

If the input values are in a column, enter the reference for the input cell in the Column Input Cell box. If the input values are in a row, enter the reference for the input cell in the Row Input Cell box.

5 Click OK.

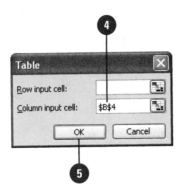

In this example, the formula is =PMT(B4/12, B5,-B3)

Asking "What If" with Goal Seek

XL03E-1-7

Create a "What-If" Scenario with Goal Seek

1. Click any cell within the list range.

2. Click the Tools menu, and then click Goal Seek.

3. Click the Set Cell box, and then type the cell address you want to change.

   You can also click the Collapse Dialog button, use your mouse to select the cells, and then click the Expand Dialog button.

4. Click the To Value box, and then type the result value.

5. Click the By Changing Cell box, and then type the cell address you want Excel to change.

   You can also click the Collapse Dialog button, use your mouse to select the cells, and then click the Expand Dialog button.

6. Click OK.

Excel's powerful functions make it easy to create powerful formulas, such as calculating payments over time. Sometimes, however, being able to make these calculations is only half the battle. Your formula might tell you that a monthly payment amount is $2,000, while you might only be able to manage a $1,750 payment. **Goal Seek** enables you to work backwards to a desired result, or goal, by adjusting the input values.

11

Creating Scenarios

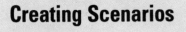

 XL03E-1-6

Because some worksheet data is constantly evolving, the ability to create multiple scenarios lets you speculate on a variety of outcomes. For example, the marketing department might want to see how its budget would be affected if sales decreased by 25 percent. Although it's easy enough to plug in different numbers in formulas, Excel allows you to save these values and then recall them at a later time. The ability to create, save, and modify scenarios means a business will be better prepared for different outcomes to avoid economic surprises.

Create and Show a Scenario

1 Click the Tools menu, and then click Scenarios.

2 Click Add.

3 Type a name that identifies the scenario.

4 Type the cells you want to modify in the scenario, or click the Collapse Dialog button, use your mouse to select the cells, and then click the Expand Dialog button.

5 If you want, type a comment.

6 Click OK.

7 Type values for each of the displayed changing cells.

8 Click OK.

9 Click Close.

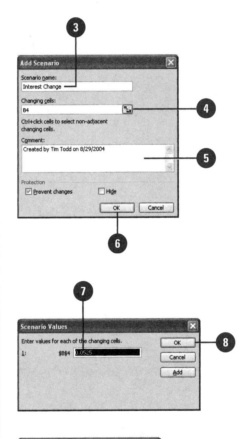

Show a Scenario

1. Click the Tools menu, and then click Scenarios.

2. Select the scenario you want to see.

3. Click Show.

4. Click Close.

Did You Know?

You can create a scenario summary report. Click the Tools menu, click Scenarios, click Summary, click the Scenario Summary option, and then click OK. A scenario summary worksheet tab appears with the report.

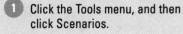

Using Solver

XL03E-1-7

The Solver is similar to Goal Seek and scenarios, but provides more options to restrict the allowable range of values for different cells that can affect the goal. The **Solver** is an add-in program, which may need to be loaded using the Add-In command on the Tools menu. The Solver is useful for predicting how results might change over time based on different assumptions. For example, suppose you have sales goals and quotas for the next three months. The Solver can take the expectations and the current quotas for each month, and determine how sales quotas for all three amounts be adjusted to achieve the goal.

Use Solver

1. Click the Tools menu, and then click Solver.

2. Select the target cell.

3. Click an Equal To option, and then, if necessary, enter a value.

4. Select the range of cells the solver uses to compare against the target cell.

5. Click Add.

6. Enter specific cell reference and constraint, and then click Add. You can specify several cell constraints.

7. Click OK.

8. Click Solve.

   If the Solver finds a solution, the Solver Results dialog box appears.

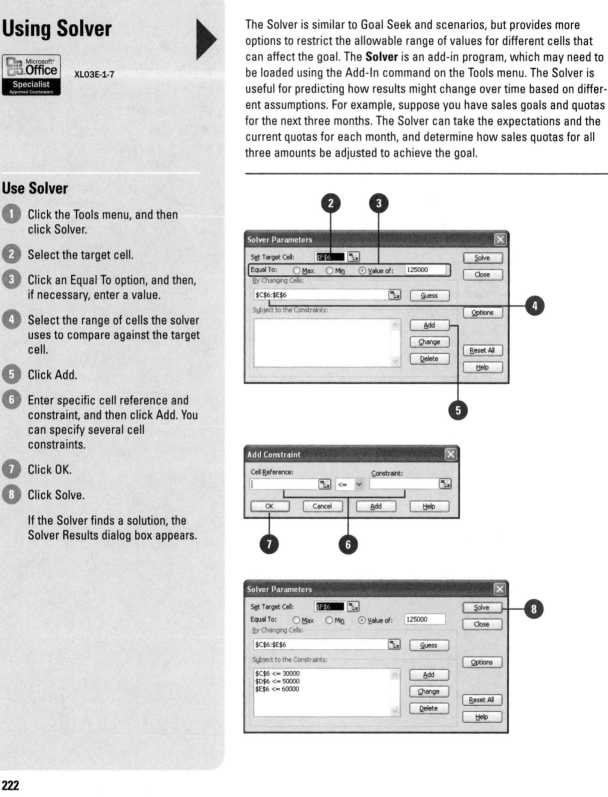

9 Click the Keep Solver Solution option.

10 Click a report type.

11 Click OK.

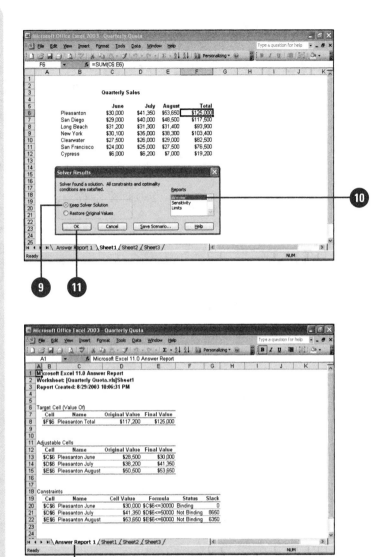

Answer report with the solver solution

11

Using Lookup and Reference Functions

XL03E-1-9

You can use lookup and reference functions in Excel to make it easy to retrieve information from a data list. The lookup functions (VLOOKUP and HLOOKUP) allow you to search for and insert a value in a cell that is stored in another place in the worksheet. The HLOOKUP function looks in rows (a horizontal lookup) and the VLOOKUP function looks in columns (a vertical lookup). Each function uses four arguments (pieces of data) as shown in the following definition: =VLOOKUP (lookup_value, table_array, col_index_num, range_lookup). The VLOOKUP function finds a value in the left-most column of a named range and returns the value from the specified cell to the right of the cell with the found value, while the HLOOKUP function does the same to rows. In the example, =VLOOKUP(12,Salary,2,TRUE), the function looks for the value 12 in the named range *Salary* and finds the closest (next lower) value, and returns the value in column 2 of the same row and places the value in the active cell. In the example, =HLOOKUP ("Years",Salary,4,FALSE), the function looks for the value "Years" in the named range *Salary* and finds the exact text string value, and then returns the value in row 4 of the column.

Use the VLOOKUP Function

1. Create a data range in which the left-most column contains a unique value in each row.

2. Click the cell you want to place the function.

3. Type **=VLOOKUP(***value, named range, column,* **TRUE** *or* **FALSE**), and then press Enter.

Use the HLOOKUP Function

1. Create a data range in which the uppermost row contains a unique value in each row.

2. Click the cell you want to place the function.

3. Type **=HLOOKUP**(*value, named range, row,* **TRUE** *or* **FALSE**), and then press Enter.

Lookup Function Arguments

Argument	Description
lookup_value	The value found in the row or the column of the named range. You can use a value, cell reference or a text string (enclosed in quotation marks).
table_array	The named range of information in which Excel looks up data.
col_index_num	The numeric position of the column in the named range (counting from the left) for the value to be returned (use only for VLOOKUP).
row_index_num	The numeric position of the row in the named range (counting from the top) for the value to be returned (use only for HLOOKUP).
range_lookup	The value returned when the function is to find the nearest value (TRUE) or an exact match (FALSE) for the lookup_value. The default value is TRUE.

11

Understanding How Macros Automate Your Work

To complete many tasks in Excel, you need to execute a series of commands and actions. To print two copies of a selected range of Sheet2 of a worksheet, for example, you need to open the workbook, switch to Sheet2, select the print area, open the Print dialog box, and specify that you want to print two copies. If you often need to complete the same task, you'll find yourself repeatedly taking the same series of steps. It can be tiresome to continually repeat the same commands and actions when you can easily create a mini-program, or macro, that accomplishes all of them with a single command.

Creating a **macro** is easy and requires no programming knowledge on your part. Excel simply records the steps you want included in the macro while you use the keyboard and mouse. When you record a macro, Excel stores the list of commands with any name you choose. You can store your macros in the current workbook, in a new workbook, or in Excel's Personal Macro workbook. Storing your macros in the Personal Macro workbook makes the macros available to you from any location in Excel, even when no workbook is open.

Once a macro is created, you can make modifications to it, add comments so other users will understand its purpose, and test it to make sure it runs correctly.

You can run a macro by choosing the Macro command on the Tools menu, or by using a shortcut key or clicking a toolbar button you've assigned to it. When you click the Tools menu, point to Macro, and then click Macros, the Macro dialog box opens. From this dialog box, you can run, edit, test, or delete any Excel macro on your system, or create a new one.

If you have problems with a macro, you can step through the macro one command at a time, known as **debugging**. Once you identify any errors in the macro, you can edit it.

Indicates the workbook(s) from which you can access the selected macro

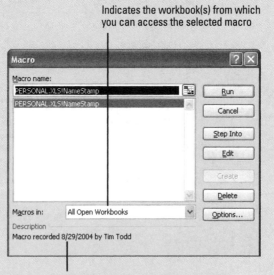

When you create a macro, you can add a description of what the macro does

Recording a Macro

XL03E-5-2

Recording a macro is almost as easy as recording your favorite CD or TV show. Once you turn on the macro recorder, Excel records every mouse click and keystroke action you execute until you turn off the recorder. Then you can "play," or run, the macro whenever you want to repeat that series of actions—but Excel will execute them at a much faster rate. You don't even need to press a rewind button when you want to run it again!

Record a Macro

1. Click the Tools menu, point to Macro, and then click Record New Macro.

2. Type a name for the macro.

3. Assign a shortcut key to use a keystroke combination instead of a menu selection to run the macro.

4. Click the Store Macro In list arrow, and then select a location.

5. Type a description, if you want. The description appears at the bottom of the Macro dialog box.

6. Click OK.

7. Execute each command or action you need to complete the macro's task. Take the time to complete each action correctly, since the macro will repeat all moves you make.

8. Click the Stop Recording button.

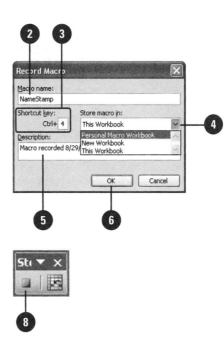

Running a Macro

XL03E-5-2

Running a macro is similar to choosing a command in Excel. When you record or edit the macro, you have the choice of making it available through a menu command, a keyboard combination, or even a toolbar button. As with other options in Excel, your choice depends on your personal preferences—and you can choose to make more than one option available. Where you store a macro when you save it determines its availability later. Macros stored in the Personal Macro workbook are always available, and macros stored in any other workbooks are only available when the workbook is open.

Run a Macro Using a Menu Command

1. Click the Tools menu, point to Macro, and then click Macros.

2. If necessary, click the Macros In list arrow, and then select the workbook that contains the macro you want to run.

3. Click the name of the macro you want to run.

4. Click Run.

   TIMESAVER *Click options to assign a Keyboard Shortcut to a macro.*

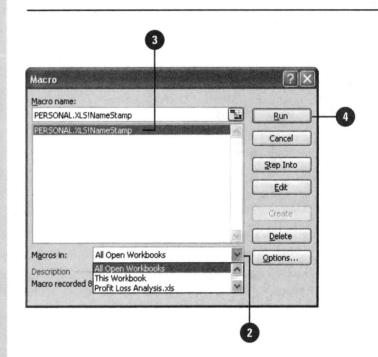

Understanding Macro Code

Macro codes may look cryptic and confusing, but they are the actual commands used within Excel. Back before tools such as the macro recorder existed, you'd create a macro by typing all the command codes necessary to perform each action in the macro.

Each action listed in a macro either performs a step or states what attributes are turned on (true) or off (false). Quotation marks are used to indicate typed text, and the terms **Sub** and **End Sub** are used to indicate the beginning and ending of subroutines, respectively.

Because not everyone wants to read through codes to figure out what a macro does, comments are often included within the code. The comments don't affect the macro; they simply clarify its purpose or actions for a person viewing the code. Comments can be used to help you remember why you took the steps you did, or to help co-workers understand what is going on in the macro and how the macro should be used. A comment always begins with an apostrophe to distinguish it from a command code.

To learn more about macro code, check out Visual Basic titles on the Que Publishing Web site at *www.quepublishing.com.*

These comments tell the name the macro was assigned when it was created and its function.

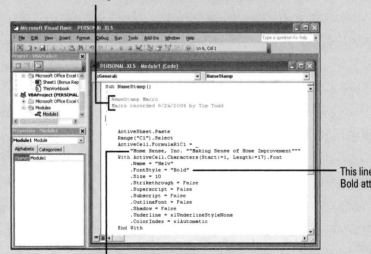

This line means that the Bold attribute is turned on.

This line indicates what to enter in the active cell.

11

Debugging a Macro Using Step Mode

XL03E-5-2

If a macro doesn't work exactly the way you want it to, you can fix the problem without re-creating the macro. Instead of recording the macro over again, Excel allows you to **debug**, or repair, an existing macro, so that you change only the actions that aren't working correctly. Excel's **step mode** shows you each action in a macro, such as a particular menu command, being executed one step at a time, and it also shows you the programming code corresponding to the action in a separate window called a Module sheet. Using step mode, you can determine which actions need modification, and then you make the necessary changes.

Debug a Macro Using Step Mode

1. Click the Tools menu, point to Macro, and then click Macros.

2. Click the name of the macro you want to debug.

3. Click Step Into.

4. Click the Debug menu, and then click Step Into to proceed through each action.

5. When you're done, click the File menu, and then click Close And Return To Microsoft Office Excel.

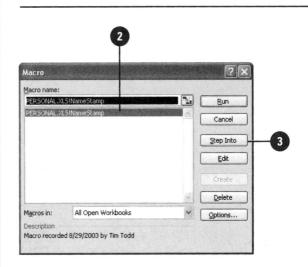

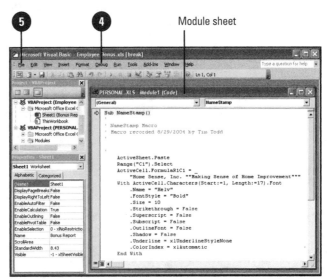

Module sheet

Editing a Macro

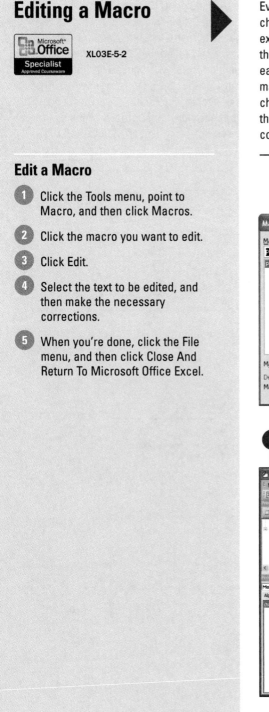

XL03E-5-2

Even if a macro works correctly, you may sometimes find that you want to change the way it runs or the steps it contains. To do so, you can edit the existing code—the list of instructions Excel recorded when you turned on the macro recorder. As you recorded the macro steps, Excel kept track of each action in a separate location called a Module sheet. You can edit macro code by opening its Module sheet and using the keyboard to make changes just as you would to a word processing document. You can use the Delete and Backspace keys to remove characters and then type the corrections.

Edit a Macro

1. Click the Tools menu, point to Macro, and then click Macros.

2. Click the macro you want to edit.

3. Click Edit.

4. Select the text to be edited, and then make the necessary corrections.

5. When you're done, click the File menu, and then click Close And Return To Microsoft Office Excel.

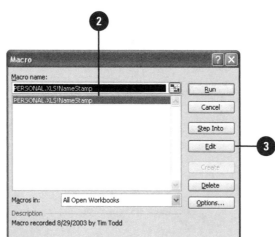

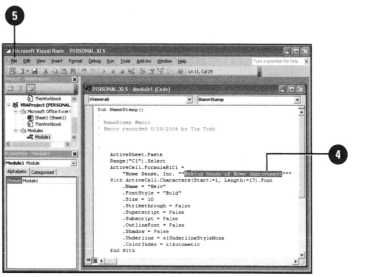

Restricting Workbook Access

You can use Information Rights Management (IRM) in Office 2003 programs to provide restricted access to Office documents. In Outlook, you can use IRM to create messages with restricted permission to help prevent worksheets from being forwarded, printed, copied, or edited by unauthorized people. If you attach an Excel workbook to an Outlook message, the workbook also contains the restriction. IRM uses a server to authenticate the credentials of people who create or receive worksheets or e-mail with restricted permission. For Microsoft Office users without access to one of these servers, Microsoft provides a free trial IRM service, which requires a .NET Passport.

Set Up Information Rights Management

① Click the File menu, point to Permission, and then click Restrict Permission As.

② Click Yes to download and install IRM. Follow the wizard instructions.

Upon completion, the Service Sign-Up Wizard opens.

③ Click the Yes, I Want To Sign Up For This Free Trial Service From Microsoft option.

④ Click Next, and then follow the remaining instructions to create a .NET Passport and complete the service sign-up.

⑤ Click Cancel.

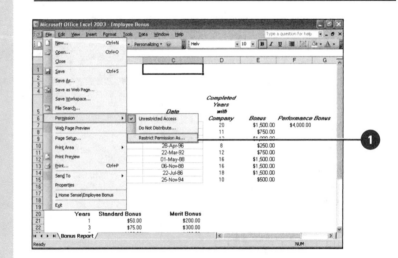

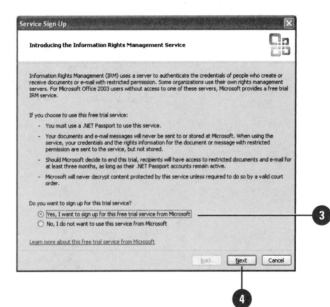

Create a Workbook with Restricted Permission

1 Open the workbook you want to restrict permission.

2 Click the File menu, point to Permission, and then click Restrict Permission As.

3 Click the user with the permissions to create or open restricted content.

4 Click OK.

5 Select the Restrict Permission To This Workbook check box.

6 Enter e-mail addresses of users in the Read and Change boxes or click the Read or Change button to select users from your Address Book.

7 Click More Options.

8 Select the check boxes with the specific permissions you want.

9 Click OK.

A restricted message appears above the address name.

Did You Know?

You can unrestrict a workbook. Click the File menu, point to Permission, and then click Unrestricted Access.

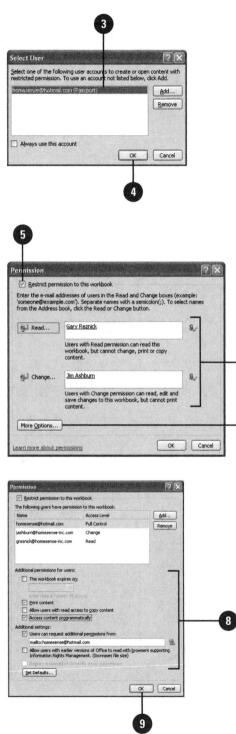

Protecting Your Data

XL03E-3-1, XL03E-3-2

To preserve all your hard work—particularly if others use your files—you can protect it with a password. You can protect a sheet or an entire workbook. In each case, you'll be asked to supply a password, and then enter it again when you want to work on the file. Passwords are case sensitive, so be sure to supply your password as it was first entered. If you forget a password, there is no way to open the file, so it's very important to write down your password(s). Keep your password in a safe place. Avoid obvious passwords such as your name, your company, or your favorite pet.

Apply a Password to a Worksheet

1. Click the Tools menu, point to Protection, and then click Protect Sheet.

2. Select the check boxes for the options you want protected in the sheet.

3. Type a password.

4. Click OK.

5. Retype the password.

6. Click OK.

Did You Know?

You can protect and share a workbook. Click the Tools menu, point to Protection, click Protect And Share Workbook, select the Sharing Track Changes check box, type a password, click OK, retype the password, and then click OK.

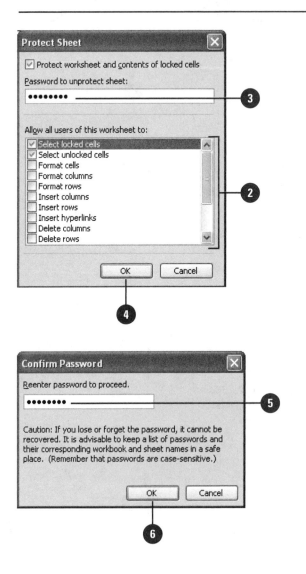

Apply a Password to Edit Parts of a Worksheet

① Select the range in which you want to apply a password.

② Click the Tools menu, point to Protection, and then click Allow Users To Edit Ranges.

③ Click New.

④ Type a range password.

⑤ Click OK.

⑥ Retype the password.

⑦ Click OK.

⑧ To modify or delete a range, click a range, and then click Modify or Delete.

⑨ Click OK.

Did You Know?

You can unprotect a worksheet or workbook quickly. Click the Tools menu, point to Protection, and then click Unprotect Worksheet or Unprotect Workbook, type the password, and then click OK.

See Also

See "Hiding and Unhiding Worksheets and Workbooks" on page 78 for information on hiding data in selected worksheets or workbooks without deleting it.

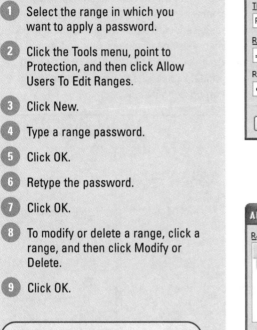

11

Using Digital Signatures

XL03E-3-2

Set Digital Signature

1. Click the Tools menu, and then click Options.

2. Click the Security tab.

3. Click Digital Signatures.

4. If necessary, click Add, select a certificate, and then click OK.

5. Click the certification you want to attach to your digital signature.

6. Click OK.

7. Click OK.

Office 2003 uses Microsoft Authenticode technology to help you protect your Office documents and macros by using a **digital signature**, or digital ID. A digital ID protects the sender's identity. It contains a private key, which stays on the sender's computer, and a digital certificate that contains a public key. The certificate is sent with digitally signed documents and it contains the key to decipher messages from the sender. Before you can add a digital signature to a document or workbook, you need to get a certificate. You can get a digital signature and more information on security options from microsoft at: *http://office.microsoft.com*.

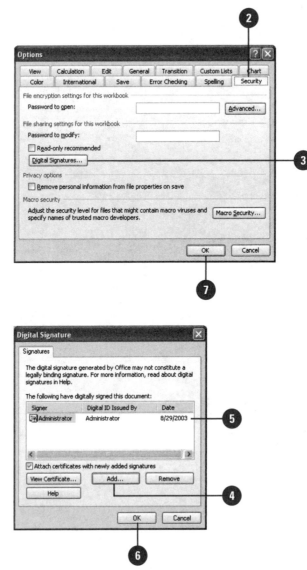

Set a Macro Security Option

① Click the Tools menu, and then click Options.

② Click the Security tab.

③ Click Macro Security.

④ Click the security option you want.

⑤ Click OK.

⑥ Click OK.

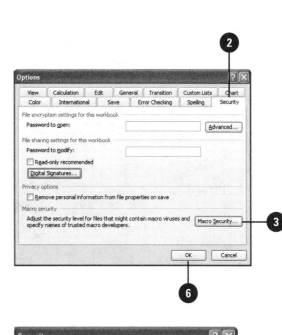

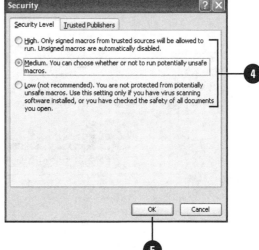

11

Applying Security Settings

XL03E-3-2

File encryption is additional security you can apply to a workbook. **File encryption** scrambles your password to protect your workbook from unauthorized people from breaking into the file. You can use the Security tab in the Options dialog box to set password protection using file encryption. If you are aware of file encryption types, you can select the one you want to use. You don't have to worry about the encryption, Excel handles everything. All you need to do is remember the password.

Apply File Encryption

1 Click the Tools menu, and then click Options.

2 Click the Security tab.

3 Type a password.

4 Click OK.

5 Retype the password.

6 Click OK.

Did You Know?

You can remove file encryption. Click the Tools menu, click Options, click the Security tab, delete the file encryption password, and then click OK.

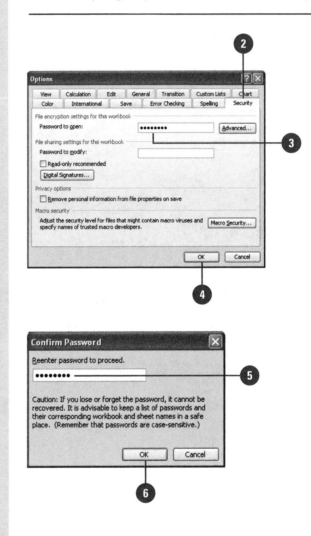

Sharing Workbook Data

Introduction

Creating successful workbooks is not always a solitary venture; you may need to share a workbook with others or get data from other programs before a project is complete. In Microsoft Office Excel 2003, you have several choices that you can use to create a joint effort. In many offices, your co-workers (and their computers) are located across the country or the world. They are joined through networks that permit users to share information by opening each other's files and to simultaneously modify data.

Microsoft Office Excel 2003 makes it easy for you to communicate with your teammates. Instead of writing on yellow sticky notes and attaching them to a printout, you can insert electronic comments within worksheet cells. You can also track changes within a workbook made by you and others. In addition to sharing workbooks, you can merge information from different workbooks into a single document, and you can link data between or consolidate data from different worksheets and workbooks.

By using a variety of techniques, you can link, embed, hyperlink, export, or convert data to create one seamless workbook that is a group effort by many co-workers.

Sharing Workbooks

XL03E-3-3

When you're working with others in a networked environment, you may want to share workbooks you created. You may also want to share the responsibilities of entering and maintaining data. **Sharing** means users can add columns and rows, enter data, and change formatting, while allowing you to review their changes. This type of work arrangement is particularly effective in team situations in which multiple users have joint responsibility for data within a single workbook. In cases in which multiple users modify the same cells, Excel can keep track of changes, and you can accept or reject them at a later date.

Enable Workbook Sharing

1. Open the workbook you want to share.

2. Click the Tools menu, and then click Share Workbook.

3. Click the Editing tab.

4. Select the Allow Changes By More Than One User At The Same Time check box.

5. Click OK, and then click OK again to save your workbook.

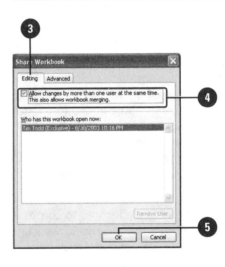

Change Sharing Options

1. Open the workbook you want to share.

2. Click the Tools menu, and then click Share Workbook.

Did You Know?

Excel alerts you if you are working in a shared file. When sharing is enabled, "[Shared]" appears in the title bar of the shared workbook.

Shared workbook

③ Click the Advanced tab.

④ To indicate how long to keep changes, select one of the Track Changes options, and then if necessary, set the number of days.

⑤ To indicate when changes should be saved, select one of the Update Changes options, and then if necessary, set a time internal.

⑥ To resolve conflicting changes, select one of the Conflicting Changes Between Users options.

⑦ Select one or both of the Include In Personal View check boxes.

⑧ Click OK.

Creating and Reading a Cell Comment

 Microsoft® Office Specialist Approved Courseware

XL03S-4-1

Any cell on a worksheet can contain a **comment**—information you might want to share with co-workers or include as a reminder to yourself without making it a part of the worksheet. (Think of a comment as a nonprinting sticky note attached to an individual cell.) A cell containing a comment displays a red triangle in the upper-right corner of the cell. By default, comments are hidden and are displayed only when the mouse pointer is held over a cell with a red triangle.

Add a Comment

1. Click the cell to which you want to add a comment.

2. Click the Insert menu, and then click Comment.

3. Type the comment in the comment box.

4. Click outside the comment box when you are finished, or press Esc twice to close the comment box.

Read a Comment

1. Position the mouse pointer over a cell with a red triangle to read its comment.

2. Move the mouse pointer off the cell to hide the comment.

   To show all the comments, click the View menu, and then click Comments. The Reviewing toolbar appears with the Show All Comments button selected.

Editing and Deleting a Cell Comment

You can edit, delete, and even format cell comments just as you do other text on a worksheet. If you are working with others online, they may want to delete a comment after reading it. You might want to format certain comments to add emphasis. You can use formatting buttons, such as Bold, Italic, Underline, Font Style, Font Color, or Font Size, on the Formatting toolbar. When you no longer need a comment, you can quickly delete it.

Edit a Comment

1. Right-click the cell containing the comment.

2. Click Edit Comment.

3. Make your changes using common editing tools, such as the Backspace and Delete keys, as well as the Formatting toolbar buttons.

4. Press Esc twice to close the comment box.

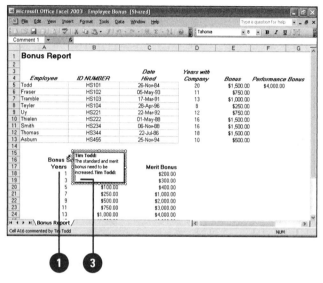

Delete a Comment

1. Right-click the cell containing the comment you want to delete.

2. Click Delete Comment.

Did You Know?

You can update comments. Add and modify comments using the Reviewing toolbar. Right-click any toolbar, and then click Reviewing to display the toolbar. Position the mouse pointer over a button to display its function.

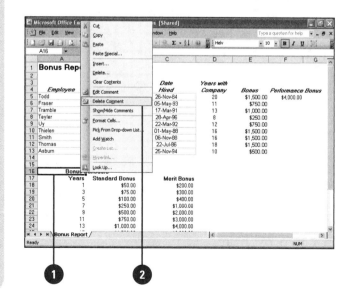

Tracking Changes

XL03E-3-5

As you build and fine-tune a workbook—particularly if you are sharing workbooks with co-workers—you can keep track of all the changes that are made at each stage in the process. The Track Changes feature makes it easy to see who made what changes and when, and to accept or reject each change. To take full advantage of this feature, turn it on the first time you or a co-worker edits a workbook. Then, when it's time to review the workbook, all the changes will be recorded. You can review tracked changes in a workbook at any point. Cells containing changes are surrounded by a blue border, and the changes made can be viewed instantly by moving your mouse pointer over any outlined cell. When you're ready to finalize the workbook, you can review each change and either accept or reject it.

Turn On the Track Changes Feature

1 Click the Tools menu, point to Track Changes, and then click Highlight Changes.

2 Select the Track Changes While Editing check box.

3 Select the When, Who, or Where check box. Click an associated list arrow, and then select the option you want.

4 Click OK.

5 Make changes in worksheet cells.

Column and row indicators for changed cells appear in red. The cell containing the changes has a blue outline.

6 To view tracked changes, position the mouse pointer over an edited cell.

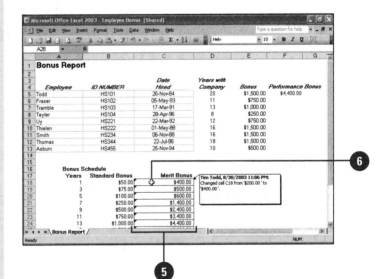

244

Accept or Reject Tracked Changes

1. Click the Tools menu, point to Track Changes, and then click Accept Or Reject Changes. If necessary, click OK in the message box.

2. Click OK to begin reviewing changes.

3. If necessary, scroll to review all the changes, and then click one of the following buttons:

   ◆ Click Accept to make the selected change to the worksheet.

   ◆ Click Reject to remove the selected change from the worksheet.

   ◆ Click Accept All to make all of the changes to the worksheet after you have reviewed them.

   ◆ Click Reject All to remove all of the changes to the worksheet after you have reviewed them.

4. Click Close.

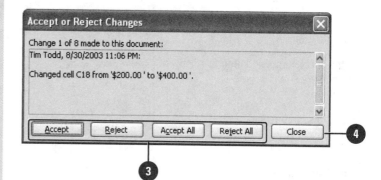

Did You Know?

You can keep track of revisions by tracking changes. Use the Track Changes feature to follow important changes in data, even if you are the only user of a worksheet.

The title bar changes to alert you of shared status. When you or another user applies the Track Changes command to a workbook, the message "[Shared]" appears in the title bar of the workbook to alert you that this feature is active.

12

Comparing and Merging Workbooks

XL03E-3-4

For one reason or another, multiple users may maintain identical workbooks. At some point, you'll want to integrate their data into one master workbook, known as the template. First, though, you need to compare the data to identify the differences between the worksheets. Excel can electronically combine the entries, which ensures the integrity of your data. When merging workbooks, all the workbooks must be identical to the file into which the data is being merged. To distribute copies of a workbook and merge the changes into the original, the workbooks must have sharing, change tracking, and change history turned on and use a different file names.

Merge Workbook Data

1 Open the shared workbook that you want to merge.

2 Click the Tools menu, and then click Compare And Merge Workbooks.

3 Click OK to save the workbook, if necessary.

4 Select the files you want merged with the active file.

To select more than one workbook to merge, press and hold Ctrl, and then click other files.

5 Click OK.

6 Click the Save button.

7 Click the Tools menu, point to Track Changes, and then click Accept Or Reject Changes.

8 Select the When check box, click the list arrow, and then click Not Yet Reviewed.

9 Clear the Who and Where check boxes.

10 Click OK.

11 Click the buttons to accept or reject changes, and then click Close.

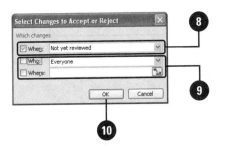

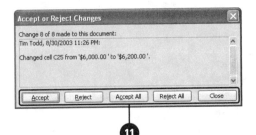

Sending a Workbook for Review

After you have completed your workbook, you can share and send it to others for review. The Mail Recipient (for Review) command makes it easy to create and send an e-mail with the workbook attachment and proper follow up settings. When a reviewer receives the e-mail with the attached file and opens the workbook, the reviewing tools are ready to use during the review process. When the reviewers return the file, Excel prompts you to merge the changes with the original workbook. You can use the reviewing tools to accept or reject the changes, or end the review cycle.

Send a Workbook for Review Using E-Mail

① Open the shared workbook you want to send out for review.

② Click the File menu, point to Send To, and then click Mail Recipient (Review). Your default e-mail program opens, displaying a new e-mail message window.

③ If a message box appears, asking you to save a shared version of the workbook for reviews, click Yes, and then click the Save button to save a shared copy of the file.

④ Click the To button, select the contacts to whom you want the message sent, and then click OK.

⑤ Type a message for the reviewers.

⑥ Click the Send button on the toolbar to send the e-mail to reviewers.

⑦ When the reviewer receives the e-mail, open the file attachment, make changes, and then click the Reply With Changes button on the Reviewing toolbar.

⑧ When you receive the e-mail back with changes, open the file, and then merge the changes.

⑨ When you're done, click the End Review button on the Reviewing toolbar.

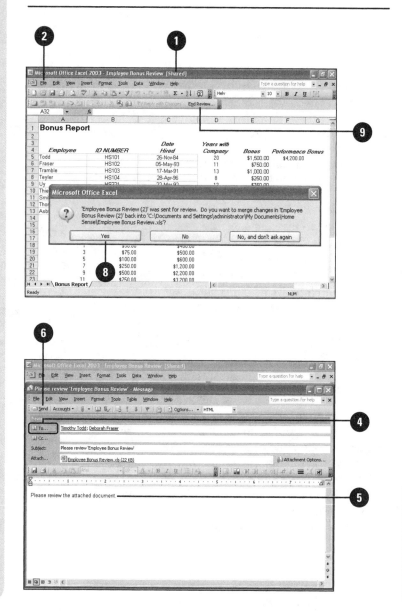

12

Sharing Information Between Programs

Office can convert data or text from one format to another using a technology known as **object linking and embedding (OLE)**. OLE allows you to move text or data between programs in much the same way as you move them within a program. The familiar cut and paste or drag and drop methods work between programs and documents just as they do within a document. In addition, Excel and all Office programs have special ways to move information from one program to another, including importing, exporting, embedding, linking, and hyperlinking.

Importing and Exporting

Importing and exporting information are two sides of the same coin. **Importing** copies a file created with the same or another program into your open file. The information becomes part of your open file, just as if you created it in that format. Some formatting and program-specific information such as formulas may be lost. **Exporting** converts a copy of your open file into the file type of another program. In other words, importing brings information into your open document, while exporting moves information from your open document into another program file.

Embedding

Embedding inserts a copy of a file created in one program into a file created in another program. Unlike imported files, you can edit the information in embedded files with the same commands and toolbar buttons used to create the original file. The original file is called the **source file**, while the file in which it is embedded is called the **destination file**. Any changes you make to an embedded object appear only in the destination file; the source file remains unchanged.

For example, if you place an Excel chart into a PowerPoint presentation, Excel is the source program, and PowerPoint is the destination program. The chart is the source file; the presentation is the destination file.

Linking

Linking displays information from one file (the source file) in a file created in another program (the destination file). You can view and edit the linked object from either the source file or the destination file. The changes are stored in the source file but also appear in the destination file. As you work, Office updates the linked object to ensure you always have the most current information. Office keeps track of all the drive, folder, and file name information for a source file. However, if you move or rename the source file, the link between files will break.

Embedding and Linking	
Term	**Definition**
Source program	The program that created the original object
Source file	The file that contains the original object
Destination program	The program that created the document into which you are inserting the object
Destination file	The file into which you are inserting the object

Once the link is broken, the information in the destination file becomes embedded rather than linked. In other words, changes to one copy of the file will no longer affect the other.

Hyperlinking

The newest way to share information between programs is hyperlinks—a term borrowed from World Wide Web technology. A **hyperlink** is an object (either colored, underlined text or a graphic) that you can click to jump to a different location in the same document or a different document.

Deciding Which Method to Use

With all these different methods for sharing information between programs to choose from, sometimes it is hard to decide which method to use. To decide which method is best for your situation, answer the following questions:

① Do you want the contents of another file displayed in the open document?

♦ **No**. Create a hyperlink. See "Creating a Hyperlink" on page 270.

♦ **Yes**. Go to question 2.

② Do you want to edit the content of the file from within the open document?

♦ **No**. Embed the file as a picture. See "Linking and Embedding Files" on page 256.

♦ **Yes**. Go to question 3.

③ Is the source program (the program used to create the file) available on your computer?

♦ **No**. Import the file. See "Exporting and Importing Data" on page 250.

♦ **Yes**. Go to question 4.

④ Do you want to use the source program commands to edit the file?

♦ **No**. Import the file. See "Exporting and Importing Data" on page 250.

♦ **Yes**. Go to question 5.

⑤ Do you want changes you make to the file to appear in the source file (the original copy of the file)?

♦ **No**. Embed the file. See "Exporting and Importing Data" on page 256.

♦ **Yes**. Link the file. See "Linking and Embedding Files" on page 256.

12

Exporting and Importing Data

XL03S-5-10, XL03E-4-1

In cases where you don't need the data you are using from another source to be automatically updated if the source data changes, the most expedient way to get the data is to copy and paste it. In cases where you want to copy data from one program to another, you can convert the data to a format that the other program accepts. If you have text you want to include on your worksheet, you can **import** a text file in a workbook.

Export Excel Data Using Copy and Paste

1. Select the cell or range that you want to copy.

2. Click the Copy button on the Standard toolbar.

3. Open the destination file, or click the program's taskbar button if the program is already open.

4. Position the pointer where you want the data to be copied.

5. Click the Paste button on the Standard toolbar.

6. Click the Paste Options button, and then click the option you want.

See Also

See "Understanding a Data Form" on page 196 for information on entering information in a predesigned form.

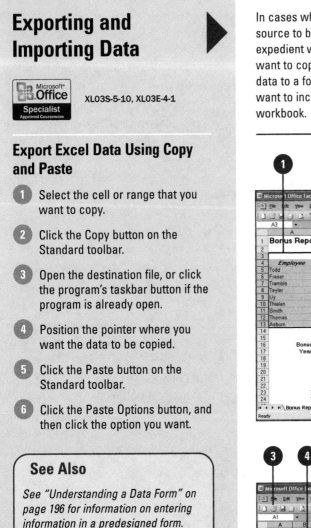

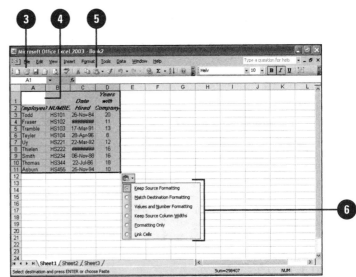

Export an Excel File to Another Program Format

1. Open the file from which you want to export data.

2. Click the File menu, and then click Save As.

3. Click the Save As Type list arrow.

4. Click the file format you want.

5. Click Save.

Did You Know?

Excel can save a file to a format only with an installed converter. If the format you want to save a file in does not appear in the Save As Type list, you'll need to install it by running Setup from the Microsoft Office 2003 CD.

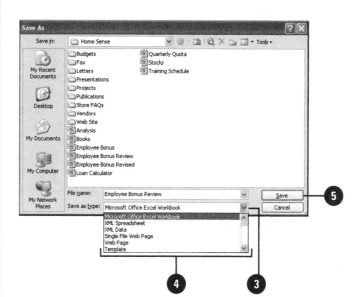

Import a Text File

1. Open the workbook in which you want to insert text data.

2. Click the Data menu, point to Import External Data, and then click Import Data.

3. Click the Files Of Type list arrow, and then click Text Files.

4. Click the Look In list arrow, and then select the folder where the text file is located.

5. Click the text file you want to import.

6. Click Open.

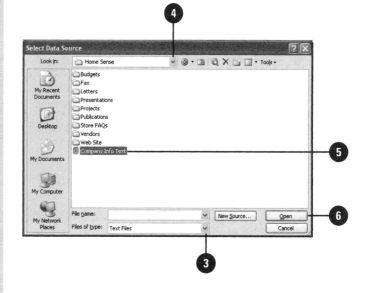

12

Working with XML

XL03E-1-15

XML (Extensible Markup Language) is a universal language that enables you to create documents in which data is stored independently of the format so you can use the data more seamlessly in other forms. XML is fully supported in Office 2003 through Word, Excel, and Access. XML allows you to work with the familiar Office interface and create and save documents as XML, without ever knowing the XML language. When you work with XML, you can attach an XML Schema—a set of rules that defines the elements and content used in an XML document. XML schemas are created by developers who understand XML. After you attach a schema, you need to map the schema elements to cells in your worksheet. When the mapping is complete, you can import the XML data related to the XML schema to populate the worksheet.

Attach a Schema

1. Click the Data menu, point to XML, and then click XML Source.

2. Click XML Maps.

3. Click Add.

4. Locate and select the XML schema file you want to attach, and then click Open.

5. If necessary, click OK to create a schema based on the XML source data.

6. To delete or rename an XML schema, select the schema, and then click Delete or Rename.

7. Click OK.

8. When you're done, click the Close button on the task pane.

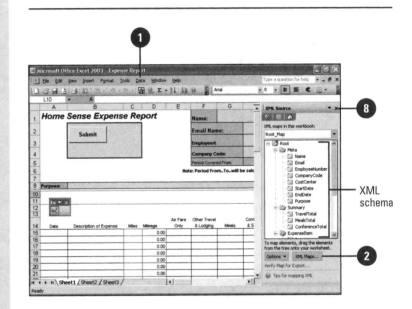

XML schema

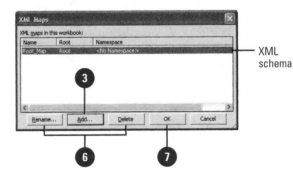

XML schema

Did You Know?

You can change XML view options. In the XML Source task pane, click Options to turn on or off options to pre-view data in the task pane, hide help text in the task pane, automatically merge elements when mapping, include data heading, and hide border of inactive lists.

Create an XML Data Map

1. Open the worksheet in which you want to map the XML data.

2. Click the Data menu, point to XML, and then click XML Source.

3. Click the Map Name list arrow, and then click the XML schema you want to use.

4. Drag the named elements from the XML Source task pane to the corresponding cells in the worksheet.

5. When you're done, click the Close button on the task pane.

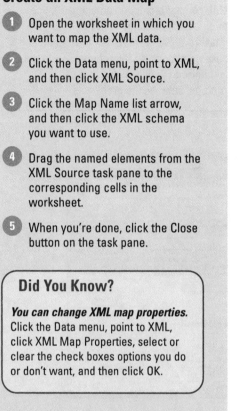

Did You Know?

You can change XML map properties. Click the Data menu, point to XML, click XML Map Properties, select or clear the check boxes options you do or don't want, and then click OK.

Import XML Data

1. Open the worksheet in which you want to map the XML data.

2. Click the Data menu, point to XML, and then click Import.

3. Click the Files Of Type list arrow, and then click XML Files.

4. Locate, and then select the XML data file you want to import.

5. Click Import.

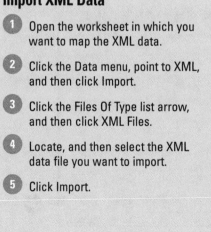

12

Exporting and Saving Data in XML

After you finish working with your XML document, you can export or save the data for use in other XML compatible documents and applications. You can save the contents of a mapped range with the XML Data format or XML Spreadsheet format. The XML Data format is an independent XML industry standard that uses a separate XML schema, while the XML Spreadsheet format is a specialized Excel XML file that uses its own XML schema to store information, such as file properties.

Export XML Data

1. Open the worksheet with the XML data.

2. Click the Data menu, point to XML, and then click Export.

3. If necessary, click the XML map you want to use, and then click OK.

4. Select a location where you want to export the XML data.

5. Type a name for the XML file.

6. Click Export.

Did You Know?

You can quickly verify a data map before you export the data. Click the Data menu, point to XML, click XML Data Source, click the Verify Map For Export link at the bottom of the task pane, and then click OK when it's done.

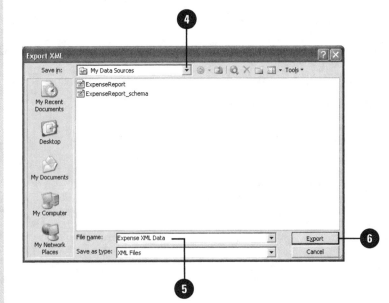

Save XML Data

1. Open the worksheet with the XML data.

2. Click the File menu, and then click Save As.

3. Click the Save As Type list arrow, and then click XML Data or XML Spreadsheet.

4. Select a location where you want to save the XML data.

5. Type a name for the XML file.

6. Click Save.

7. If necessary, click Continue, click the XML map you want to use, and then click OK.

   IMPORTANT *When you save with the XML Data format, the active worksheet is now the XML data. To work with the original worksheet, you need to re-open it.*

Did You Know?

You can also open an XML data file. Click the File menu, click Open, click the Files Of Type list arrow, click XML Files, select the XML data file, click Open, click the As An XML List, As A Read-Only Workbook, or Use The XML Source Task Pane option, and then click OK.

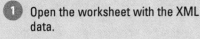

12

Linking and Embedding Files

Information created using other Office programs can be shared among them. This means that data created in an Excel workbook, can be included in a Word document without being retyped. This makes projects such as annual or departmental reports simple to create. Information can be either **linked** or **embedded**. Data that is linked has the advantage of always being accurate because it is automatically updated when the linked document is modified.

Create a Link to Another File

1. Open the source file and any files containing information you want to link.

2. Select the information in the source file, and then click the Copy button on the Standard toolbar.

3. Click the insertion point in the file containing the link.

4. Click the Edit menu, and then click Paste Special.

5. Click Paste Link.

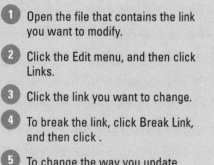

Modify a Link

1. Open the file that contains the link you want to modify.

2. Click the Edit menu, and then click Links.

3. Click the link you want to change.

4. To break the link, click Break Link, and then click .

5. To change the way you update data, click Startup Prompt, click a startup option, and then click OK.

6. To manually update the data, click Update Values.

7. Click Close.

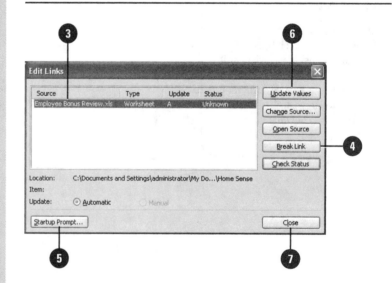

Embed a New Object

1. Click the Insert menu, and then click Object.

2. Click the Create New tab.

3. Click the object type you want to insert.

4. Click OK.

5. Follow the necessary steps to insert the object.

   The steps will vary depending on the object type.

Embed or Link to an Existing Object

1. Click the Insert menu, and then click Object.

2. Click the Create From File tab.

3. Click Browse, and then locate the file that you want to link.

4. To create a link to the object, select the Link To File check box.

5. Click OK.

Did You Know?

You can edit an embedded object. Edit an embedded object only if the program that created it is installed on your computer.

You can update links each time you open a linked document. When you open a workbook that contains links, a warning dialog box opens asking you if you want to update all linked information (click Yes) or to keep the existing information (click No).

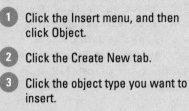

12

Linking Data

A link can be as simple as a reference to a cell on another worksheet, or it can be part of a formula. You can link cells between sheets within one workbook or between different workbooks. Cell data to be linked is called the source data. The cell or range linked to the source data is called the destination cell or destination range. If you no longer want linked data to be updated, you can break a link easily. Create links instead of making multiple identical entries; it saves time and ensures your entries are correct.

Create a Link Between Worksheets or Workbooks

1 Select the cell or range that contains the source data.

2 Click the Copy button on the Standard toolbar.

3 Click the sheet tab where you want to link the data.

4 Select the destination cell or destination range.

5 Click the Paste button on the Standard toolbar.

6 Click the Paste Options button, and then click Link Cells.

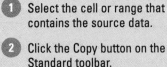

Break a Link

1. Click the cell containing the linked formula you want to break.

2. Click the Copy button on the Standard toolbar.

3. Click the Edit menu, and then click Paste Special.

4. Click the Values option.

5. Click OK.

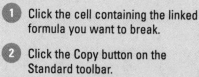

Did You Know?

You can include a link in a formula and treat the linked cell as one argument in a larger calculation. Enter the formula on the formula bar, and then select a cell in the worksheet or workbook you want to link. A cell address reference to a worksheet is =tab name!cell address (=Orders!A6). A cell reference to a workbook is ='[workbook name.xls]tab name'!cell address (='[Product Orders.xls]Orders'!A6).

You can arrange worksheet windows to make linking easier. To arrange open windows, click the Window menu, click Arrange, and then click the option for the window arrangement you want.

12

Consolidating Data

XL03E-4-5

In some cases, you'll want to consolidate data from different worksheets or workbooks into one workbook, rather than simply linking the source data. For instance, if each division in your company creates a budget, you can pull together, or **consolidate**, the totals for each line item into one company-wide budget. If each divisional budget is laid out in the same way, with the budgeted amounts for each line item in the same cell addresses, then you can very easily consolidate the information without any retyping. If data in individual workbooks change, the consolidated worksheet or workbook will always be correct.

Consolidate Data from Other Worksheets or Workbooks

1. Open all the workbooks that contain the data you want to consolidate.

2. Open or create the workbook that will contain the consolidated data.

3. Select the destination range.

4. Click the Data menu, and then click Consolidate.

5. Click the Function list arrow, and then select the function you want to use to consolidate the data.

6. Type the location of the data to be consolidated, or click the Reference Collapse Dialog button, and then select the cells to be consolidated.

Did You Know?

You can include all labels. Make sure you select enough cells to accommodate any labels that might be included in the data you are consolidating.

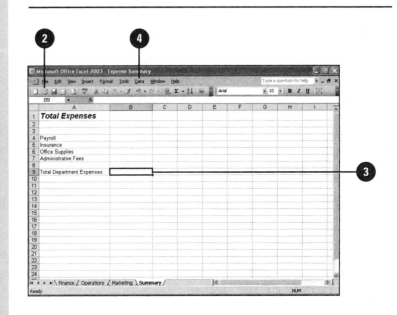

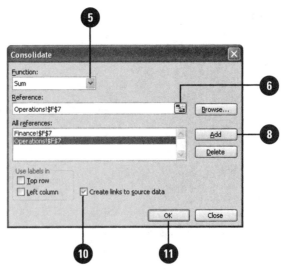

⑦ Click the Expand Dialog button.

⑧ Click Add to add the reference to the list of consolidated ranges.

⑨ Repeat steps 6 through 8 until you have listed all references to consolidate.

⑩ Select the Create Links To Source Data check box.

⑪ Click OK.

Did You Know?

You can consolidate worksheets even if they are not laid out identically. If the worksheets you want to consolidate aren't laid out with exactly the same cell addresses, but they do contain identical types of information, select the Top Row and Left Column check boxes in the Consolidate dialog box so that Excel uses labels to match up the correct data.

You can arrange multiple workbooks. Use the Window menu to move between workbooks or to arrange them so they are visible at the same time.

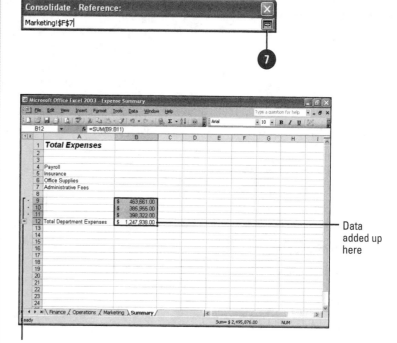

Data added up here

Click to collapse the data

12

Getting Data from a Database

If you have data in a database, you can use functions in Excel to retrieve data from a table in a database. To retrieve the data, you can select or create a data source, build a query to create a link to the data, and optionally, create a filter to limit the information. When you select or create a data source, you need to identify the database type and then connect to it. To build a query, you can use the Query wizard to step you through the process, or you can manually create a query the same way you do in Microsoft Access. If you use the same table in a database for data, you can define and save the data source for use later.

Define a New Data Source

1. Click the Data menu, point to Import External Data, and then click New Database Query.

2. Click the Databases tab.

3. Click <New Data Source>.

4. Click OK.

5. Type the name of the source.

6. Click the second box list arrow, and then click Microsoft Access Driver (*.mdb).

7. Click Connect.

8. Click Select.

9. Navigate to the folder with the database you want to use, and then click OK.

10. Click OK again.

11. Click the fourth box list arrow, and then click the default table for the data source.

12. Click OK.

   Follow the steps to create a query on the next page, starting with step 4.

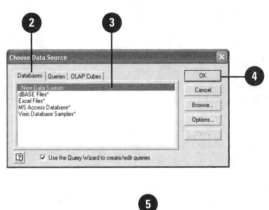

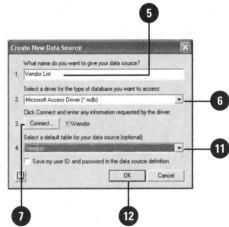

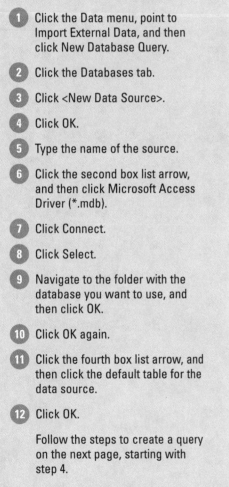

262

Create a Database Query

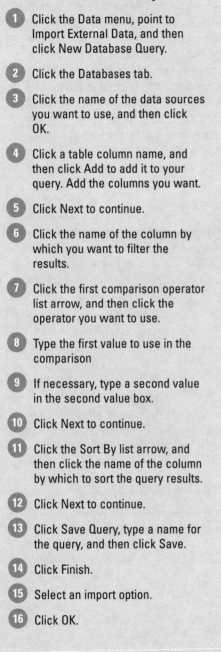

1. Click the Data menu, point to Import External Data, and then click New Database Query.

2. Click the Databases tab.

3. Click the name of the data sources you want to use, and then click OK.

4. Click a table column name, and then click Add to add it to your query. Add the columns you want.

5. Click Next to continue.

6. Click the name of the column by which you want to filter the results.

7. Click the first comparison operator list arrow, and then click the operator you want to use.

8. Type the first value to use in the comparison

9. If necessary, type a second value in the second value box.

10. Click Next to continue.

11. Click the Sort By list arrow, and then click the name of the column by which to sort the query results.

12. Click Next to continue.

13. Click Save Query, type a name for the query, and then click Save.

14. Click Finish.

15. Select an import option.

16. Click OK.

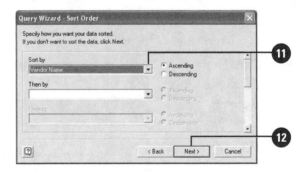

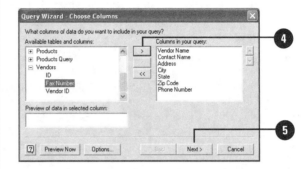

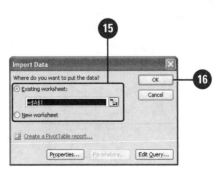

12

Getting Data from Another Program

XL03E-4-1

Information you want to analyze may not always exist in an Excel workbook; you might have to retrieve it from another Office program, such as Access. Access table data can be easily converted into Excel worksheet data. Before you can analyze Access data in a workbook, you must convert it to an Excel file. You can either use the Analyze It With Microsoft Office Excel command in Access to export data as an Excel table file, or use the PivotTable And PivotChart Report wizard in Excel to use the Access data as a **PivotTable**, a table you can use to perform calculations with or rearrange large amounts of data. Once you determine what fields and criteria you want to use to summarize the data and how you want the resulting table to look, the wizard does the rest.

Export an Access Database Table into an Excel Workbook

1. Click Start on the taskbar, point to All Programs, click Microsoft Office, and then click Microsoft Office Access 2003.

2. Open the database you want, and then click Tables on the Objects bar.

3. Click the table you want to analyze.

4. Click the OfficeLinks button list arrow on the Database toolbar.

5. Click Analyze It With Microsoft Office Excel to save the table as an Excel file, start Excel, and open the workbook.

6. Use Excel tools to edit and analyze the data.

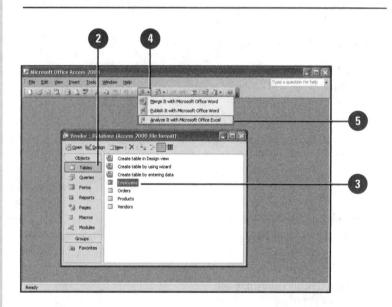

Create an Excel Workbook PivotTable from an Access Database

1. Click the Data menu, and then click PivotTable And PivotChart Report.

2. Click the External Data Source option.

3. Click Next to continue.

4. Click Get Data.

5. On the Databases tab, click MS Access Database, or click Browse, and then locate and open the Access data source you want.

6. Click OK, and then if necessary follow the wizard to select the data you want to use.

7. Click Next to continue.

8. Click a location option for the new PivotTable.

9. If you want, click Layout or Options to change the way the PivotTable looks or functions, and then click OK.

10. Click Finish.

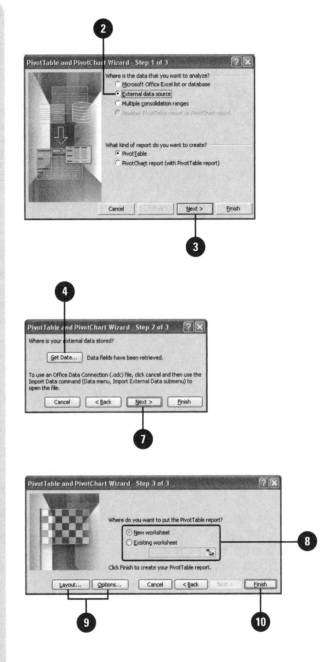

Publishing Data on the Web

Introduction

With the creation of your workbook, and all the various elements that you've added, why not share it with others? You can save your workbook as a Web page, and then preview it as a Web page to be sure you have the right look.

Incorporating hyperlinks within your Microsoft Office Excel 2003 worksheet adds an element of connectivity to your work. You can create a worksheet, and then have a hyperlink with supporting research to add to the content of your data. Or, you can copy data from a Web page and incorporate it into your Excel workbook. Either way, using the Web to publish Excel data or incorporate research into your workbook, is a great resource.

A single worksheet can become an extensive connection to other data elements, with added hyperlinks. And, given Excel's ability to exchange information, you can analyze data and hold on-line meetings. You can also send files using e-mail, all while maintaining Excel's functionality.

Opening a Workbook as a Web Page

After saving a workbook as a Web page, you can open the Web page, an HTML file, in Excel. This allows you to quickly and easily switch from HTML to the standard Excel format and back again without losing any formatting or functionality. For example, if you create a formatted chart in an Excel worksheet, save the workbook file as a Web page, and then reopen the Web page in Excel, the chart will look the same as the original chart in Excel. Excel preserves the original formatting and functionality of the workbook.

Open a Workbook as a Web Page in Excel

1. Click the Open button on the Standard toolbar in the Excel window.

2. Click the Files Of Type list arrow, and then click All Web Pages.

3. Click one of the icons on the Places bar for quick access to frequently used folders.

4. If the file is located in another folder, click the Look In list arrow, and then select the folder where the file is located.

5. Click the name of the workbook file.

6. Click Open.

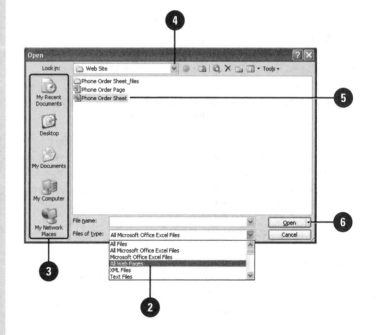

Did You Know?

You can optimize Web pages for a specific browser. Click the Tools menu, click Options, click the General tab, click Web Options, click the Browser tab, click the list arrow, select a browser, clear or select the options you want, and then click OK twice.

Previewing a Web Page

Microsoft Office Specialist Approved Courseware XL03S-5-5

You can view any Excel worksheet as if it were already on the Web by previewing the Web page. By previewing a file you want to post to the Web, you can see if there are any errors that need to be corrected, formatting that needs to be added, or additions that need to be made. Just as you should always preview a worksheet before you print it, you should preview a Web page before you post it. Previewing the Web page is similar to using the Print Preview feature before you print a worksheet. This view shows you what the page will look like once it's posted on the Internet. You do not have to be connected to the Internet to preview a worksheet as a Web page.

View the Web Page

1. Open the workbook file you want to view as a Web page.

2. Click the File menu, and then click Web Page Preview.

   Your default Web browser starts and displays the Web page.

3. Click the Close button to quit your Web browser, and then return to Excel.

Creating a Hyperlink

Microsoft Office Specialist
Approved Courseware

XL03S-5-3

With instant access to the Internet, your worksheet can contain links to specific sites so you and anyone else using your worksheet can access Web information. An Internet link that is embedded on a worksheet is called a **hyperlink**—because when it is clicked, you are instantly connected to the link's defined address on the Web. If your worksheet contains a hyperlink, the link appears in the worksheet as blue text. To connect to the Web site, just click the hyperlink.

Create a Hyperlink

1. Select a cell where you want the hyperlink to appear.

2. Click the Insert Hyperlink button on the Standard toolbar.

3. Click one of the icons on the Link To bar for quick access to frequently used files, Web pages, and links.

4. Type or select the name and location of the file or Web page you want to link to.

5. Click OK.

Did You Know?

You can create a custom ScreenTip for a hyperlink. Select the hyperlink you want to customize, click the Insert Hyperlink button on the Standard toolbar, click ScreenTip, type the ScreenTip text you want, click OK, and then click OK again.

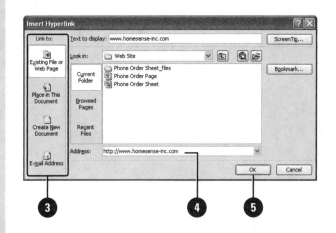

Jump to a Hyperlink

1. Click the hyperlink on your worksheet.

   Excel opens your Web browser.

2. Establish an Internet connection.

   The Web page associated with the hyperlink is displayed.

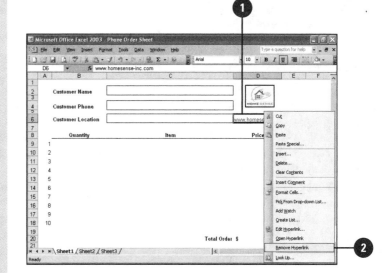

Remove a Hyperlink

1. Right-click the cell containing the hyperlink you want to remove.

2. Click Remove Hyperlink.

Did You Know?

Web addresses and URLs mean the same thing. Every Web page has a Uniform Resource Locator (URL), or Web address. Each URL contains specific parts that identify where a Web page is located. For example, the URL for Perspection's Web page is: *http://www.perspection.com/index.htm* where "http://" shows the address is on the Web, "www.perspection.com" shows the computer that stores the Web site, and "index.htm" is a Web page on the Web site.

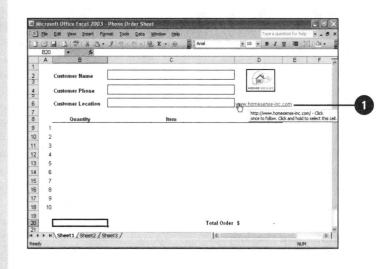

Saving a Worksheet as a Web Page ▶

 XL03S-5-10

You can place an existing Excel worksheet on the Internet for others to use. In order for any document to be placed on the Web, it must be in **HTML** (Hypertext Markup Language) format. This format enables you to post, or submit, Excel data on a Web site for others. You don't need any HTML knowledge to save an Excel worksheet as a Web page. When you save a worksheet as a Web page, you can save it using the Web Page or Single File Web Page format. The Web Page format saves the worksheet as an HTML file and a folder that stores supporting files, such as a file for each graphic, worksheet, and so on. Excel selects the appropriate graphic format for you based on the image's content. A single file Web page saves all the elements of a Web site, including text and graphics, into a single file in the MHTML format, which is supported by Internet Explorer 4.0 or later.

Save a Workbook or Worksheet as a Web Page

1 Click the File menu, and then click Save As Web Page.

2 Click the Save As Type list arrow, and then click Web Page.

3 Select the drive and folder in which you want to save the Web page.

4 Type the name for the Web page.

5 Select the Entire Workbook or the Selection: Sheet option.

6 If you want to change the title of your Web page, click Change Title, type a new title, and then click OK.

7 Click Save.

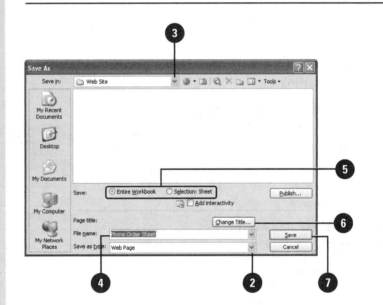

Did You Know?

You can publish a Web page to an FTP site on the Internet. In the Save As dialog box, click the Save In list arrow, click Add/Modify FTP Locations, fill in the FTP site information, click Add, click OK, and then click the FTP site.

272

Save a Workbook or Worksheet as a Single File Web Page

1 Click the File menu, and then click Save As Web Page.

2 Click the Save As Type list arrow, and then click Single File Web Page.

3 Select the drive and folder in which you want to save the Web page.

4 Type the name for the Web page.

5 Select the Entire Workbook or the Selection: Sheet option.

6 If you want to change the title of your Web page, click Change Title, type a new title, and then click OK.

7 Click Save.

The Web page is saved as a single file.

Publishing a Web Page

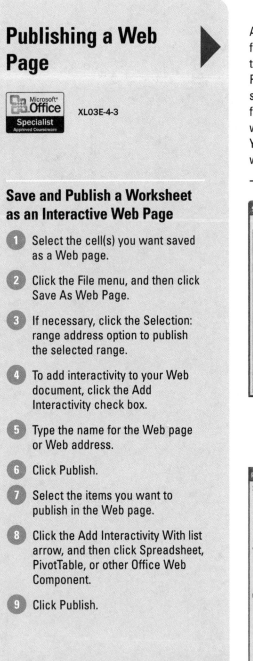
At times, you'll want to publish a copy of your current workbook in HTML format directly to a **Web server** (a computer on the Internet or intranet that stores Web pages) so others can view and manipulate your data. Publishing to a Web server is as simple as saving a file. A worksheet saved as a Web page retains all its spreadsheet, charting, or PivotTable functionality and formatting properties. This **interactivity** means that while your worksheet is on the Web, others can manipulate your data. You can elect to let anyone using Internet Explorer 4.01 or later interact with your data from Excel.

Save and Publish a Worksheet as an Interactive Web Page

1. Select the cell(s) you want saved as a Web page.

2. Click the File menu, and then click Save As Web Page.

3. If necessary, click the Selection: range address option to publish the selected range.

4. To add interactivity to your Web document, click the Add Interactivity check box.

5. Type the name for the Web page or Web address.

6. Click Publish.

7. Select the items you want to publish in the Web page.

8. Click the Add Interactivity With list arrow, and then click Spreadsheet, PivotTable, or other Office Web Component.

9. Click Publish.

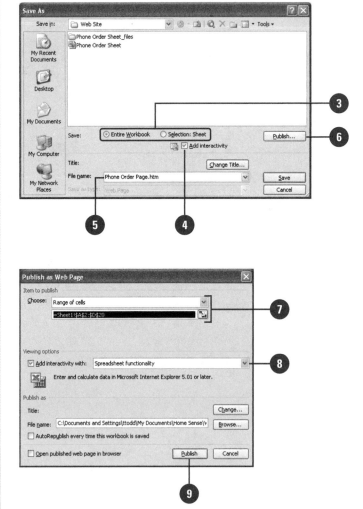

Getting Data from the Web

You can look up data on the Web and insert it into Excel using the Web toolbar. You can jump from Web site to Web site, gathering data to include on your own worksheets. You might, for example, want to include text from a Web site containing information relevant to your company, department, or research project. The Web is also a great source of free clip art. Using Microsoft's Clip Gallery Live or other online resources, you can illustrate a worksheet with almost any product, theme, or idea.

Get Data from the Web Using the Web Toolbar

1. Click the View menu, point to Toolbars, and then click Web.

2. Click the Search The Web button on the Web toolbar.

   Excel opens your Web browser.

3. Establish an Internet connection.

4. Follow the directions to search for Web sites that contain the data you want.

5. To get text data from a Web page, select the text, click the Edit menu, and then click Copy. Switch to Excel, and then paste the text on your worksheet.

6. To download a file, click the download hyperlink, click the Save This File To Disk option, click OK, select a location, and then click Save.

7. When you're done, click the Close button.

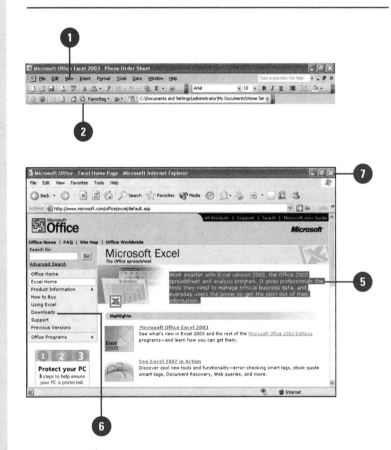

Did You Know?

You can hide and display other tool-bars. To hide the other toolbars, click the Show Only Web Toolbar button on the Web toolbar. Click the button again to display the other toolbars.

Copying a Web Table to a Worksheet

You can copy tabular information on a Web page and paste or drag the information into an Excel worksheet. It's an easy way to transfer and manipulate Web-based table data using Excel. Excel simplifies access to table data by making it available to anyone with a browser. If you need to make changes to the table, you can use normal editing techniques in Excel.

Copy a Web Table to a Worksheet

1. Open your Web browser.

2. In the Address bar, type the location of the Web page with the table data you want to copy, and then press Enter.

3. Select the table data in the Web page you want to copy.

4. Open the Excel worksheet where you want to paste the table data.

5. Right-click the taskbar, and then click Tile Windows Vertically.

6. Drag the table data from the Web browser window to the location on the worksheet where you want the table data, and then release the mouse button.

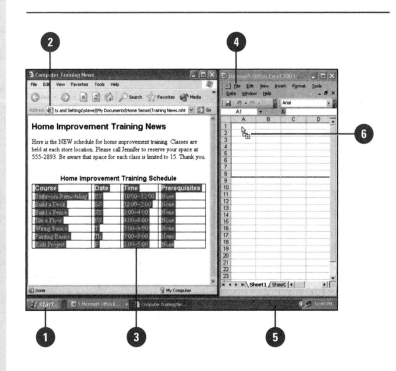

Did You Know?

You can use copy and paste to transfer table data to Excel. In your browser, select the table data you want, click the Edit menu, click Copy, switch to Excel, click the cell where you want to place the table data, and then click the Paste button on the Standard toolbar.

Creating Refreshable Web Queries

XL03E-4-1

If you need to analyze Web data in a worksheet, you can use the copy and paste commands to bring the data from a Web page into the worksheet. The Paste Options button allows you to specify whether you want the information to keep the data as it is right now or make it refreshable to the current data on the Web. As the data changes on the Web, you can use the Refresh Data button to quickly update the data in you worksheet. You don't need copy and copy the information again.

13

Copy and Paste Refreshable Data from the Web

1. Open the Web page with the information you want to copy into a worksheet, and then select the data.

2. Click the Edit menu, and then click Copy.

3. Switch to Excel, and then click the active cell where you want the data.

4. Click the Paste button on the Standard toolbar.

5. Click the Paste Options button, and then click Create Refreshable Web Query.

6. Click the arrow buttons to select the information you want.

7. Click Import.

Did You Know?

You can quickly refresh a Web query. Click a cell in the worksheet with the query data, and then click the Refresh Data button on the External Data toolbar. A spinning refresh icon appears in the status bar to indicate that the query is running. You can double-click the icon to check the status of the query.

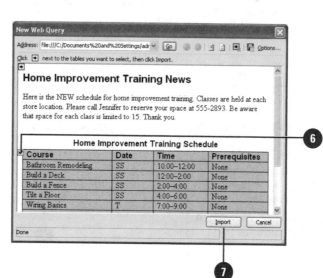

Getting Data from Web Queries

You can import data into Excel through database and Web queries and analyze data with formulas and formatting. You can insert columns within query tables and apply formulas and formatting. When data is refreshed, the formatting and analysis are retained. Excel helps you through the process of bringing data from a Web page to your worksheet. You can create a new Web query as you choose the URL and parameters for how you want to import the Web data. Once you save the query, you can run it again at any time.

Get Data from a New Web Query

1. Click the Data menu, point to Import External Data, and then click New Web Query.

2. Type the address for the Web page that contains the data you want.

3. Click the arrow buttons to select the information you want.

4. Click Options to select the formatting you want your data to keep.

5. Click Import.

6. Click the Existing Worksheet option and specify a starting cell, or click the New Worksheet option.

7. Click OK.

Did You Know?

You can change Web options. Click the Tools menu, click Options, click the General tab, and then click Web Options. Click the tab with the options you want to change, make the changes, and then click OK.

You can get data from an existing Web query. Click the Data menu, point to Get External Data, click Run Saved Query, select the query file, and then click Get Data.

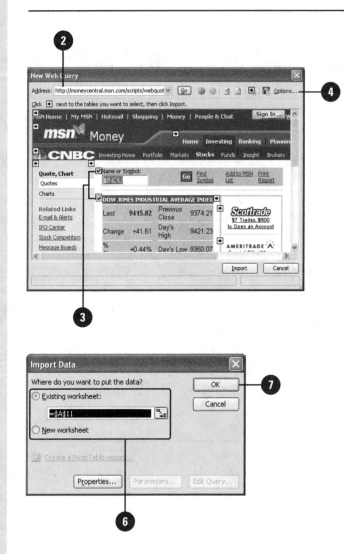

Saving Web Queries

When you create a Web query, it is automatically saved for use in the current workbook. If you need the same query in another workbook, you can save the Web query in a separate file. When you save a query, the file uses the .iqy extension, which you can import into another workbook.

Save a Web Query

① Click the Data menu, point to Import External Data, and then click Edit Query.

② Click the Save Query button.

③ Select the drive and folder in which you want to save the query.

④ Type a name for the query.

⑤ Click Save.

⑥ Click Cancel.

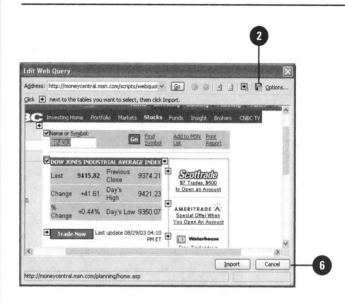

Import a Query

① Click the Data menu, point to Import External Data, and then click Import Data.

② Locate and select the query file (.iqy).

③ Click Open.

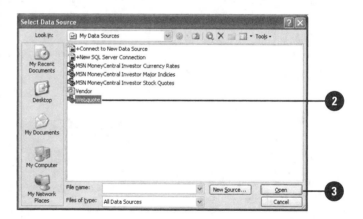

Holding an Online Meeting

Excel helps you to collaborate with others online not only by sharing information but by scheduling meetings using Outlook 2003, and holding meetings online using a program called Microsoft NetMeeting. Participants share and exchange information as if they were in one room. The **host** starts the meeting and controls access to the document. When the host allows editing, participants can work on the document one at a time. Otherwise, they cannot make changes, but they can see any changes the host makes. All participants can talk to each other, video conference, share programs, collaborate on documents, send files, exchange messages in Chat, transfer files, and draw in the Whiteboard.

Schedule a Meeting

1. Click the Tools menu, point to Online Collaboration, and then click Schedule Meeting.

2. Enter participants' names or e-mail addresses, a subject, and the meeting location.

3. Click Browse, and then double-click a document you want to send.

4. Select a start and end date and time.

5. Type a message.

6. Click the Send button.

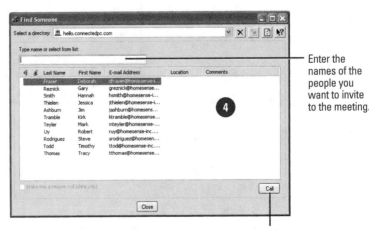

Hold a Meeting

1. Open the document you want to share.

2. Click the Tools menu, point to Online Collaboration, and then click Meet Now.

3. If this is your first meeting, enter your personal information, select a server, and then click OK.

4. Select the participants for the meeting, and then click Call.

Enter the names of the people you want to invite to the meeting.

Click to start NetMeeting running in the background.

Collaborate in an Online Meeting

1. As the host, click the Allow Others To Edit button on the Online Meeting toolbar.

2. When collaboration is turned on, click anywhere in the document to gain control. If you are a participant, double-click anywhere in the document to gain control.

3. Click the Allow Others To Edit button again to turn off the collaboration, or press Esc if you don't have control of the document.

Participate in an Online Meeting

◆ Use the buttons on the Online Meeting toolbar to participate in an online meeting.

Did You Know?

You can join an online meeting. If you receive an online meeting call, click Accept in the Join Meeting dialog box. If you receive an Outlook reminder for the meeting, click Start This NetMeeting (host), or Join This NetMeeting (participant). To receive an Outlook reminder to join a meeting, you need to have accepted the meeting from an e-mail message.

Online Meeting Toolbar

Button	Description
	Allows the host to invite additional participants to the online meeting
	Allows the host to remove a participant from the online meeting
	Allows participants to edit and control the presentation during the online meeting
	Allows participants to send messages in a Chat session during the online meeting
	Allows participants to draw or type on the Whiteboard during the online meeting
	Allows either the host to end the online meeting for the group or a participant to disconnect

Sending Workbooks Using E-Mail

E-mail is a great way to send timely information to friends and business colleagues. You can send a worksheet in an e-mail message or an entire workbook as a file attachment using your favorite e-mail program. Route a workbook through e-mail, rather than send it, when you want others to review a copy of it online. As the workbook is routed, you can track its status. After all of the recipients have reviewed the workbook, it is automatically returned to you.

Send a Worksheet in an E-Mail Message

1. Open the worksheet you want to send.

2. Click the E-Mail button on the Standard toolbar.

3. Click the To or Cc button. Select the contacts to whom you want the message sent, and then click OK.

4. Click the Send This Sheet button on the toolbar.

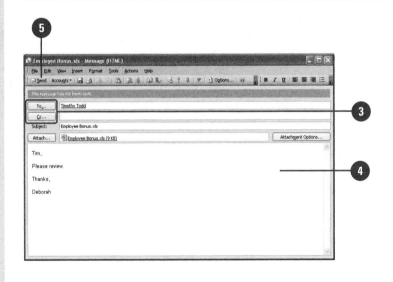

Send a Workbook as an E-Mail Attachment

1. Open the workbook you want to send.

2. Click the File menu, point to Send To, and then click Mail Recipient (As Attachment). Your default e-mail program opens, displaying a new e-mail message window.

3. Click the To or Cc button. Select the contacts you want, and then click OK.

4. Type a related message.

5. Click the Send button on the toolbar.

Route a Workbook in an E-Mail Message

1. Open the workbook you want to send.

2. Click the File menu, point to Send To, and then select Routing Recipient.

3. Click Address. Select the contacts to whom you want the message routed, click the To or Cc button, and then click OK.

4. Type the topic of the message.

5. If you want, type a related message.

6. Select other routing options you want.

7. Click Route.

   The workbook is sent as an attachment in an e-mail message.

Did You Know?

You can select a group alias as the recipient. Select a group alias as the recipient. However, all members of the group alias are considered one recipient and receive one e-mail message.

You can route a workbook at a later time. Open the workbook you want to route. Click the File menu, point to Send To, click Routing Recipient, click Addresses, select contact names, click the To or Cc button, click OK, and then click Add Slip. At a later time, click the File menu, point to Send To, and then click Next Routing Recipient.

Routing Slip

From: Deborah Fraser

To:
1 - Jim Ashburn
2 - Gary Reznick
3 - Kirk Tramble

Move

Add Slip
Cancel
Route
Clear

Address... Remove

Subject:
Routing: Employee Bonus

Message text:
Please review. Thanks!

Route to recipients
- One after another
- All at once

☑ Return when done
☑ Track status

13

Getting Documents from the Web

File Transfer Protocol (FTP) is an inexpensive and efficient way to transfer files between your computer and others on the Internet. You can download or receive any kind of file, including text, graphics, sound, and video files, from an FTP site—an Internet site dedicated to file transfer. To download a file, you need an ID and password to identify who you are. Anonymous FTP sites are open to anyone; they usually use anonymous as an ID and your full e-mail address as a password. You can also save the FTP site address to revisit the site later.

Add or Modify FTP Locations

1. Click the Open button on the Standard toolbar.

2. Click the Look In list arrow, and then click Add/Modify FTP Locations.

3. Type the complete address for an FTP site.

4. Type a password.

5. Click Add.

6. Click OK.

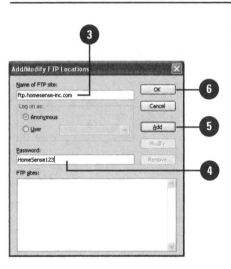

Access an FTP Site

1. Click the Open button on the Standard toolbar.

2. Click the Look In list arrow, and then click the FTP site you want to log in to.

3. Select a Log On As option.

4. Enter a password (your E-mail address or personal password).

5. Click OK.

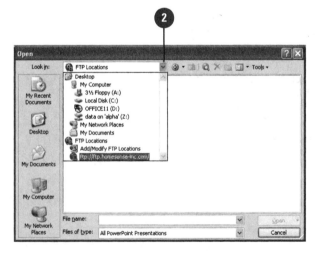

Tools for Working More Efficiently

Introduction

Microsoft Office Excel 2003 offers many tools that help you make the best use of your time. You can customize several settings in the Excel work environment to suit the way you like to work. You can make general changes that affect every workbook, or specific editing options.

You can increase your efficiency by customizing the look of the Excel window, the way you execute commands, and the way you create and arrange worksheets in a window. You can maximize your view of the work area, so you spend less time scrolling through a sheet or switching from sheet to sheet, and more time working with data.

Creating your own custom toolbar, or enhance the one you use most often, can save you both time and workspace. You can create your own menu with a list arrow and add all your favorite commands. You can also use speech recognition that lets Excel respond to voice commands.

Have you ever wondered how those automated phone messages work? Well, with the playback tool in Excel, you can have Excel speak the value of cell contents. You can initiate commands with your voice and have them performed in Excel. This is very helpful when you want to dictate text or numbers directly into your workbook. Using multiple languages can assist you in translation areas of a workbook that you might be sharing with others. You can also have Excel translate your handwriting into text or numbers. When problems arise, and they usually do, Excel has a repairing and recovery feature to try and get your lost workbooks.

Modifying Workbook Properties

 XL03E-4-6

If you're not sure when you created or last printed a workbook, or if you need statistical information about a workbook, such as the number of revisions or total editing time, you can use the Properties dialog box to quickly find this information. If you can't remember the name of a range in a workbook, the Properties dialog box keeps track of this information for you. You can also create custom file properties to help you manage and track files. If you associate a file property to an item in the document, the file property updates when you change the item. When you enter information for a property, you can use the Search command on the Tools menu in the Open dialog box or the Advanced File Search task pane to find a workbook with the desired property.

Display Workbook Properties

1. Open the workbook you want to see properties on. Click the File menu, and then click Properties.

2. Click the tabs (General, Summary, Statistics, or Contents) to view information about the worksheet:

   ◆ **General.** To find out file location or size.

   ◆ **Summary.** To add title and author information for the document.

   ◆ **Statistics.** To display date related information about a workbook.

   ◆ **Contents.** To display the tab names and the named ranges.

3. Click OK.

Did You Know?

You can view properties in the Open dialog box. In the Open dialog box, select the file you want to view properties, click the View button, and then click Properties.

Customize Workbook Properties

① Click the File menu, and then click Properties.

② Click the Custom tab.

③ Type a name for the custom property or select a name from the list.

④ Click the data type for the property you want to add.

⑤ Type a value for the property that matches the type you selected in the Type box.

⑥ Click Add.

⑦ Click OK.

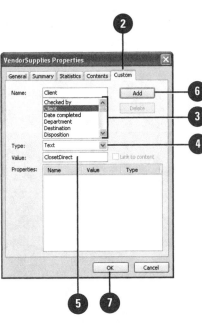

Link to Workbook Properties

① Name the cell or range in which you want to link the property.

② Click the File menu, and then click Properties.

③ Click the Custom tab.

④ Type the name for the custom property.

⑤ Select the Link To Content check box.

⑥ Click the defined content to which you want to link.

⑦ Click Add.

⑧ Click OK.

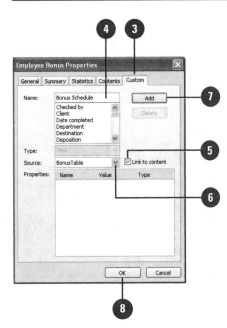

14

Finding a File or Contents in a File

The search feature available in the Open dialog box is also available using the Search task pane. You can use the Search task pane to find a file's name or location as well as search for specific text or property in a workbook. This becomes handy when you recall the content of a document, but not the name. When you perform a search, try to use specific or unique words to achieve the best results.

Find a File or Contents in a File

1. Click the File menu, and then click File Search.

2. Type the name of the file you are looking for or any distinctive words or phrases in the worksheet.

3. Click the Search In list arrow, and then select or clear the check boxes to indicate where you want the program to search.

   Click the plus sign (+) to expand a list.

4. Click the Results Should Be list arrow, and then select or clear the check boxes to indicate the type of files you want to find.

5. Click Go.

6. To revise the find, click Modify.

7. When the search results appear, point to a file, click the list arrow, and then click the command you want.

8. When you're done, click the Close button on the task pane.

Did You Know?

You can use wildcards to search for file names. When you recall only part of the file name you want to open, type a question mark (?) for any one unknown character or an asterisk (*) for two or more unknown characters.

Find a Property in a File

1. Click the File menu, and then click File Search.

2. Click Advanced File Search.

3. Click the Property list arrow, and then select the property in which you want to search.

4. If necessary, click the Condition list arrow, and then select a criteria.

5. Type the value in which you want to search.

6. Click Add.

7. Click the Search In list arrow, and then select or clear the check boxes to indicate where you want the program to search.

   Click the plus sign (+) to expand a list.

8. Click the Results Should Be list arrow, and then select or clear the check boxes to indicate the type of files you want to find.

9. Click Go.

10. To revise the find, click Modify.

11. When the search results appear, point to a file, click the list arrow, and then click the command you want.

12. When you're done, click the Close button on the task pane.

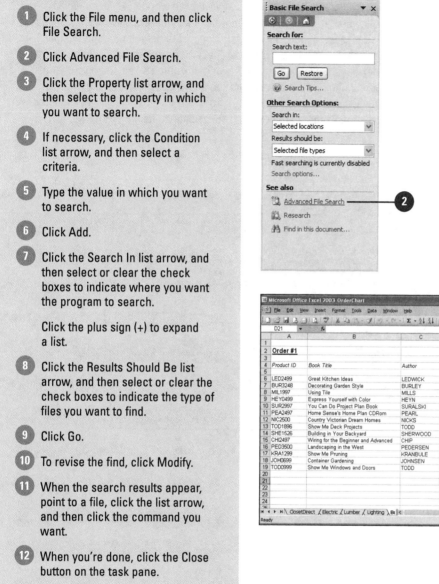

Changing Options

XL03E-5-3

You can customize several settings in the Excel work environment to suit the way you like to work. If you always save workbooks in a specific folder, you can change the default location where workbooks are saved. You can make general changes, including the default font and the number of sheets in a new workbook. If your workbooks usually contain five sheets, you could make five the workbook default. You can also change editing options, such as whether the active cell moves after you enter data, and whether to allow drag-and-drop moving. Taking a few minutes to change Excel's default setting saves time in the long run.

Change General Options

1. Click the Tools menu, and then click Options.

2. Click the General tab.

3. To change the number of recently used files listed at the bottom of the File menu, click the up or down arrow to set the number of files you want.

4. To change the default number of sheets in a new workbook, click the up or down arrow to set a number.

5. To change the default font, click the Standard Font list arrow, and then select a new font.

6. To change the default font size, click the Size list arrow, and then select a new font size.

7. To specify where Excel should automatically look for existing files or newly saved files, enter the location of your default folder.

8. Click the User Name box, and then edit its contents.

9. Click OK.

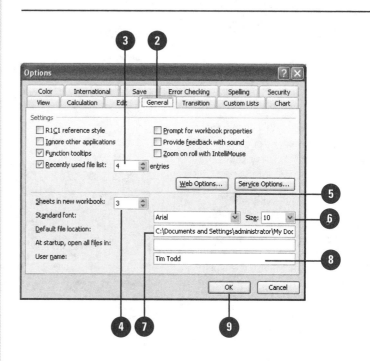

Change Edit Options

① Click the Tools menu, and then click Options.

② Click the Edit tab.

③ Click to select or clear any of the check boxes to change the editing options you want, some options include:

- ◆ Make edits directly in a cell.

- ◆ Use drag-and-drop to copy cells.

- ◆ Determine the direction the active cell takes once you press Enter.

- ◆ Determine the number of decimals to the right of the decimal point if using a fixed number format.

- ◆ Choose to cut, copy, and sort objects with cells.

- ◆ Have Excel ask whether links should be updated.

- ◆ Have Excel provide animated feedback.

- ◆ Enable the AutoComplete feature to make data entry easier and more accurate.

④ Click OK.

②

Options   ? ✕

| Color | International | Save | Error Checking | Spelling | Security |
| View | Calculation | Edit | General | Transition | Custom Lists | Chart |

Settings

☑ Edit directly in cell

☑ Allow cell drag and drop

　☑ Alert before overwriting cells

☑ Move selection after Enter

　Direction:　Down ▾

☐ Fixed decimal

　Places:　2

☑ Cut, copy, and sort objects with cells

☑ Ask to update automatic links

☐ Provide feedback with Animation

☑ Enable AutoComplete for cell values

☑ Extend data range formats and formulas

☑ Enable automatic percent entry

☑ Show Paste Options buttons

☑ Show Insert Options buttons

③

OK　　Cancel

④

14

Changing Your Worksheet View

You can customize the way Excel appears when you work on a worksheet. If you typically don't need the task pane when you first start Excel, you can hide it when you start the program. If you need more room to view another row of data, you can hide the status bar. If you are creating a custom spreadsheet, you can change the color of the gridlines or hide them all together. The View tab in the Options dialog box allows you to change the way you view a worksheet or workbook in Excel to suit your needs.

Change View Options

1. Click the Tools menu, and then click Options.

2. Click the View tab.

3. Select or clear any of the check boxes to change the view options you want.

   ◆ Startup Task pane

   ◆ Formula bar

   ◆ Status bar

   ◆ Windows in Taskbar

   ◆ Row & column headers

   ◆ Comment indicators

   ◆ Show placeholders

   ◆ Page breaks

   ◆ Sheet tabs

4. Click OK.

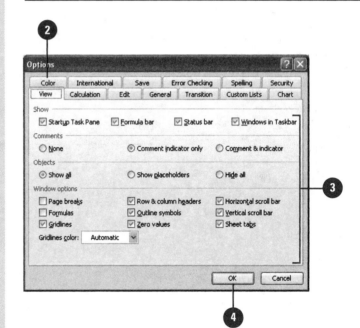

Did You Know?

You can arrange multiple views of one workbook. To view different parts of the active workbook in multiple windows, select the Windows Of Active Workbook check box in the Arrange Windows dialog box.

Creating a Custom View

If you continually change your view and print settings for a specific worksheet, you can create a customize view and quickly switch to it at any time. When you display a view, Excel switches to the active worksheet when you created the view. You can use the Custom Views dialog box to quickly view all views in a workbook and show the one you want. If you no longer need a custom view, you can use the Custom Views dialog box to remove it.

Create a Custom View

1 Open the workbook with the view and print settings you want to save in the view.

2 Click the View menu, and then click Custom Views.

3 Click Add.

4 Type a name for the view.

5 Click OK.

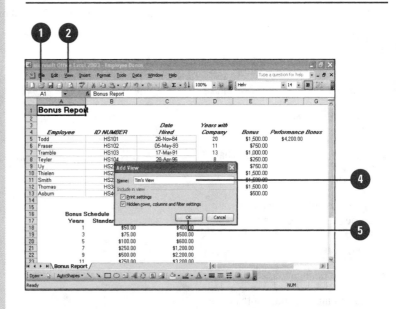

Create a Custom View

1 Click the View menu, and then click Custom Views.

2 Click the view you want to display.

3 Click Show.

Creating a Toolbar

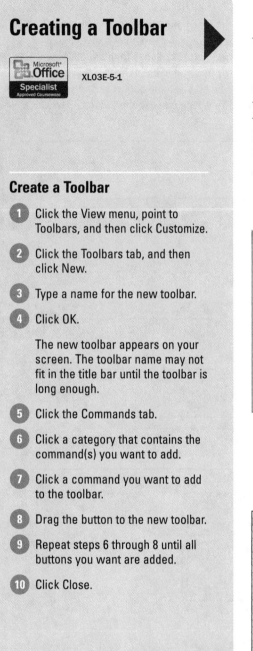

XL03E-5-1

If none of the existing Excel toolbars fits your needs or if you just want a toolbar to call your own, you can create a new toolbar. You might use the Page Break command very often. Wouldn't it be easier if you had that button on your own toolbar? Perhaps your workbooks require a lot of formatting. Wouldn't it be more convenient if you had a special toolbar containing a variety of formatting buttons? Creating a toolbar that contains the buttons necessary for your most common tasks can dramatically increase your efficiency. Besides creating toolbars, you can change toolbar and menu options to best meet your working habits.

Create a Toolbar

1. Click the View menu, point to Toolbars, and then click Customize.

2. Click the Toolbars tab, and then click New.

3. Type a name for the new toolbar.

4. Click OK.

   The new toolbar appears on your screen. The toolbar name may not fit in the title bar until the toolbar is long enough.

5. Click the Commands tab.

6. Click a category that contains the command(s) you want to add.

7. Click a command you want to add to the toolbar.

8. Drag the button to the new toolbar.

9. Repeat steps 6 through 8 until all buttons you want are added.

10. Click Close.

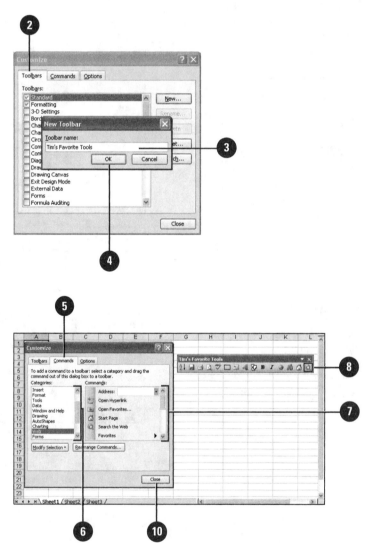

Change Toolbars and Menus Options

1. Click the View menu, point to Toolbars, and then click Customize.

2. Click the Options tab.

3. Select Personalized Menus and Toolbars options as needed.

4. Select Other options as needed.

5. To animate your menus, click the Menu Animations list arrow, and then select an animation.

6. Click Close.

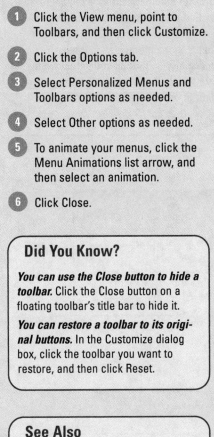

Did You Know?

You can use the Close button to hide a toolbar. Click the Close button on a floating toolbar's title bar to hide it.

You can restore a toolbar to its original buttons. In the Customize dialog box, click the toolbar you want to restore, and then click Reset.

See Also

See "Changing Your Worksheet View" on page 292 for information on customizing the way your worksheet appears.

14

Customizing a Toolbar ▶

XLO3E-5-1

Excel contains predesigned toolbars; by default, the Standard and Formatting toolbars appear on the screen at all times. These two toolbars contain buttons for commonly used Excel commands. However, since everyone works differently, you may find that these toolbars display some buttons you never use, while they do not display others you want available on your screen. The Toolbar Options menu makes these toolbars inherently customizable by displaying buttons you select from the list menu. You can also customize the toolbar display by displaying different Excel toolbars and by adding or deleting different buttons on any toolbar.

Personalize a Toolbar Quickly

1. Click the Toolbar Options list arrow on a toolbar.

2. To move a button from Toolbar Options to the toolbar, click the toolbar button you want.

   The toolbar button is displayed on the toolbar.

3. To quickly add or remove a button from a toolbar, point to Add Or Remove Buttons, point to a toolbar, and then click the button you want to add or remove.

Delete a Button from a Toolbar

1. Click the View menu, point to Toolbars, and then click Customize.

2. Click the Toolbars tab.

3. Make sure the toolbar you want to change is selected.

4. Drag the button you want to delete off the toolbar.

5. Click Close.

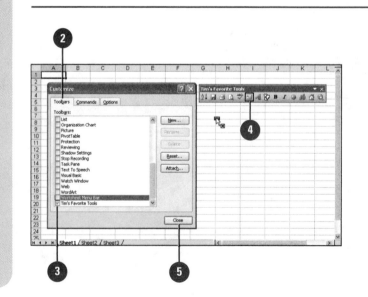

Add a Button to a Toolbar

① Click the View menu, point to Toolbars, and then click Customize.

② Make sure the toolbar you want to change is selected.

③ Click the Commands tab.

④ Click the category that contains the command you want to add.

⑤ Click the command you want to add.

⑥ Drag the button you want to add to any location on the selected toolbar.

⑦ Repeat steps 4 through 6 until all the buttons you want are added.

⑧ Click Close.

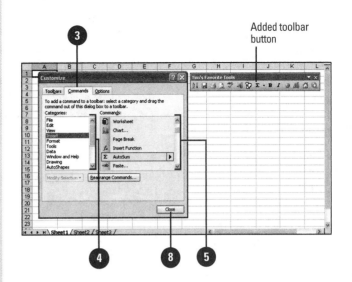

Added toolbar button

Did You Know?

You can assign a button to a macro. In the Customize dialog box, click the Commands tab, click Macros in the Categories list, click Custom Button in the Commands list, drag the button to a toolbar, click Modify Selection, click Assign Macro, click the macro you want to use, click OK, and then click Close.

14

Adding Menus and Menu Items

XL03E-5-1

Just as you can add toolbar buttons to toolbars, you can add menu commands to any existing menus. You can even create your own menu and add just the commands you want. If, for example, you design a specific worksheet that will be used by others, you can create a specific menu just for their use. This menu can contain the commands they'll need while using your worksheet.

Add a Menu Item

1. Click the Tools menu, click Customize, and then click the Commands tab.

2. Click the category that contains command(s) you want to add to the menu.

3. Click the command you want.

4. Drag the command to the desired location on the menu.

5. Click Close.

Create a New Menu

1. Click the Tools menu, click Customize, and then click the Commands tab.

2. Click the New Menu category, and then drag New Menu to the desired location on the menu bar.

3. Right-click the new menu on the menu bar.

4. Type a name for the menu, and then press Enter.

5. Click a category, and then drag the commands you want on the new menu, and then click Close.

New Menu location

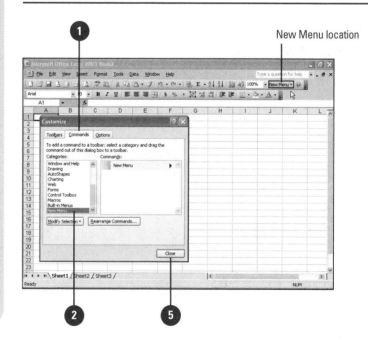

Playing Back Worksheet Data

With Excel, you can have the computer read back data entered on a worksheet. The Text To Speech toolbar gives you options to read back data you select on a worksheet for verification. You can hear the contents of all the cells in a worksheet continuously or each individual cell after you enter data in it. Each cell is selected by row or column and the value or formula is read by the computer. If you hear an error or you're done listening to the data, you can stop the computer from speaking at any time.

Speak the Value of Cells

1 Click the Tools menu, point to Speech, and then click Show Text To Speech Toolbar.

2 Select the group of cells you want to hear spoken.

3 Click the By Rows button or By Columns button on the Text To Speech toolbar to indicate how you want the computer to read the cells in the worksheet.

4 Click the Speak Cells button on the Text To Speech toolbar. The computer reads the value of the current cells and moves to the next one.

5 When you're done, click the Stop Speaking button on the Text To Speech toolbar, and then click the Close button.

Did You Know?

You can choose from computer generated voices. You can double-click the Speech icon in the Control Panel to choose between different voices and customize settings.

You can hear the value of a spoken cell. To hear the value of a cell spoken after you enter data in the cell, click the Speak On Enter button on the Text To Speech toolbar.

Controlling Excel with Your Voice

The Office Language bar allows you to dictate text directly into your document and also to control buttons, menus, and toolbar functions by using the Voice Command option. When you first install an Office program, the Language bar appears at the top of your screen. If you are using English as a default language, the toolbar is denoted by the letters EN. (Other languages have appropriate abbreviations as well.) Before you can use speech recognition, you need to install it first. You can choose the Speech command on the Tools menu in Excel, or you can use Add Or Remove Programs in the Control Panel to change the Office 2003 installation. Before you can use the Language bar for either dictation or voice commands, you need to connect a microphone to your computer, and you must train your computer to your voice using the Speech Recognition Wizard.

Work with the Language Bar

◆ **Open.** Right-click a blank area on the taskbar, point to Toolbars, and then click Language Bar.

◆ **Minimize.** Right-click the Language bar, and then click Minimize. The Language bar docks in the taskbar at the bottom right of the screen, near the system clock.

◆ **Restore.** Right-click the Language bar, and then click Restore The Language Bar.

◆ **Display or hide option buttons.** Click the Options button (the list arrow at the right end of the toolbar), and then click an option to display or hide.

◆ **Change speech properties.** Click the Speech Tools button, and then click Options.

◆ **Change Language Bar properties.** Click the Options button (the list arrow at the right end of the toolbar), and then click Settings.

Speech Tools button   Minimize button

EN English (United States) | Microphone | Dictation | Voice Command | Too loud | Tools | Handwriting

- Learn from document…
- Options…
- Training…
- Add/Delete Word(s)…
- Current User ▶

Options button

EN English (United States) | Microphone | Dictation | Voice Command | Too loud | Tools | Handwriting

- Correction
- ✓ Dictation
- ✓ Voice Command
- Speak Text
- Pause Speaking
- ✓ Speech Tools
- Handwriting
- ✓ Help
- Settings…
- Restore Defaults

Train Your Computer to Your Voice

1 Click the Speech Tools button on the Language bar, and then click Training.

2 Click Next, read the instructions, ensure you are in a quiet place, and then click Next again.

3 Read the sentence provided to automatically set the proper volume of the microphone, and then click Next.

4 Read the text with hard consonants to help determine whether or not the microphone is positioned too closely to your mouth. Repeat the process until you have a clear, distinct audio playback, and then click Next.

5 After you are reminded to ensure that your environment is suitable for recording again, read the instructions, and then click Next.

6 Read the following series of dialog boxes. The words on the screen are highlighted as the computer recognizes them. As each dialog box is completed, the program will automatically move to the next one, and the process meter will update accordingly.

7 At the end of the training session, click Finish and your voice profile is updated and saved automatically.

Did You Know?

You can create additional speech profiles. Click the Speech Tools button on the Language bar, click Options, click New, and then follow the Profile Wizard instructions.

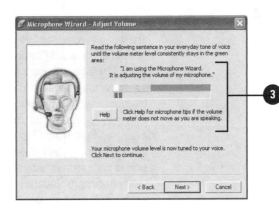

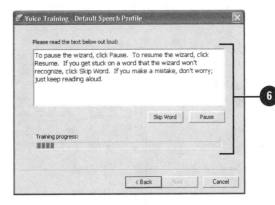

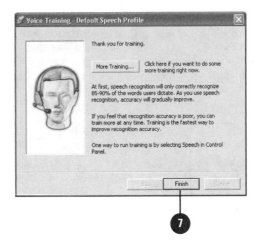

Executing Voice Commands

The two modes, Dictation and Voice Command, are mutually exclusive of one another. You do not want the word File typed, for example, when you are trying to open the File menu. Neither do you want the menu to open instead of the word File being typed when you are in the middle of a sentence. As such, you must manually click either mode on the Language bar to switch between them. The Voice Command mode allows you to talk your way through any sequence of menus or toolbar commands, simply by reading aloud the appropriate text instead of clicking it. For example, if you wanted to print the current selection of the workbook you are working on, you would simply say File, Print, Selection, OK (without saying the commas between the words as written here). You need not worry about remembering every command sequence because as you say each word in the sequence, the corresponding menu or submenu appears onscreen for your reference.

Execute Voice Commands

1. If necessary, display the Language bar.

2. Click the Microphone button on the Language bar. The toolbar expands so that the Voice Command button becomes available on the toolbar.

3. Click the Voice Command button to shift into that mode.

4. Work with your Office document normally. When you are ready to issue a command, simply speak the sequence just as you would click through it if you were using the menus or toolbar normally (ie. with the mouse or via keyboard shortcuts).

Say "File" to display the menu.

Did You Know?

You can have text read back to you. Display the Speak Text button on the Language bar. Select the text you want read back to you, and then click Speak Text.

Dictating Text ▶

Dictating the text of a letter or other document using Office speech recognition functions may be easier for some users than typing, but don't think that it is an entirely hands free operation. For example, you must manually click the Voice Command button when you want to format anything that has been input, and then click again on Dictation to resume inputting text. Additionally, the Dictation function is not going to be 100% accurate, so you will need to clean up mistakes (such as inputting the word *Noir* when you say *or*) when they occur. Finally, although you can say punctuation marks, such as comma and period, to have them accurately reflected in the document, all periods are followed by double spaces (which may not be consistent with the document formatting you want between sentences) and issues of capitalization remain as well. Nevertheless, it is fun and freeing to be able to get the first draft of any document on paper simply by speaking it.

14

Dictate Text

1 If necessary, display the Language bar.

2 Click the Microphone button the Language bar. The toolbar expands so that the Dictation button becomes available on the toolbar.

3 Click to position the insertion point inside the Office document where you want the dictated text to appear, and then begin speaking normally into your microphone. As you speak, the words will appear on the page.

4 When you have finished dictating your text, click the Microphone button again to make the speech recognition functions inactive.

Recognizing Handwriting

Although entering information into an Office document through the keyboard is fast and efficient, you may find that you need to enter information in handwritten form. Office provides handwriting recognition to help you convert handwriting into text. Before you can insert handwritten text into a document, you need to have a mouse, a third party electronic stylus, an ink device, or a handwriting tablet, such as Tablet PC attached to your computer. Although you can use the mouse, for best results you should use a handwriting input device. When you insert handwritten text into a document that already contains typed text, the handwritten text is converted to typed text and then inserted in line with the existing text at the point of the cursor. The program recognizes the handwriting when there is enough text for it to do so, when you reach the end of the line, or if you pause for approximately two seconds. In addition, the converted text will take on the same typeface attributes as the existing text.

Insert Handwritten Text into a Document

1. If necessary, display the Language bar.

2. Click the Handwriting button on the Language bar, and then click Write Anywhere.

3. Move the mouse over a blank area of your Office document, and then write your text.

   After recognition, the characters that you write appear as text in the Office document.

4. Use the additional handwriting tools to move the cursor, change handwriting modes, and correct text.

Handwriting changed to text

Insert Handwritten Text on a Writing Pad

1. If necessary, display the Language bar.

2. Click the Handwriting button on the Language bar, and then click Writing Pad.

3. Move the cursor over the writing area of the Writing Pad dialog box. (The cursor turns into a pen.)

4. Write your text with the pen.

   After recognition, the characters that you write appear in the Office document.

5. Use the additional handwriting tools to move the cursor, change handwriting modes, and correct text.

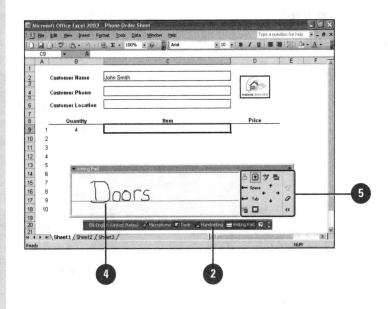

For Your Information

Using Additional Handwriting Tools

When you click the Handwriting button on the Language bar and then click the Writing Pad or Write Anywhere option, a dialog box opens on your screen with another toolbar. It has the same options that are available through the Handwriting button on the Language bar. In addition, the toolbar has the following buttons: Ink, Text, Backspace, Space, directional cursors, Enter, Tab, Recognize Now, and Write Anywhere. You use these buttons to control the input.

Repairing and Recovering Office Programs

Never again do you need to worry when Office stops working for no apparent reason. All the Office programs are now self-repairing, which means that Office checks to see if essential files are missing or corrupt as a program opens and fixes the files as needed. You may never even realize there was a problem. Other times, Office starts fine but might have another problem, such as a corrupted font file or a missing template. These kinds of problems used to take hours to identify and fix. Now Office does the work for you with the Detect And Repair feature, which locates, diagnoses, and fixes any errors in the program itself. If you need to add or remove features or remove Office entirely, you can use Office Setup's maintenance feature.

Detect and Repair Problems

1. Click the Help menu, and then click Detect And Repair.

2. Click Start.

   Insert the Office 2003 CD in your CD-ROM drive.

3. If the Detect And Repair command does not fix the problem, you might need to reinstall Microsoft Office.

4. Click Finish.

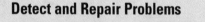

Click to restore shortcuts to the Start menu.

Recover an Office Program

1. Click the Start button on the taskbar, point to All Programs, point to Microsoft Office, point to Microsoft Office Tools, and then click Microsoft Office Application Recovery.

2. Select the application you want to recover.

3. Click Recover Application or End Application.

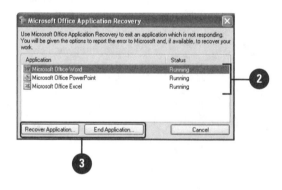

Perform Maintenance on Office Programs

1 In Windows Explorer, double-click the Setup icon on the Office CD.

2 Click one of the following maintenance buttons:

◆ **Add Or Remove Features** to determine which and when features are installed or removed.

◆ **Reinstall or Repair** to repair or reinstall Office.

◆ **Uninstall** to uninstall Office.

3 Follow the wizard instructions to complete the maintenance.

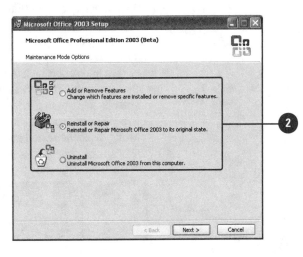

Using Multiple Languages

International Microsoft Office users can change the language that appears on their screens by changing the default language settings. Users around the world can enter, display, and edit text in all supported languages, including European languages, Japanese, Chinese, Korean, Hebrew, and Arabic, just to name a few. You'll probably be able to use Office programs in your native language. If the text in your document is written in more than one language, you can automatically detect languages or designate the language of selected text so the spelling checker uses the right dictionary.

Add a Language to Office Programs

① Click Start on the taskbar, point to All Programs, point to Microsoft Office, point to Microsoft Office Tools, and then click Microsoft Office 2003 Language Settings.

② Click to select the languages you want to use.

③ Click Add.

④ Click OK, and then click Yes to quit and restart Office.

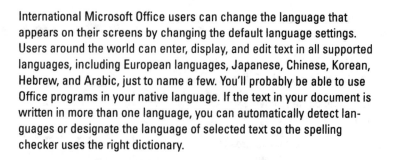

Did You Know?

There is a Multilingual AutoCorrect. Office supports an AutoCorrect list for each language. For example, the English AutoCorrect list capitalizes all cases of the single letter "i;" in Swedish however, "i" is a preposition and is not capitalized.

You can check your keyboard layout. After you enable editing for another language, such as Hebrew, Cyrillic, or Greek, you might need to install the correct keyboard layout so you can enter characters for that language. In the Control Panel, double-click the Regional And Language icon, click the Language tab, and then click Details to check your keyboard.

Working Together on Office Documents

Introduction

Microsoft SharePoint technology, known as SharePoint Team Services, is a collection of products and services which provide the ability for people to engage in communication, document and file sharing, calendar events, sending alerts, tasks planning, and collaborative discussions in a single community solution. SharePoint enables companies to develop an intelligent application which connects their employees, teams, and information so that users can be part of a Knowledge Community.

Before you can use SharePoint Team Services, SharePoint needs to be set up and configured on a Windows 2003 Server by your network administrator or Internet service provider.

SharePoint is integrated into Office 2003 and enables you to share data and documents using the Shared Workspace task pane directly from Office Excel 2003, Office Word 2003, or Office PowerPoint 2003. The Shared Workspace task pane allows you to see the list of team members collaborating on the current project, find out who is online, send an instant message, and review tasks and other resources. You can use the Shared Workspace task pane to create one or more document workspaces where you can collect, organize, modify, share, and discuss Office documents. The Shared Workspace task pane displays information related to the document workspaces stored on SharePoint Team Services. In addition, you can also publish a data list in Excel to a SharePoint server so that other team members with the appropriate privileges can view and make changes to the list.

Viewing SharePoint Team Services

Microsoft SharePoint displays the contents of its home page so you can work efficiently with your site. The available pages are: The Home Page, Manage Content Page, Manage Users Page, Change Portal Site Navigation Page, Change Settings Page, and Site Settings Page. You can navigate within the site by clicking on each of the links within the home page. Certain Administrative Access rights are needed in order to view these pages.

Home Page view is the first page your users see when they access the URL for Microsoft SharePoint Server. If you are within a Windows 2003 Active Domain and have a Domain Account, you will not be prompted to type in your user credentials and password. If you do not have an account you will be asked to type in your credentials to have the page display your SharePoint Site. Please contact your Systems Administrator if you do not have access to the SharePoint Server.

Documents and Lists Page view allows you to manage content to your SharePoint Site. You can create Portal sites, a Document Library, Upload Graphic Images in an Image Library Site, Create Calender Events, Create an Address Book of Contents, Setup Project Events, Create a Web Discussion site, and setup Surveys. Within your Document and Lists page you will be able to administer your content to provide users with content management capabilities.

Manage Users Page view allows you to add users to your SharePoint Site. If their e-mail address is located within their Domain Account on Windows 2003, then SharePoint will e-mail the users you created and invite them to join in to the SharePoint Server. From the Manage Users Page you can add, delete, and change the permissions of a user for your site.

Home Page

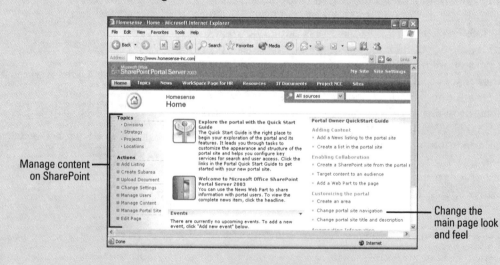

Manage content on SharePoint

Change the main page look and feel

Documents and Lists Page

Adds a new portal site

Adds documents to the site

Adds graphics to the site

Manage Users Page

Adds new users

List of users

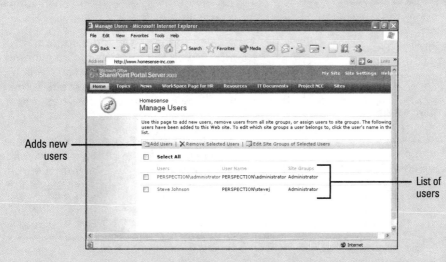

Administering SharePoint Team Services

Administering Microsoft SharePoint is easy within the site settings. The available pages are: The Home Page, Manage Content Page, Manage Users Page, Change Portal Site Navigation Page, Change Settings Page, and Site Settings Page. You can navigate within the site by clicking on each of the links within the home page. Certain Administrative Access rights are needed in order to view these pages.

Change Portal Site Navigation Page gives you a hierarchy structure to make changes to other portal sites within SharePoint. If you want to move your site to the top-level within SharePoint or modify your sub-level pages, you can do so with the SharePoint Portal Site Navigation Page.

Change Settings Page allows you to swiftly customize the look and feel of your portal site. You can change the title, description, and logo for the site. You can change the URL for creating sites based on the published templates for your site. You can also add a change management process by having the site approved by a manager before being published, and allowing you to change your contact information for your site.

Site Settings Page has four different categories: General Settings, Portal Site Content, Search Settings and Indexed Content, and User Profile, Audiences, and Personal Sites.

◆ **General Settings** offers additional security features, which allows you to manage the alerts settings, change your default SMTP e-mail server, change the location of your SharePoint Site, and modify the Regional Language Settings to your site.

◆ **Portal Site Content** allows you to manage the site structure, view your site lists and document libraries, import data into your SharePoint Server, and add link listings to your site.

◆ **Search Settings and Indexed Content** allows you to create Meta tags within your SharePoint Server, create search crawlers to investigate your site for new key words which will create better search results within your site.

◆ **User Profile, Audiences, and Personal Sites** allows you to change and manage your user profiles within your site. You can also manage your audiences and personal settings.

Quick Launch bar

Location of the site logs

Name of the SharePoint server

Change Settings Page

Change publishing settings

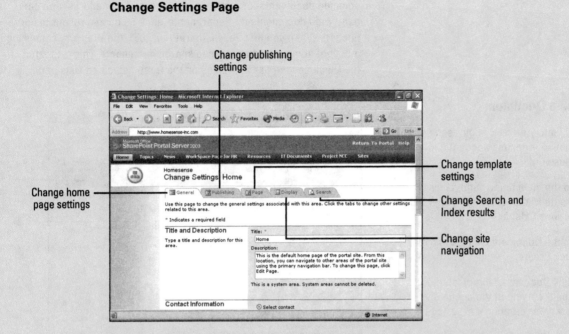

Change home page settings

Change template settings

Change Search and Index results

Change site navigation

Site Settings Page

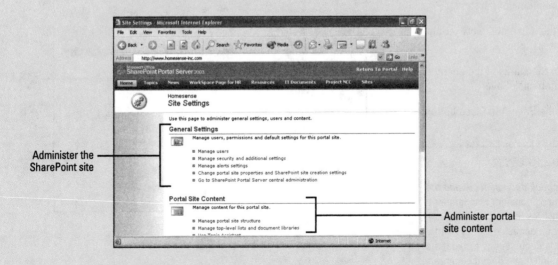

Administer the SharePoint site

Administer portal site content

Storing Documents in the Library

A SharePoint **Document Library** is a central depository of files you can share with company employees, team members and permissible members with access. Within the Document Library you can create a list of common documents for a project, documented procedures, and company wide documents for departments, such as human resources or finance. When you first install SharePoint 2003, the Web site comes with a built-in document library called **shared documents**. This is located on the Quick Launch bar as well as on the Documents and Lists page.

Upload a Document

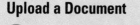

① Log into your SharePoint server with your domain account and password.

② On the main home page, click Create Manage Content under the Actions Sidebar.

③ On the Documents and Lists page, click Create.

④ Click Document Library, and then type the name of the document library for creating a new page.

⑤ Click Upload Document.

⑥ Type the location of the document, or click Browse to search for the document on your system.

⑦ Type the name of the owner and a brief description.

⑧ Select the status of the document, and then click Save.

⑨ Click the Save And Close button.

Did You Know?

You can check documents in and out.
SharePoint's document management system ensures that only one person at a time can access a file. You can check out a document by clicking the Content menu in the document library, and then clicking Check Out.

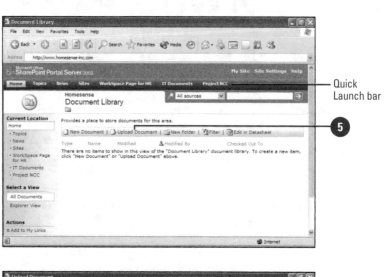

Quick Launch bar

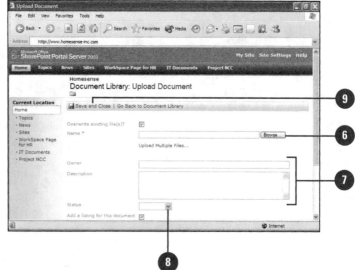

Viewing Team Members

After you have setup a portal page, you need to specify a user access list to the site. Specifying a user access list controls who can access the site, as well as who has administrative privileges. With integration to Microsoft Active Directory, users can be managed with the same groups as your domain. The access will allow your users to perform a specific action in your site by assigning them to the appropriate groups.

Add New Members to the Site

1. Log into your SharePoint server with your domain account and password.

2. On the main home page, click Give User Access To The Portal.

3. On the Manage Users page, click Add Users.

4. Type the name of their domain account.

5. Click the type of permissions you want to give this user:

   ◆ **Reader.** Gives the user read-only access to the portal site.

   ◆ **Contributor.** Gives the user write access to the document libraries and lists.

   ◆ **Web Designer.** Gives the user the ability to create lists and document libraries and customize the overall look and feel of the site.

   ◆ **Administrator.** Gives the user full access of the portal site.

   ◆ **Content Manager.** Gives the user the ability to manage lists, libraries, sites and moderate the discussions.

   ◆ **Member.** Gives the user the ability to personalize the portal site content and create lists.

6. Click Next, fill out any additional information, and then click Finish.

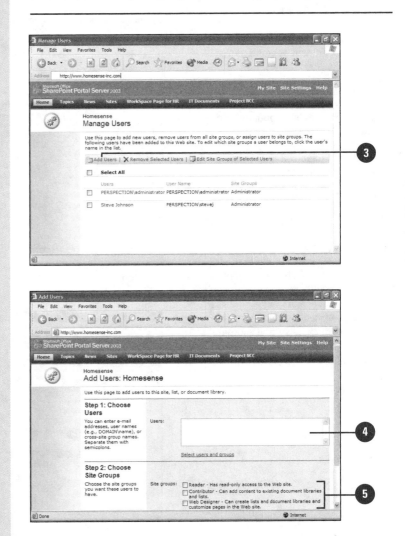

15

Setting Up Alerts

An Alert notifies you when there is new information which has been changed on the portal site. You can customize your areas of interests and define when you want to be notified after the site has been updated. You can define an alert to track new matches to a search query, changes to the site page, or a new site addition.

Create Your E-Mail Alert

1. Log into your SharePoint server with your domain account and password.

2. In a Portal Site, click Alert Me.

3. Define your delivery options, and then click Next.

4. Click Advanced Options if you want to set up filters.

5. Click OK.

Did You Know?

You can use the following filter categories to be alerted with: Search queries, document and listings, areas, new listings, sites added to the site directory, sharepoint lists and libraries, list items, portal site users, and backward compatible document library folders.

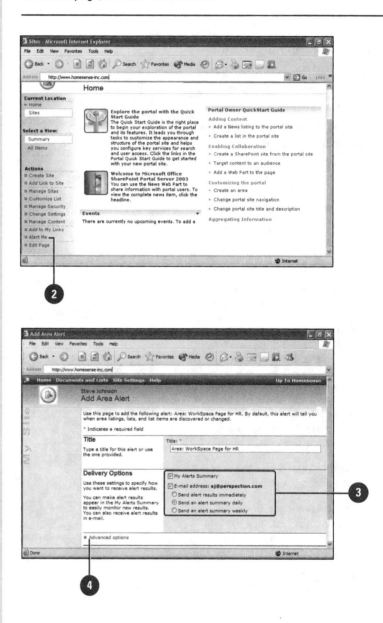

Assigning Project Tasks

Assigning a project task is another way you can use SharePoint to collaborate on the site. By creating a task, you can manage your team with status updates. You can also provide a central way to manage the effectiveness of a project. Since this is a Web based system, everyone can access this with a simple Web browser.

Add a Task Item to Your Site

1. Log into your SharePoint server with your domain account and password.

2. On the main home page, click Create Manage Content under the Actions Sidebar.

3. Click Create, and then click Tasks.

4. Type the name of the task, add in an optional description, click Yes, if you want to add the task to the menu bar, and then click Create.

5. Click New Item.

6. Type the title, set the priority, status, and completion percentage, assign your resource, add a description, and then set your due date.

7. Click the Save And Close button.

Did You Know?

You can use the Upload button to add an attachment. A general rule of thumb would be to keep your attachments under 1 MB, however, unless your administrator has set rights on your site, you are free to upload as much as you want.

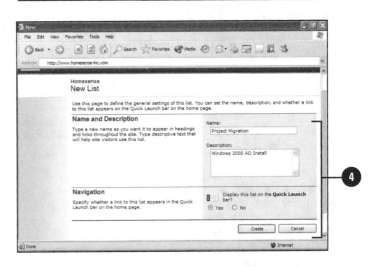

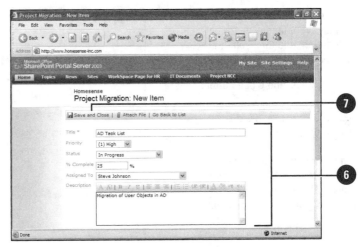

Creating an Event

Creating an event allows you to send out notices on upcoming meetings, deadlines, and other important events. This is helpful if you need to send out information to a wide range of people or in a project you are working on. If you are looking to set up a meeting to a large group of people, you may want to set up an event which is seen by everyone who logs in.

Set Up New Events

① Log into your SharePoint server with your domain account and password.

② On the main home page, click Create Manage Content under the Actions Sidebar.

③ Click Create, and then click Events.

④ Type the name of the event, add in an optional description, click Yes if you want to add the event to the menu bar, and then click Create.

⑤ Click New Item.

⑥ Type the event title, select a begin and end event time, a description, the location, and then select a recurrence option.

⑦ Click the Save And Close button.

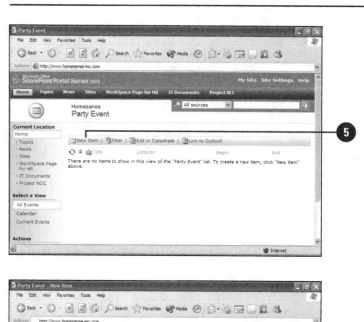

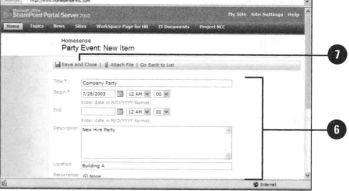

Did You Know?

You can use a new collaboration feature in Outlook 2003 called Meeting Workspace. Meeting Workspace allows you to gather information and organize everyone when you create a scheduled meeting event. To create a Meeting Workspace in Outlook 2003, prepare a calender event and set up your attendees for the event. Then click Meeting Workspace to link this to your SharePoint Server. You may need to type in the URL of your SharePoint server. Please get this from your System Administrator.

Link to Events in Outlook

 On the Events Page, click Link To Outlook.

 If a security dialog box appears asking for your approval prior to adding a folder, click Yes.

You will be prompted to type in the credentials of your user account.

 Type in your Domain User credentials and password, and then click OK.

 Click Other Calendars to view your SharePoint calendar.

Did You Know?

You will not be able to change the events in your SharePoint calendar folder within Outlook 2003. You will only have read access rights within Outlook 2003. To change the SharePoint calendar information, return to your SharePoint Site, and then modify the information under your Events Site.

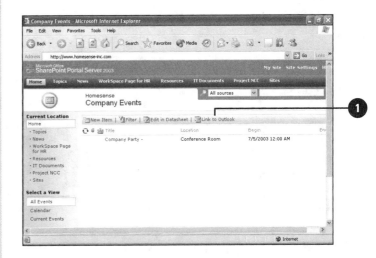

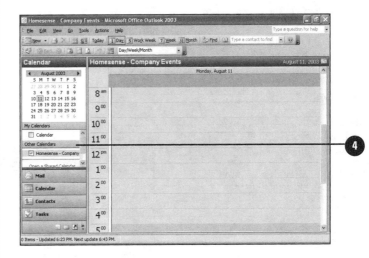

Creating Contacts

You can create a contact list when you want to have a central database of your team information. You will have the ability to manage information about sales contacts, vendors, and employees that your team has involvement with.

Create a Contact List

① Log into your SharePoint server with your domain account and password.

② On the main home page, click Create Manage Content under the Actions Sidebar.

③ Click Create, and then click Contacts.

④ Type the name of the contact, add an optional description, click Yes, if you want to add the contacts list to the menu bar, and then click Create.

⑤ Click New Item.

⑥ Type the contact name, and then add in all the appropriate information on your contact.

⑦ Click the Save And Close button.

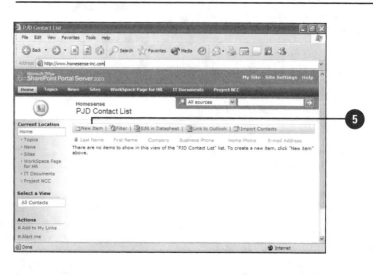

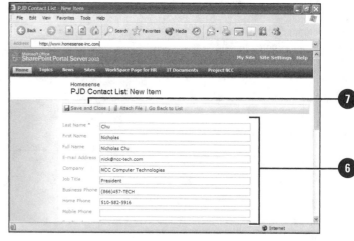

Link to Contacts in Outlook

① On the Contacts page, click Link To Outlook.

② If a security dialog box appears asking for your approval prior to adding a folder, click Yes.

You will be prompted to type in the credentials of your user account.

③ Type your Domain User credentials and password, and then click OK.

④ Click Other Contacts to view your SharePoint contacts.

Did You Know?

You will not be able to change the contact information in your SharePoint contacts folder within Outlook 2003. You will only have read access rights within Outlook 2003. To change the SharePoint contacts information, return to your SharePoint Site, and then modify the information under your Contacts Site.

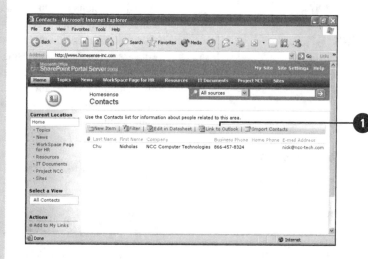

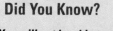

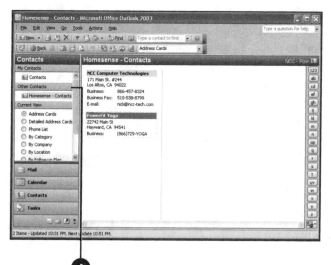

15

Holding Web Discussions

Web discussions are threaded discussions which allow users to collaborate together in a Web environment. Users can add and view discussion items, add in documents during the discussion and carry on conversations. Since the discussions are entered into a different area than the shared document, users can modify the document without effecting the collaborative discussion. Users can add changes to read-only documents and allow multiple users to create and edit discussion items simultaneously.

Hold a Web Discussion

1. Log into your SharePoint server with your domain account and password.

2. On the main home page, click Create Manage Content under the Actions Sidebar.

3. Click Create, and then click Discussion Boards.

4. Type the name of the Discussion Board, add an optional description, click Yes, if you want to add this to the menu bar, and then click Create.

5. Click New Discussion.

6. Type the subject name, and then add in all the appropriate information on your discussion.

7. Click the Save And Close button.

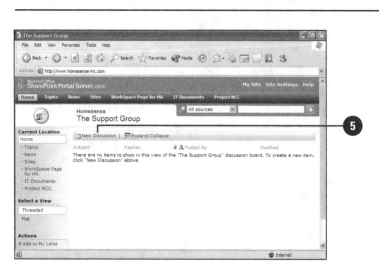

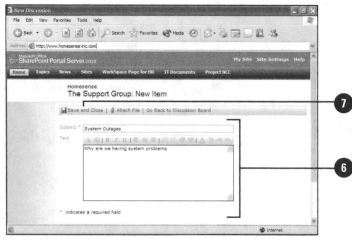

Working with Shared Workspace

Using Shared Workspace icons allow you to connect to your SharePoint Server in an Office 2003 program: Word, Excel and PowerPoint. Each icon displays different information on your document. Users can view the status of a document, see the availability of a document, display properties of a document, and list additional resources, folders, and access rights of a document. You can also show the current tasks which are assigned for your document, display the online team members of your group, and display the workspace information.

Use Shared Workspace in an Office 2003 Program

1. Log into your SharePoint server with your domain account and password.

2. In an Office 2003 program (Word, Excel and PowerPoint), click on the Tools menu, and then click Shared Workspace.

   If you open Shared Workspace for the first time you may be prompted to create a new workspace area.

3. Use the Shared Workspace Navigation bar tools.

   ◆ **Status.** Displays the checked-in/checked-out status of your current document.

   ◆ **Members**. Shows you who is online from your Team Members Group.

   ◆ **Tasks**. Shows you the current tasks assigned for this current document and the completion status.

   ◆ **Documents**. Displays the name and workspace of the selected document.

   ◆ **Links**. Displays additional resources, folders, and lists the access of files.

   ◆ **Document Info**. Displays the author of the document and the properties of the document.

15

Publishing a List

If you have a list of data in Excel, you can publish the list to a SharePoint server so others can view and edit the data. To use this feature, you must have a Microsoft Windows SharePoint Services site, which needs to be created by your system administrator. Excel uses the Publish List To SharePoint Site Wizard to step you through the process. As you publish the data list, you have the option to link the data list to SharePoint so that the data can be quickly updated, or synchronized, between Excel and the SharePoint server. During the process, the wizard tries to determine the data type for each column list and match it to one of the following SharePoint data types: Text (single lines), Text (multiple lines), Currency, Date, Number, and Hyperlink. If you use formulas in a list, the SharePoint server converts them to calculated values. After you publish the list, you can view the list from the SharePoint server.

Publish a Data List

1. Open the workbook with the list you want to publish, and then click a cell in the data list.

2. Click the Data menu, point to List, and then click Publish List.

3. Type the name of the SharePoint server.

4. To establish a link, select the Link To The New SharePoint List check box.

5. Type the name of the list.

6. Type a description about the list.

7. Click Next to continue.

8. Verify the data types are correct, and then click Finish.

   TROUBLE? *If the data types are not correct, click Cancel, and then make changes.*

   An ID column is added to the list as the first column to make sure all the records are unique.

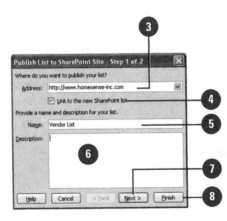

Work with a Published Data List on the SharePoint Server

1. Select a cell in a published data list on a worksheet.

2. Click the Data menu, and then point to List.

3. Click the command you want to perform.

   ◆ View List On Server

   ◆ Unlink List

   ◆ Synchronize List

   ◆ Discard Changes And Refresh

   ◆ Hide Border Of Inactive Lists

See Also

See "Creating a List" on page 195 for information on creating and working with data lists.

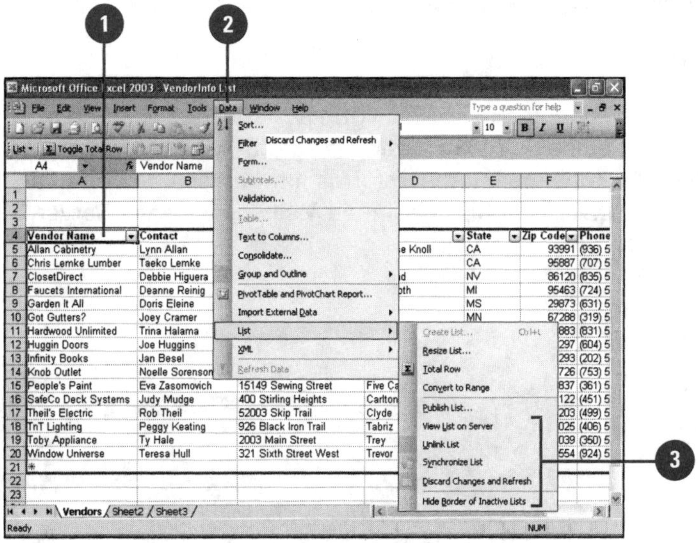

15

Installing Windows 2003 and SharePoint Server 2003

In order for you to install the new version of SharePoint, you must Install Windows 2003 Server. Windows 2003 Server uses the new .NET Architecture Internet Information Server (IIS) 6.0, Microsoft SMTP (Simple Mail Transport Protocol) Service and Microsoft SQL Server 2000 Desktop Engine (MSDE 2000) or Microsoft SQL Server 2000 Enterprise or Standard Edition (64-bit), with Microsoft SQL Server 2000 SP3 or later.

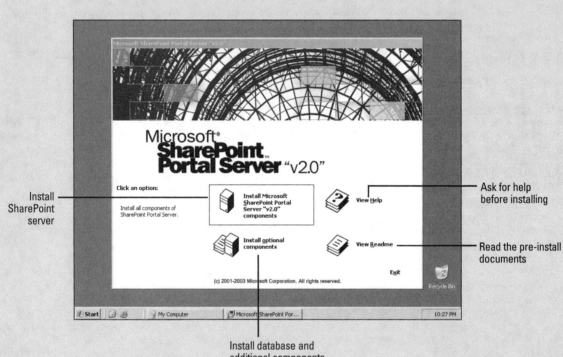

Install SharePoint server

Ask for help before installing

Read the pre-install documents

Install database and additional components

Microsoft Office Specialist

About the Microsoft Office Specialist Program

The Microsoft Office Specialist certification is the globally recognized standard for validating expertise with the Microsoft Office suite of business productivity programs. Earning an Microsoft Office Specialist certificate acknowledges you have the expertise to work with Microsoft Office programs. To earn the Microsoft Office Specialist certification, you must pass one or more certification exams for the Microsoft Office desktop applications of Microsoft Office Word, Microsoft Office Excel, Microsoft Office PowerPoint, Microsoft Office Outlook, or Microsoft Office Access. The Microsoft Office Specialist program typically offers certification exams at the "specialist" and "expert" skill levels. (The availability of Microsoft Office Specialist certification exams varies by program, program version, and language. Visit *www.microsoft.com/officespecialist* for exam availability and more information about the program.) The Microsoft Office Specialist program is the only Microsoft-approved program in the world for certifying proficiency with Microsoft Office programs.

What Does This Logo Mean?

It means this book has been approved by the Microsoft Office Specialist program to be certified courseware for learning Microsoft Office Excel 2003 and preparing for the certification exam. This book will prepare you fully for the Microsoft Office Specialist exam at the specialist and expert levels for Microsoft Office Excel 2003. Each certification level has a set of objectives, which are organized into broader skill sets. Throughout this book, content that pertains to a Microsoft Office Specialist objective is identified with the Microsoft Office Specialist logo and objective number below the title of the topic:

 XL03S-1-1
XL03E-2-2

Excel 2003 Specialist Objectives

Objective	Skill	Page
XL03S-1	**Creating Data and Content**	
XL03S-1-1	Enter and edit cell content	30-36
XL03S-1-2	Navigate to specific cell content	8-9, 46-47, 114
XL03S-1-3	Locate, select and insert supporting data	128-129
XL03S-1-4	Insert, position, and size graphics	130-131, 156-157
XL03S-2	**Analyzing Data**	
XL03S-2-1	Filter lists using AutoFilter	202
XL03S-2-2	Sort lists	200-201
XL03S-2-3	Insert and modify formulas	34, 54-57, 59-61, 64
XL03S-2-4	Use statistical, date and time, financial, and logical functions	71-72
XL03S-2-5	Create, modify, and position diagrams and charts based on worksheet data	146-147, 177-179
XL03S-3	**Formatting Data and Content**	
XL03S-3-1	Apply and modify cell formats	92-93, 96-97, 101-107
XL03S-3-2	Apply and modify cell styles	110-113
XL03S-3-3	Modify row and column formats	81-85, 98-99
XL03S-3-4	Format worksheets	74, 78-79, 108-109
XL03S-4	**Collaborating**	
XL03S-4-1	Insert, view and edit comments	242-243
XL03S-5	**Managing Workbooks**	
XL03S-5-1	Create new workbooks from templates	4-5
XL03S-5-2	Insert, delete and move cells	39-45
XL03S-5-3	Create and modify hyperlinks	270-271
XL03S-5-4	Organize worksheets	74-77
XL03S-5-5	Preview data in other views	116-117, 123, 269
XL03S-5-6	Customize Window layout	15, 78-79, 86-87
XL03S-5-7	Setup pages for printing	116-120, 122
XL03S-5-8	Print data	120-121, 124
XL03S-5-9	Organize workbooks using file folders	20-21
XL03S-5-10	Save data in appropriate formats for different uses	22-23, 250-251, 254-255, 272-273

Excel 2003 Expert Objectives

Objective	Skill	Page
XL03E-1	**Organizing and Analyzing Data**	
XL03E-1-1	Use subtotals	66-67
XL03E-1-2	Define and apply advanced filters	203
XL03E-1-3	Group and outline data	212-213
XL03E-1-4	Use data validation	214
XL03E-1-5	Create and modify list ranges	195, 204-205
XL03E-1-6	Add, show, close, edit, merge, and summarize scenarios	220-221
XL03E-1-7	Perform data analysis using automated tools	216-219, 222-223
XL03E-1-8	Create PivotTable and PivotChart reports	206, 210-211
XL03E-1-9	Use Lookup and Reference functions	224-225
XL03E-1-10	Use Database functions	213
XL03E-1-11	Trace formula precedents, dependents and errors	70
XL03E-1-12	Locate invalid data and formulas	68-69
XL03E-1-13	Watch and evaluate formulas	68-69
XL03E-1-14	Define, modify and use named ranges	62-64
XL03E-1-15	Structure workbooks using XML	252-253
XL03E-2	**Formatting Data and Content**	
XL03E-2-1	Create and modify custom data formats	92-93
XL03E-2-2	Use conditional formatting	94
XL03E-2-3	Format and resize graphics	134-136, 156-159
XL03E-2-4	Format charts and diagrams	148, 180-181, 184-185, 190-191
XL03E-3	**Collaborating**	
XL03E-3-1	Protect cells, worksheets, and workbooks	234-235
XL03E-3-2	Apply workbook security settings	234-238
XL03E-3-3	Share workbooks	240-241
XL03E-3-4	Merge workbooks	246
XL03E-3-5	Track, accept, and reject changes to workbooks	244-245
XL03E-4	**Managing Data and Workbooks**	
XL03E-4-1	Import data to Excel	250-251, 264-265 277-278

Excel 2003 Expert Objectives *(continued)*

Objective	Skill	Page
XL03E-4-2	Export data from Excel	254-255
XL03E-4-3	Publish and edit Web worksheets and workbooks	274
XL03E-4-4	Create and edit templates	88-90
XL03E-4-5	Consolidate data	260-261
XL03E-4-6	Define and modify workbook properties	286-287
XL03E-5	**Customizing Excel**	
XL03E-5-1	Customize toolbars and menus	294-298
XL03E-5-2	Create, edit, and run macros	227-228, 230-231
XL03E-5-3	Modify Excel default settings	290-291

Preparing for a Microsoft Office Specialist Exam

Every Microsoft Office Specialist certification exam is developed from a list of objectives, which are based on studies of how Microsoft Office programs are actually used in the workplace. The list of objectives determine the scope of each exam, so they provide you with the information you need to prepare for Microsoft Office Specialist certification. Microsoft Office Specialist Approved Courseware, including the Show Me series, is reviewed and approved on the basis of its coverage of the objectives. To prepare for the certification exam, you should review and perform each task identified with a Microsoft Office Specialist objective to confirm that you can meet the requirements for the exam.

Taking a Microsoft Office Specialist Exam

The Microsoft Office Specialist certification exams are not written exams. Instead, the exams are performance-based examinations that allow you to interact with a "live" Office program as you complete a series of objective-based tasks. All the standard menus, toolbars, and keyboard shortcuts are available during the exam. Microsoft Office Specialist exams for Office 2003 programs consist of 25 to 35 questions, each of which requires you to complete one or more tasks using the Office program for which you are seeking certification. A typical exam takes from 45 to 60 minutes. Passing percentages range from 70 to 80 percent correct.

The Exam Experience

After you fill out a series of information screens, the testing software starts the exam and the Office program. The test questions appear in the exam dialog box in the lower right corner of the screen.

◆   The timer starts when the first question appears and displays the remaining exam time at the top of the exam dialog box. If the timer and the counter are distracting, you can click the timer to remove the display.

◆   The counter at the top of the exam dialog box tracks how many questions you have completed and how many remain.

◆   If you think you have made a mistake, you can click the Reset button to restart the question. The Reset button does not restart the entire exam or extend the exam time limit.

◆   When you complete a question, click the Next button to move to the next question. It is not possible to move back to a previous question on the exam.

◆   If the exam dialog box gets in your way, you can click the Minimize button in the upper right corner of the exam dialog box to hide it, or you can drag the title bar to another part of the screen to move it.

Tips for Taking an Exam

◆ Carefully read and follow all instructions provided in each question.

◆ Make sure all steps in a task are completed before proceeding to the next exam question.

◆ Enter requested information as it appears in the instructions without formatting unless you are explicitly requested otherwise.

◆ Close all dialog boxes before proceeding to the next exam question unless you are specifically instructed otherwise.

◆ Do not leave tables, boxes, or cells "active" unless instructed otherwise.

◆ Do not cut and paste information from the exam interface into the program.

◆ When you print a document from an Office program during the exam, nothing actually gets printed.

◆ Errant keystrokes or mouse clicks do not count against your score as long as you achieve the correct end result. You are scored based on the end result, not the method you use to achieve it. However, if a specific method is explicitly requested, you need to use it to get credit for the results.

◆ The overall exam is timed, so taking too long on individual questions may leave you without enough time to complete the entire exam.

◆ If you experience computer problems during the exam, notify a testing center administrator immediately to restart your exam where you were interrupted.

Exam Results

At the end of the exam, a score report appears indicating whether you passed or failed the exam. An official certificate is mailed to successful candidates in approximately two to three weeks.

Getting More Information

To learn more about the Microsoft Office Specialist program, read a list of frequently asked questions, and locate the nearest testing center, visit:

www.microsoft.com/officespecialist

New! Features

Microsoft Office Excel 2003

Microsoft Office Excel 2003 is the spreadsheet program that gives you support for XML and new features that make it easier to analyze and share information.

- **Compare workbooks side by side (p. 14-15)** Comparing workbooks side by side allows you to see the differences between two workbooks more easily, without having to constantly switch back and forth between windows. You can scroll through both workbooks at the same time to identify differences between the two workbooks.

- **Person Names Smart Tag menu (p. 50-51)** Quickly locate contact information such as a person's phone number and complete tasks such as scheduling a meeting using the Person Names Smart Tag menu. The menu is available in Excel wherever a person's name appears.

- **Enhanced statistical functions (p. 71-72)** Use enhanced statistical functions, including enhancements to rounding results and precision, in your workbooks:

  BINOMDIST, CHIINV, CONFIDENCE, CRITBINOM, DSTDEV, DSTDEVP, DVAR, DVARP, FINV, FORECAST, GAMMAINV, GROWTH, HYPGEOMDIST, INTERCEPT, LINEST, LOGEST, LOGINV, LOGNORMDIST, NEGBINOMDIST, NORMDIST, NORMINV, NORMSDIST, NORMSINV, PEARSON, POISSON, RAND, , RSQ, SLOPE, STDEV, STDEVA, STDEVP, STDEVPA, STEYX, TINV, TREND, VAR, VARA, VARP, VARPA, and ZTEST.

- **Research task pane (p. 128-129)** The new Research task pane offers a wide variety of reference information and expanded resources if you have an Internet connection. You can conduct research on topics using an encyclopedia, Web search, or by accessing third-party content.

- **Enhanced list functionality (p. 195, 200-202, 205)** Create lists in your worksheet to group and manage related data. You can create a list on existing data or create a list from an empty range. A new user interface and a corresponding set of functionality are exposed for ranges that are designated as a list. Every column in a list has AutoFilter enabled by default in the header row which allows you to quickly filter or sort your data. A dark blue list border clearly outlines the range of cells that compose your list. A row in the list frame that contains an asterisk is called the insert row. Typing information in this row automatically adds data to the list. A total row can be added to your list. When you click on a cell within the total row, you can pick from a drop-down list of aggregate functions. The size of a list can be modified by dragging the resize handle found on the bottom right corner of the list border.

◆ **List integration with Windows SharePoint Services (p. 324-325)** Share the information contained within an Excel list by using Windows SharePoint Services. You can create a Windows SharePoint Services list based on your Excel list on a Windows SharePoint Services site by publishing the list. If you choose to link the list to the Windows SharePoint Services site, any changes you make to the list in Excel will be updated on the Windows SharePoint Services site when you synchronize the list.

◆ **Information Rights Management (p. 232-233)** Create or view content with restricted permission using Information Rights Management (IRM). IRM allows individual authors to specify permission for who can access and use workbooks or e-mail messages, and helps prevent sensitive information from being printed, forwarded, or copied by unauthorized people.

◆ **XML support (p. 252-253)** Organize and work with workbooks and data in ways that were previously impossible or very difficult. By using your XML schemas, you can now identify and extract specific pieces of business data from ordinary business documents. You can also attach a custom XML schema to any workbook by using the XML Source task pane to map cells to elements of the schema. Once you have mapped the XML elements to your worksheet, you can import and export XML data into and out of the mapped cells.

◆ **Support for ink devices, such as the Tablet PC (p. 304-305)** Quickly provide input by adding your own handwriting to Office documents on a Tablet PC as you would using a pen and a printout. Additionally, view task panes horizontally to help you do your work on the Tablet PC.

◆ **Document Workspaces (p. 309-323)** Create a Document Workspace to simplify the process of co-writing, editing, and reviewing workbooks with others in real time. A Document Workspace site is a Windows SharePoint Services site that is centered around one or more documents and is typically created when you use e-mail to send a workbook as a shared attachment.

◆ **Smart documents** Smart documents are programmed to extend the functionality of your workbook by dynamically responding to the context of your actions. Several types of workbooks, especially workbooks that are used as part of a process such as forms and templates, work well as smart documents. Smart documents can help you reuse existing content and can make it easier to share information. They can even interact with other Office programs such as Microsoft Office Outlook, all without leaving the workbook or starting Outlook.

Troubleshooting

Worksheets and workbooks

Index

P

source data, 258

source files, 248

source programs, 248

speech profiles, creating, 301

speech recognition, installing, 300

spelling, checking/correcting, 48-49, 52

spin boxes, in dialog boxes, 12

spinning 3-D objects, 164

splitting the screen into panes, 86, 87

squares, drawing, 152

stacking order, changing, 168

Standard toolbar

    buttons, 37, 57, 66

    combining with the Formatting toolbar, 295

Start menu

    opening recently opened workbooks from, 7

    starting Excel from, 2

starting

    Excel, 2

    workbooks, 4

status bar (Excel window), 3

step mode, debugging macros in, 230

stock quotes, inserting, 51

storing cell contents, 39

storing documents in SharePoint document libraries, 314

storing macros, 226

Style dialog box, and the Format Cells dialog box, 111

styles, 110-113

    applying, 111

    creating, 110, 113

    deleting, 113

    merging from another workbook, 112, 113

    modifying, 112

subtotals, calculating, 66

subtraction operator (-), 54

SUM function, 71

surfaces for 3-D objects, setting, 165

T

Tab key, navigating worksheets, 9

tables

    Access database tables, 264

    data tables, 218

    Web tables, 276

    See also PivotTables

tabs, in dialog boxes, 12

    See also sheet tabs

task panes (Excel window), 3, 13

    opening/closing, 13

    starting workbooks from, 4

taskbar (Windows), switching between Office documents, 14

tasks (on SharePoint servers), adding, 317

templates

    creating, 23, 88

    creating files with, 5

    default, 89, 90

    downloading from the Web, 5

    vs. macros, 88

    modifying/customizing, 89, 90

    opening, 89

    saving workbooks as, 23, 88

    testing, 88

text

    in charts. *See* chart text

    dictating, 300, 303

    spell checking/correcting, 48-49, 52

    in workbooks, finding, 288

    in worksheets. *See* text (in worksheets)

    See also WordArt text

text (in worksheets)

    aligning, 98-99

    coloring, 101

    entering, 30-31, 48

    flow control, 100

    formatting, 92, 96-97, 101, 106, 111

    wrapping, 100

    See also cell comments; labels

W